How
Architecture
Works

How Architecture Works

A HUMANIST'S TOOLKIT

Witold Rybczynski

FARRAR, STRAUS AND GIROUX   NEW YORK

Farrar, Straus and Giroux
18 West 18th Street, New York 10011

Library of Congress Cataloging-in-Publication Data
Rybczynski, Witold.
    How architecture works : a humanist's toolkit /
Witold Rybczynski. — First edition.
        pages   cm
    Includes bibliographical references and index.
    ISBN 978-0-374-21174-5 (hardcover)
    1. Architecture.   I. Title.

NA2550 .R965 2013
720—dc23
                                              2013006524

Designed by Jonathan D. Lippincott

Farrar, Straus and Giroux books may be purchased for educational, business,
or promotional use. For information on bulk purchases, please contact the
Macmillan Corporate and Premium Sales Department at 1-800-221-7945,
extension 5442, or write to specialmarkets@macmillan.com.

www.fsgbooks.com
www.twitter.com/fsgbooks • www.facebook.com/fsgbooks

1   3   5   7   9   10   8   6   4   2

To the students of my freshman seminar class,
who taught me to look anew at architecture through youthful eyes

Of the many doorways we pass in a short walk, most are fulfilling their purpose, most of them are well-enough built. How many are worth a second look? It seems that there is something more than merely "function," something more than good construction, something more difficult to achieve, if so few can achieve it. It is precisely the pursuit of this *something* that makes of architecture a thing apart . . . —Paul Philippe Cret

Architecture starts when you carefully put two bricks together. There it begins. —Ludwig Mies van der Rohe

CONTENTS

How
Architecture
Works

INTRODUCTION

A Jacobean Revival chapel that I attended in high school was my first intimate experience of architecture: timber arches, dark paneling, stained-glass windows depicting suffering Jesuit martyrs—and hard wooden pews. The carved pulpit was like a fo'c'sle overlooking a sea of restless schoolboys. Exactly what makes a building memorable is hard to pin down. It's certainly not merely fulfilling a practical function—all buildings do that. Beauty? Architecture is an art, yet we rarely concentrate our attention on buildings as we do on plays, books, and paintings. Most architecture, a backdrop for our everyday lives, is experienced in bits and pieces—the glimpsed view of a distant spire, the intricacy of a wrought-iron railing, the soaring space of a railroad station waiting room. Sometimes it's just a detail, a well-shaped door handle, a window framing a perfect little view, a rosette carved into a chapel pew. And we say to ourselves, "How nice. Someone actually thought of that."

Despite this familiarity, most of us lack a conceptual framework for thinking about the experience of architecture. Where are we to find this framework—in the intentions and theories of architects, in the pronouncements of critics, in some kind of pure aesthetic judgment, or in our own experience of buildings? The rationalizations of architects are usually unreliable, intended to persuade rather than to explain. The judgments of critics are frequently little more than partisan opinions. Nor are architectural terms always clear, whether it is the dentils, squinches, and ogee curves of historical styles, or the impenetrable poststructuralist jargon of the contemporary avant-garde. Of course, all professions have their technical terminology, but while television and the movies have made the languages of law and medicine familiar, the infrequent appearance of architects on the big screen is rarely enlightening, whether it's the fictional Howard Roark in *The Fountainhead* or the real Stanford White in *The Girl in the Red Velvet Swing*.

Why does this matter? Because architecture is for the most part a public art. Despite the media's trumpeting of "signature" buildings, architecture isn't—or at least shouldn't be—a personality cult. Gothic cathedrals were not built for architecture buffs or the cognoscenti but for the medieval man in the street, who could gape at the grotesque gargoyles, be inspired by the carvings of devout saints, marvel at the glowing rose windows, or be transported by the hymns reverberating in the cavernous nave. Architecture, if it is any good, speaks to all of us.

EXPERIENCING ARCHITECTURE

What counts as architecture? In the Middle Ages the answer was simple; cathedrals, churches, monasteries, and a few public buildings were architecture, the rest was simply building. Today, the scope of architecture has broadened. Architecture is the setting for many ordinary activities, and it may be small or large, modest or grand, special or mundane. Ultimately, we recognize the spirit of architecture in any building that exhibits a coherent visual language. As Mies van der Rohe observed, "Architecture starts when you carefully put two bricks together."

The language of built architecture is not a foreign tongue—

you shouldn't need a phrase book or a user's manual—but it can be complicated, since buildings must accomplish many tasks, practical as well as artistic. The architect is thinking of function as well as inspiration, of construction as well as visual expression, and of details as well as spatial effects. He must take into account the building's long-term use as well as its immediate impact, and consider its surroundings as well as its interior environment. "The architect is a sort of theatrical producer, the man who plans the setting for our lives," wrote Steen Eiler Rasmussen. "When his intentions succeed, he is like the perfect host who provides every comfort for his guests so that living with him is a happy experience."

Rasmussen, a Danish architect and planner, wrote that in 1959 in his classic *Experiencing Architecture*. It is a deceptively simple book. "My object is in all modesty to endeavor to explain the instrument the architect plays on, to show what a great range it has and thereby awaken the senses to its music." The accomplished author of numerous books on cities and urban history— and a friend of Karen Blixen—Rasmussen was not a polemicist. "It is not my intention to attempt to teach people what is right or wrong, what is beautiful or ugly." He visited most of the buildings he described, and the bulk of the photographs in the book are his own. *Experiencing Architecture* takes the reader behind the scenes, so to speak, and reveals how architecture works its magic.

I was introduced to *Experiencing Architecture* by Norbert Schoenauer, my favorite teacher when I was an architecture student at McGill University. A Hungarian postwar refugee, he had studied under Rasmussen at the Royal Danish Academy of Fine Arts in Copenhagen. The experience turned Schoenauer into a Scandinavian humanist, and while he taught me the craft of architecture—how to draw and plan and design—he never let me forget that buildings were foremost settings for everyday life.

In developing a conceptual toolkit for thinking about the experience of architecture, I follow in Rasmussen's—and

Schoenauer's—footsteps. Such a toolkit should reflect our daily experience of buildings, which is practical as well as aesthetic. This book moves between the two poles, sometimes emphasizing one, sometimes the other. This requires occasionally changing the focus—zooming in to a small detail, zooming out to consider a building in its overall surroundings. Along the way, I aim to provide practical answers to theoretical questions or, to paraphrase James Wood, to ask a critic's questions and offer an architect's answers. What is the meaning of a particular form? How does a detail contribute to the whole? Why does this building touch us?

Some readers will look in vain for their favorite building. Like Rasmussen, I have generally confined myself to buildings I have visited—and buildings that have spoken to me—so the range is hardly comprehensive; in any case, this is not meant to be a catalog of buildings and architects, but of ideas. My book is likewise a personal exploration, and while the Dane was a committed modernist who brought a functionalist's sensibility to his task, I've lived through both the decline and resurgence—in altered form—of modern architecture, and along the way have lost many of my youthful certainties. I consider history a gift, rather than an imposition, for example, and find historians to be more reliable guides than many architectural thinkers. As someone who has practiced architecture, I find it difficult to excuse technical incompetence in the name of experimentation, or to overlook functional deficiencies for the sake of artistic purity. Architecture is an applied art, and it is in the application that the architect often finds inspiration. I confess to a partiality for those who face this challenge squarely, rather than withdraw to hermetic theories or personal quests.

VERTICAL AESTHETIC

Experiencing Architecture has one striking omission. Except for a brief and unexplained allusion to the "great monotony" of Rockefeller Center, Rasmussen had nothing to say about the twentieth century's most distinctive addition to the architectural lexicon: the skyscraper. It's a curious oversight. Admittedly, there were few high-rise buildings in Europe in 1959, but he might have mentioned the KBC Tower, a twenty-six-story Art Deco building in Antwerp and Europe's first skyscraper, or the interesting Torre Velasca, a medieval-looking postwar high-rise in Milan. Nor did he refer to a skyscraper being built in his native Copenhagen, the SAS Royal Hotel designed by Arne Jacobsen, Denmark's leading modernist. Rasmussen, who was a visiting professor at the Massachusetts Institute of Technology and traveled widely in the United States, included several American buildings in his book, but not Lever House, the office building that had inspired Jacobsen, nor the most talked-about skyscraper of the 1950s, Mies van der Rohe's Seagram Building. Despite his rather conventional modernist leanings, Rasmussen was a traditional urbanist, and I have the impression that he disapproved of the idea of cities dominated by commercial towers.

Our cities are full of tall buildings. Skyscrapers have become so ubiquitous that we take them for granted and easily forget what unusual structures they really are, feats of engineering designed to resist major wind forces (and earthquakes), integrating environmental and communications systems, and transporting people quickly and efficiently hundreds of feet into the air. Functionally, nothing could be simpler than an office or apartment tower: repetitive floors stacked up one on top of the other surrounding an elevator core. But skyscrapers represent a thorny architectural problem. For one thing, they are very big. You can stand back and take in the Leaning Tower of Pisa, or the clock tower of the Palace of Westminster in London, just as you would any other building, but a skyscraper is different. Architects are often pictured with maquettes of tall buildings: Frank Lloyd Wright posed in his studio in front of a seven-foot-high model of the proposed San Francisco Call Building; *Life* magazine depicted Mies van der Rohe as an architectural Gulliver peering out between the twin towers of the Lake Shore Drive apartments; and a *Time* magazine cover showed Philip Johnson cradling a model of the AT&T Building like a proud father. But actual skyscrapers are much too big to be experienced all of a piece. They are perceived in two quite different ways: from a great distance, as part of the urban skyline, and close up, as part of the street.

The other problem with office towers is their lack of architectural variety. Traditionally, architects have made large buildings interesting compositions by introducing different-size windows, projecting bays, balconies, gables, turrets, dormers, and chimneys. But a high-rise office building consists of floor after floor of undifferentiated space. It took architects some time to find a satisfying solution. In 1896, twenty-six years after the first elevatored office building—the seven-story Equitable Life Assurance Building in New York City, which resembled a pumped-up Parisian mansion—the Chicago architect Louis Sullivan wrote a groundbreaking essay titled "The Tall Office Building Artistically Considered." Sullivan described skyscrapers as the crude combination of technology (elevators and steel construction) and economics (putting more rentable space on a building lot). "How shall we impart to this sterile pile, this crude, harsh, brutal agglomeration, this stark, staring exclamation of eternal strife, the graciousness of these higher forms of sensibility and culture that rest on the lower and fiercer passions?" he asked in his somewhat flowery prose. His answer, simply put, was to divide the tall building into different parts. The lowest two floors would be richly ornamented and relate visually to the street; the upper floors would express Sullivan's dictum that "form ever follows function." He explained: "Above this, throughout the indefinite number of typical office tiers, we take our cue from the individual cell, which requires a window with its separating pier, its sill and lintel, and we, without more ado, make them look all alike because they are all alike." He also suggested that the top of the building should be finished off with an attic floor, a frieze, or a large cornice, to indicate that the tiers of offices had definitely come to an end. At the time he wrote the essay, Sullivan had already demonstrated his concept in the Wainwright Building in St. Louis. The ten-story block of red brick and ornamented terra-cotta is hardly a skyscraper by our standards, but it nevertheless is generally considered to be the prototype for the modern high-rise office building. The piers between the rows of identical windows run straight up uninterrupted to the frieze, and produce what Sullivan called a "vertical aesthetic."

Sullivan's tripartite formula, based on a classical sense of architectural order, influenced many later skyscrapers, including the famous Flatiron Building, designed by his Chicago colleague, Daniel Burnham. While Sullivan designed organic decorations akin to European Art Nouveau, Burnham favored historical models; for example, his and John Root's Masonic Temple Building in Chicago, once the tallest in the world, was topped by a vaguely Tudor pitched roof, while their Rookery Building includes Byzantine, Venetian, and Romanesque motifs.

The Gothic style was common in early skyscrapers such as the Woolworth Building in New York, the Cathedral Building in Oakland, and the Chicago Tribune Tower. The proportions and attenuated ornament of Perpendicular Gothic are tailor-made for very tall buildings, since they emphasize verticality and upward thrust. The top of the Chicago Tribune Tower, for example, with its flying buttresses and pinnacles, was based on the Butter Tower of Rouen Cathedral. The architect, Raymond Hood, later designed commercial towers that were progressively less ornamented, but he maintained the pronounced sense of vertical massing. His magnificent RCA Building at Rockefeller Center, which creates the impression of a soaring stalagmite, remains one of the best skyscrapers in Manhattan—despite Rasmussen's reservations.

Modern tall buildings can still be loosely categorized as either classical or Gothic, depending on how they deal with structure.

Consider the recently completed Comcast Center in Philadelphia, designed by Robert A. M. Stern. From a distance, the all-glass tower looks like a tapering obelisk. The base of the building, which faces a pedestrian plaza, is fronted by a tall winter garden leading to the lobby. Stern is known as the architect of Shingle Style houses and Georgian campus buildings, and while Comcast is modernist in execution, it is classical in composition, adhering to Sullivan's formula of base-shaft-crown.

There is nothing in the Comcast Center's sleek glass walls that reveals what holds up the tower. In fact, its steel frame surrounds a high-strength reinforced concrete elevator and stair core (a post-9/11 safety feature), and the top of the building houses the world's largest tuned damper, a water-filled pendulum that acts to minimize swaying of the building in high winds. But these devices are hidden. In the Hongkong and Shanghai Bank headquarters in Hong Kong, on the other hand, Norman Foster reveals the elements of the core, since he places them on the exterior of the building. The main structural components—clusters of columns, massive trusses, and crisscrossing girders—are similarly exposed. Unlike most Hong Kong skyscrapers, which have discreet, solid forms, the bank is composed of several stepped-back sections of different heights, giving the impression that the building is still under construction. "There is a lot more that is Gothic than classical in all this structural and spatial magic," wrote the British architecture critic Chris Abel. "If the 'medieval' service towers, 'flying braces' and 'incomplete' appearance of the building had not already prompted the idea, then the soaring proportions of the atrium (read nave) and the great translucent eastern window easily justify the building's popular description as a 'cathedral of commerce.'" "Cathedral of Commerce" was the nickname of the Woolworth Building, whose architect, Cass Gilbert, created little gargoyles in the lobby in the likeness of persons involved in the building, including himself (with a slide rule), and Frank Woolworth, the "5¢ and 10¢ store" magnate, counting his nickels and dimes. Gilbert had a lighter touch than Foster, whose austere style is never humorous, but Abel is correct to draw the parallel. Like a medieval cathedral, the Hongkong Bank celebrates its construction.

In the New York Times Building on Eighth Avenue, Renzo Piano achieves something unusual: he combines classical and Gothic. From a distance, the tall building appears to be a simple cruciform shaft. The all-glass form is almost entirely shrouded by a sunscreen that gives the tower an oddly insubstantial appearance from a distance. But the impression of delicacy changes when the building is approached at street level. From the prominent steel rods that suspend the glass canopy over the sidewalk, to the exposed columns and beams and crisscrossing tension members at the corners, the Times Building flexes its structural muscles in plain view. Engineering hasn't been celebrated this boldly in Manhattan since the George Washington Bridge.

These three buildings are corporate symbols as well as workplaces. The sleek glass Comcast Center, as smooth—and as mute—as a computer chip, houses a high-tech communications company; the façade of the Hongkong Bank is uniformly matte gray, like a banker's pin-striped suit; and the New York Times Building, home of the nation's newspaper of record, emphasizes openness and transparency. Symbolism in corporate towers is a reminder that large commercial buildings are not expressions of an architect's personal vision. Of course, Stern's interest in history, Foster's fascination with technology, and Piano's respect for craftsmanship influence their respective designs. But these buildings also have a lot to say about the corporations that built them, and even more about the *societies* that built them. Discussing the New York Times Building, Renzo Piano observed: "I like the idea that this century is opening up with a discovery that the earth is fragile and the environment is vulnerable. Fragility, breathing with the earth and the environment, is part of a new culture. I thought the Times Building should have the qualities of lightness, vibrancy, transparency, and immateriality." This is what makes architecture interesting in a different way than sculpture or painting; buildings can sometimes be an expression of what Mies van der Rohe once called the "will of the epoch."

The three skyscrapers are also a reminder that while buildings respond to economic and cultural forces, they are primarily local. They are built in specific cities—Philadelphia, Hong Kong, New York—and they respond to their urban surroundings. They also occupy distinctly different sites. The Comcast Center is next to a Presbyterian church and faces a large plaza. It is no coincidence that the plaza is on the south side of the building—it is always best to enter a building on its sunny side if possible, for that is where the façade will appear to best advantage, with sharply de-fined shadow lines and contrasts, and in Comcast's case a sun-filled winter garden. The Hongkong Bank also faces a plaza—Statue Square—which connects to the Kowloon ferry terminal. Thus, Foster's tower occupies a unique site in the city, visible from a great distance, first from the deck of the ferry, then while walking through the park, and finally from the square itself. Piano's build-ing, by contrast, is almost lost in midtown Manhattan's forest of tall buildings. From the narrow canyon of Eighth Avenue, and the even narrower confines of Fortieth and Forty-First Streets, its ar-chitecture is experienced in snatched glimpses.

The three skyscrapers demonstrate how differently different architects use similar materials. The all-glass skin of the Com-cast Center is stretched tautly across the façade; two different kinds of glass—one more and one less transparent—define the obelisk. The glass wall of the Hongkong Bank, by contrast, is seen through a steel filigree, whose large and small structural compo-nents create a rich and deeply articulated façade. The all-glass New York Times Building is cloaked in sunscreens. The way that these architects handle details is different, too. Stern's details are elegant but don't call attention to themselves. Foster makes details that are smooth and precise, like a luxury automobile. Piano's details tend to be articulated, beautifully crafted nuts and bolts.

We often describe exciting new buildings as unique and fresh. Indeed, to say that a building is groundbreaking has become the highest form of praise, as if architecture, like fashion, should avoid any reference to the past. Yet, as Philip Johnson wisely observed, "you cannot *not* know history." I can't look at the Comcast Center without thinking of the ancient Egyptian monument whose form it mimics. When I first saw the Hongkong Bank it reminded me of Victorian engineering and steel railroad bridges. The New York Times Building makes me think of the nearby Seagram Building, and how, by simply adding a sunscreen, Piano altered Mies's classic steel-and-glass idiom. None of these three buildings can be described as historicist, yet none can escape history.

THE TOOLKIT

It helps to have a sense of what architects are trying to do, both practically and aesthetically, to understand how architecture works. In this book I describe ten essential topics of architectural concern, and the different ways in which contemporary architects do—and sometimes intentionally don't—address them.

The first third of the book deals with the fundamentals. I begin by discussing how buildings can be the expression of a single, often very simple, *idea*. But buildings are more than intellectual creations; that's what Frank Lloyd Wright meant when he remarked to Philip Johnson: "Why, Philip, little Phil, all grown up, building buildings and leaving them out in the rain." All buildings are left out in the rain; that is, a building is always part of a climate, a geography, a particular place. The immediate *setting*—what architects call the context—plays an important role in shaping a building's design, although some buildings fit in while others stick out. Sometimes, the setting is an existing building that must be added on to. Equally important is the *site*, which is not exactly the same thing. The site affects the way that a building is seen from afar, the way it is approached, the views it offers, the position of the sun.

The middle third of the book explores various aspects of the architect's craft. In most buildings, the resolution of the site and its surroundings is manifested in the building's *plan*, which is the designer's chief organizing tool. A work of architecture, however profound its generating idea, has to be built, and in a digital age buildings remain resolutely physical—bricks and mortar. I describe three essential aspects of the material presence of a building: *structure*, *skin*, and *details*. To the nonarchitect, these might seem to be purely technical subjects, determined by objective science, or at least engineering, but in truth they are as subjective and individual as an architect's sketch.

The final third of the book broadens the discussion. For most people, architectural *style* is one of the most interesting—and pleasurable—rewards of looking at buildings, yet for many architects, especially modernist architects, style is a delicate subject, sometimes skirted, often flatly denied. "Style is like a feather in a woman's hat, nothing more," stated Le Corbusier, and yet, as his own work shows, a sense of style is an important ingredient in all successful buildings. The *past* is an ever-present concern for architects, because buildings last a long time, which means that new buildings almost always have old neighbors. Moreover, new designs must recognize that cultural ideas about how buildings are used last a long time, too, hence the durable notions of front door and back door, upstairs and downstairs, inside and outside. Here, too, there is a divergence of opinion, some treating the past as an inspiration, others as a burden. *Taste* is equally in dispute: Picasso called good taste "a dreadful thing . . . the enemy of creativeness," whereas Goethe wrote, "Nothing is more fearful than imagination without taste."

The ways that buildings reflect the past, use materials, and deploy details vary considerably, of course, and as the three skyscrapers previously discussed demonstrate, there is happily no one right way to build—although there are many wrong ways. I write "happily" because I welcome architectural diversity. While the practitioner needs a solid conceptual foundation in order to create—and it is important to understand that foundation in order to better appreciate a building—I do not consider that there is only one correct architectural approach. As Rasmussen observed, "That which may be right for one artist may well be wrong for another."

Such an ecumenical position is out of step with the intense debate—the so-called discourse—that besets the architectural world today. Around the turn of the century, in music, painting, and literature, classic forms of representation broke down and with this came the need for theoretical manifestos to accompany works of art. Architecture has attempted to follow suit, producing architects better known for their writing than their built work, and practitioners whose work is accompanied by long—and often labored—explanations. However, unlike music, painting, and literature, which can exist purely in the imagination, architecture cannot be separated from the physical world: floors must be level, doors must swing open, a stair is always a stair. Architecture, grounded firmly as it is in the world, is not an academic discipline, and attempts to impose intellectual theories on buildings always run up against these irritating practicalities.

I have no grand theory to advance, no polemical agenda, no school to champion. Architecture, good architecture, is rare enough; there is no need to create artificial schisms. In any case, I believe that architecture emerges from the act of building; theories, if they have any place at all, are an indulgence of the scholar, not a need of the practitioner. All architects, no matter their professed ideology, share a concern with program, site, materials, and construction. Lest this sound too mundane, all architects are also in pursuit of that ineffable *something*, the quality, as Paul Cret wisely pointed out, that is the essence of architecture. Understanding that essence is what this book is about.

1

IDEAS

The École des Beaux-Arts in Paris, which dominated architectural education in the nineteenth and the early twentieth centuries, developed a strict method of teaching building design. After being assigned a problem, the student was isolated in a cubicle without the benefit of books or external advice, and given twelve hours to produce an *esquisse*, or preliminary design sketch. The chief purpose of this exercise was to decide on a *parti*, the governing idea that the student would turn into a detailed design over the next two months. A student handbook advised, "Selecting a *parti* for a problem is to take an attitude toward a solution in the hope that a building developed on the lines indicated by it will give the best solution of the problem." Although the *esquisse* is a thing of the past, the term *parti* has survived, for it embodies an enduring truth: great buildings are often the result of a single—and sometimes very simple—idea.

When you enter the Pantheon in Rome, you take it all in at a single glance: a vast drum supporting a coffered dome, illuminated from above by an oculus, or circular aperture. Nothing could be simpler, yet no one would describe the Pantheon as a one-liner. Finished by Hadrian in the first century A.D., it is one of the most influential buildings of Western architecture, having inspired Bramante at St. Peter's, Christopher Wren at St. Paul's,

Pantheon, Rome, A.D. 126

and Thomas Ustick Walter at the U.S. Capitol. King's College Chapel of Cambridge University, begun by Henry VI in 1446, is another building whose design expresses a singular idea: a tall space whose dematerialized walls are almost entirely stained glass. Modeled on a cathedral choir, the narrow chapel is eighty feet high and almost three hundred feet long. There is no apse, no crossing, no rose window, just a numinous, soaring space. In buildings, the idea also informs the details. While the coffers of the Pantheon emphasize the solidity and weight of the dome and lead the eye up to the oculus, the lacy fan vaults of the Perpendicular Gothic chapel harmonize with the delicate tracery of the windows.

A more recent example of a building whose design is driven by an idea is Frank Lloyd Wright's Solomon R. Guggenheim Museum in New York. Wright started with the insight that, given the high cost of Manhattan real estate, the museum had to be vertical. He explored four schemes, one of them octagonal, and settled on a spiral ramp coiling around a tall skylit space. The museumgoer would take the elevator to the top of the ramp, viewing the art as he descended. Uncomplicated in conception, yet no matter how often I go there I am always surprised—and delighted—anew. Wright kept the details in the background: the spiraling balustrade, for example, is a plain concrete parapet with a rounded top; the ramp floor is simply painted concrete. "The eye encounters no abrupt change," he explained, "but is gently led and treated as if at the edge of a shore watching an unbreaking wave."

Another modern museum that is based on a simple idea is the Sainsbury Centre for Visual Arts at the University of East Anglia in Norwich, a building designed by Norman Foster in the mid-1970s. Although the building was to house a variety of uses—exhibition spaces, a school of art history, a student cafeteria, and a faculty club—Foster accommodated them in what was basically an extremely long shed that recalls an elegant aircraft hangar.

Frank Lloyd Wright, Guggenheim Museum, New York, 1959

The long space, glazed at each end, does not feel tunnel-like, thanks to the daylight that filters down from skylights. The Sainsbury Centre has no architectural antecedents, it is as if Foster had asked himself: What if many different university functions were contained in one large space?

CONCEPT HOUSES

Ludwig Mies van der Rohe's house for Dr. Edith Farnsworth in Plano, Illinois, and Philip Johnson's own residence in New Canaan, Connecticut, are single spaces that ask an unusual question: What if all the walls of a house were glass? Both houses were designed as weekend retreats in the late 1940s; both are one-story boxes, the Farnsworth twenty-eight by seventy-seven feet, the Johnson thirty-two by fifty-six feet; and both are constructed of steel I-beams. A transparent house should be as open as possible, and in both cases the interior is a column-free space divided

Ludwig Mies van der Rohe, Farnsworth House, Plano, Illinois, 1951

Philip Johnson, Glass House, New Canaan, Connecticut, 1949

only by freestanding elements containing closets, kitchen counters, bathrooms, and other necessities. There are no conventional rooms.

Although Johnson finished his house first, he always credited Mies with the original idea.* Johnson considered the German architect his model: "I have been called Mies van der Johnson," he once told Yale students; "it doesn't bother me in the slightest." But of his own house he said, "I won't say it's imitation Mies, because it's quite different." Johnson was not just being defensive— Mies's house sits in a floodplain and is elevated five feet in the air, which makes it appear to hover, while Johnson's house is planted firmly on the ground. And there are other differences. While Mies uses luxurious materials—travertine floors and tropical hardwood paneling—Johnson uses plain red brick. The bathroom is a cylinder, "which would of course be anathema to Mies,"

*The Farnsworth House was designed in 1946 but was not completed until five years later.

said Johnson. Mies purposely designed the exterior of his glass house to be unsymmetrical—the roof and floor extend at one end to form a covered terrace—while Johnson made his four façades essentially identical, each with a door in the center. A final telling difference: Mies's steel is painted glossy white, the traditional color of garden pavilions, while Johnson's I-beams are matte black, making his house a machinelike presence in the natural landscape.

The architect and writer Peter Blake observed that Johnson's house is European in conception, like a small classical palazzo, while the Farnsworth House is free, light, and airy in a way that makes it more American—despite that Mies had arrived in Chicago from Berlin only a decade earlier. Mies visited Johnson's glass house several times when they were working together on the Seagram Building. Johnson recounted that during his last visit, although Mies was supposed to stay overnight in the guesthouse, late in the evening he announced, "I'm not staying here tonight. Find me another place to stay." Johnson said that he didn't know what had set Mies off, whether it was a small disagreement that they had had earlier, or whether he simply didn't like the architecture.

Philip Johnson was an art collector and his house contained two freestanding works of art: Nicolas Poussin's landscape painting *Burial of Phocion* and a sculpture by Elie Nadelman. Mies, on the other hand, specified that no art was to be hung on the Primavera-paneled walls. My friend Martin Pawley spent a night in the Farnsworth House and recounted that the owner, Peter Palumbo, a London developer, respected the architect's wishes and hung paintings (I think they were by Paul Klee) only inside the bathroom. A sign asked guests to make sure to leave the bathroom door open after showering to avoid creating condensation that would damage the art. Martin described a memorable episode that occurred during his visit. The Fox River had overflowed its banks, as it did annually, and in the morning he was greeted by the sight of the butler bringing breakfast from the nearby main house (where Palumbo stayed) in a canoe. On that occasion, the terrace did double duty as a boat dock.

Of the Farnsworth House, Mies's biographer Franz Schulze observed that it "is more nearly a temple than a dwelling, and it rewards aesthetic contemplation before it fulfills domestic necessity." That's a scholarly way of saying that a glass house is not very practical. Privacy was not the problem, since the Farnsworth House, like Johnson's home, is in the country, without close neighbors. Nor was the absence of separate rooms an issue, as both houses had only one occupant. The chief practical drawback of these glass houses was environmental: with unshaded plate glass and no air-conditioning, the interiors overheated in the summer, and were difficult to keep warm in the winter.* Mies and Johnson made minimal provisions for ventilation: the Farnsworth House has two hopper windows at the bedroom end; the Johnson house has no openable windows at all, and is ventilated by opening one or more of the four doors. Since neither of the houses had insect screens, mosquitoes and flies were a problem, especially at night, when they were attracted by the light.

In the 1920s, Mies had designed a residence in Czechoslovakia—the Tugendhat House—in which large sections of a glass wall were lowered into the floor to open the living room to the outdoors, without the benefit of insect screens. Are mosquitoes, moths, and flies a lesser nuisance in Europe than in America? Perhaps, for woven-wire insect screens are an American invention that came into widespread use in the second half of the nineteenth century when the screened porch became a domestic fixture. The most elegant solution I have seen to accommodate insect screens in a modern house is in a Vero Beach, Florida, residence designed by Hugh Newell Jacobsen, in which windows and insect screens

---

*When Johnson's house got too hot or cold, he simply decamped to one of the other, more conventional, houses on his estate.

both slide out of sight into wall pockets, allowing the tall openings to be glazed, screened, or fully open.

There is no place for wall pockets in a glass house. Of course, Mies and Johnson could easily have installed screens but they faced an aesthetic problem: metal screens appear opaque compared with glass, which works against the sense of reflectivity that, as Mies frequently said, is a glass building's special quality. It is a measure of both architects' single-mindedness—or of their stubbornness?—that they refused to compromise. But that's the nature of a strong idea: it tends to impose its own rules. The architect must either observe those rules or start over.

Eventually, Mies grudgingly acceded to Edith Farnsworth's demand to screen the covered terrace of her house. Johnson, who occupied his house for almost sixty years until his death, never installed screen doors and simply put up with the inconvenience of bugs. "I'd rather sleep in Chartres Cathedral with the nearest john three blocks down the street," he once told a Yale class, "than I would in a Harvard house with back-to-back bathrooms." Does great architecture trump practicality? Johnson's statement is cavalier, but his point is a serious one. The experience of great architecture is rare and precious, while convenience is commonplace—and fungible. I live in an old stone house, designed by the Philadelphia architect H. Louis Duhring Jr. in 1907. In the last few years I have had moisture problems in one of the walls, the result of a stepped parapet that absorbs water in driving rain. The house gives me pleasure daily; the leaks require occasional patching and repainting. Life's imperfect.

Frank Lloyd Wright—a more practical architect than his reputation suggests—provided insect screens and screen doors in Fallingwater, the famous house that he designed for Edgar J. Kaufmann in the Allegheny Mountains of Pennsylvania. This house was also a weekend retreat, although it is functionally more demanding than Mies's and Johnson's glass houses, since it was occupied by a family of three with frequent guests.* Wright's novel idea was to situate the house on a large rock outcropping and cantilever the structure over a waterfall. He is said to have designed the house in one morning but he must have been thinking about it for a long time, as the overlapping terraces and interlocking spaces are anything but simple. The range of materials is limited—creamy-colored reinforced concrete with rounded edges, rough stone walls and floors, and steel window frames painted his favorite color, Cherokee Red. With this simple palette, the "old magus," as his biographer Brendan Gill called him, cast his spell.

The most famous concept house in history is an Italian Renaissance villa on the outskirts of Vicenza called the Villa Rotonda, after the circular domed room at its center—a miniature Pantheon. Most Renaissance architects used axially symmetrical plans—that is, if an imaginary line is drawn through the center of the house, all the rooms on the right mirror those on the left. Andrea Palladio went one step further and created *two* intersecting main axes, producing a square house with *four* identical fronts. Each front has a columned portico, and since the house is on a hilltop, each portico has a different view. Such a rigidly symmetrical plan is not as impractical as it sounds. Each of the eight rooms has direct access to the outside without interfering with whatever is going on in the domed chamber, which is the main reception room and can be reached from any of the four porticos.

Ever since the Villa Rotonda was built, it has been an inspiration for other architects. Vincenzo Scamozzi, Palladio's student who completed the villa after his master's death, was the first to have a go, designing the four-sided villa La Rocca on a dramatic hilltop site. The English architect Inigo Jones, who admired Palladio, designed several biaxial houses, though none was built. In

---

*Yet Fallingwater is not a large house. The enclosed area is only half again as large as the Farnsworth House.

Frank Lloyd Wright, Fallingwater, Bear Run, Pennsylvania, 1935

Andrea Palladio, Villa Rotonda, Vicenza, 1571

the eighteenth century there were four famous Rotonda-like British houses, including one by the Scottish architect Colen Campbell, and another, Chiswick House, designed by Lord Burlington, a devout Palladian. To this day, architects have continued to be fascinated by Palladio's idea, and there are recent examples in the United States and England, and an exceptionally faithful facsimile that stands among olive terraces in the Palestinian West Bank.

Architects playing variations on old themes are similar to composers and painters inspired by their predecessors: Brahms revisiting Haydn, Liszt and Rimsky-Korsakov returning to Bach, Picasso painting versions of Goya, and both Picasso and Francis Bacon revisiting Velázquez. Such re-creations are a nod to genius, and also a recognition that some creative ideas—a house with four fronts, for example—are rich enough to merit further exploration.

WINNING IDEAS

To be considered for high-profile commissions, architects—even celebrated architects—are often required to enter competitions, in effect, beauty contests. The first American architectural competition was held in 1792, to choose a design for the President's House in Washington, D.C. Competition juries generally consist of architects, although they may also include a representative of the client or sponsor. In this case, the judges were the three commissioners of the new federal city and the house's future occupant, President George Washington. Thomas Jefferson, a recognized authority in architectural matters, took second place with a design based on the Villa Rotonda, but the winner was James Hoban, an Irish-born architect who just happened to be a protégé of the president.

There were only nine entries in the President's House competition, but most modern competitions have hundreds of contestants. The judging of such competitions follows a well-established pattern. The members of the jury first quickly review all the submissions, with an eye on eliminating projects that have ignored competition requirements, are incomplete, are obviously flawed, or simply look uninteresting. Once the long list is winnowed down to a manageable number, the judges spend the remainder of their time studying these designs in detail to see how well they have resolved the competition requirements. The bulk of the time may be spent discussing the final two or three submissions. Some competitions are organized in stages, a group of entrants from the first stage being chosen to elaborate their projects in a second stage. The entries to open competitions are always anonymous, as opposed to closed or invited competitions, whose participants are known to the jury. Participants in invited competitions are generally paid a fee; participants in open competitions receive no remuneration, except for the winner and the runners-up.

The challenge in entering a competition is not how to devise a project that will stand up to close scrutiny—that goes without saying—but rather how to make the first cut; that is, how to stand out from the crowd. The best way to do this is to present the jury with an easy-to-understand, compelling solution, which is why competitions often result in buildings organized around a simple— and striking—idea. One of the most famous modern examples is the Sydney Opera House. The open competition, announced in 1956, attracted more than two hundred international entries. All the finalists addressed the complex functional requirements of two large performance halls (despite its name, this is really a multipurpose performing arts complex), but only the winner, Jørn Utzon, a Danish architect, provided a lyrical solution to the dramatic site, a spit of land jutting into Sydney Harbour. Utzon, thirty-eight, had built no major projects, but he had apprenticed with Alvar Aalto and Frank Lloyd Wright, and had absorbed their organic approach to design. While most of the finalists in the Sydney competition housed the two music halls in International Style boxes, Utzon enclosed them in a sculptural composition of billowing concrete shells.

The Sydney competition jury consisted of the head of the New South Wales public works department, a local architecture professor, and two prominent practitioners: Sir Leslie Martin, a respected British architect who had recently designed the Royal Festival Hall in London, and Eero Saarinen, then the leading member of the younger generation of American architects. Saarinen arrived late, after the first round of project selection had already been made. Leafing through the pile of rejects he pulled out Utzon's project and announced, "Gentlemen, here is the winner."

Saarinen was interested in concrete shell construction and had just started work on the TWA Terminal in New York, which may have inclined him to Utzon's unconventional design. Although the construction of the opera house would have a troubled history, leading to cost overruns, compromises to the design, and the architect's resignation, Utzon's idea of a collection of sail-like forms

Jørn Utzon, Sydney Opera House, Sydney, 1973

on a podium has been vindicated, and the building has become one of the great architectural icons of the twentieth century.*

The story of Saarinen imposing his will on a jury is not apocryphal. The following year he was invited to judge an international competition for a new city hall in Toronto. The other jury members were the well-known Italian modernist architect Ernesto Rogers; Ned Pratt of the respected Vancouver firm Thompson, Berwick & Pratt; Sir William Holford, a planning expert from London; and Gordon Stephenson, a British-born planner living in Toronto. Once again Saarinen arrived late—a day and a half after the others had started to winnow down the 520 entrants to the 8 who would continue on to a second stage. Their choices were boxy, mostly low-rise buildings. Once again Saarinen asked to look at the discarded projects, and as before, an unusual design caught his eye: two curved high-rise slabs enfolding a circular council chamber. He convinced the jury to advance the project to the second stage. The two British planners remained skeptical, but Saarinen's forceful advocacy convinced Rogers and Pratt and the project was declared the winner. Viljo Revell's design has functional drawbacks—splitting a municipal bureaucracy in two makes little organizational sense—but the building and its popular plaza have become a Toronto icon.

Architects are ambivalent about competitions. On a practical level, competitions are extremely expensive: entering a large competition can cost millions of dollars. More important, competitions oblige the architect to work in a vacuum. In later life, I. M. Pei refused to enter competitions, since he considered that the best architecture could emerge only from a considered dialogue between architect and client. Competition juries often favor the dramatic over the thoughtful, the simplistic over the well-resolved, the eye-catching over the subtle. Buildings such as memorials,

*Utzon, too, was vindicated when he received the Pritzker Prize, and when the opera house was declared a World Heritage Site, although he never returned to Australia to see the finished building.

Viljo Revell, Toronto City Hall, Toronto, 1965

where a simple idea can carry the whole project, lend themselves to competitions; on the other hand, when the program or the site requires a nuanced solution, a single-idea building often falls flat. Buildings based on a single idea, like the Pantheon, can be wonderful, but an idea that is intended mainly to catch the attention of a jury often proves one-dimensional when the project is actually built. Nevertheless, the public favors competitions, since they provide an opportunity for young talent to be recognized in a field that tends to privilege age and experience. Clients like competitions, since they provide an opportunity to choose between several designs—and several architects—while fund-raisers use competitions as a way to raise public interest in a building project. Everyone loves a horse race—except, perhaps, the horses.

WHAT IS AN
AFRICAN AMERICAN MUSEUM?

In July 2008, the Smithsonian Institution announced that it was looking for an architect to design a $500 million National Museum of African American History and Culture, to be built on the Mall in Washington, D.C. The selection process involved two steps. First, interested architects, or teams of architects, submitted their professional qualifications and demonstrated experience in museum design, and then the Smithsonian selected six firms to participate in a design competition. This type of closed competition is increasingly common, as clients seek design options but want to avoid the practical and financial problems that can occur when open competitions are won by neophytes, or by small firms that do not have the resources to execute large, demanding commissions. Nevertheless, small or young practices may enter closed competitions by teaming up with larger, more established firms.

The Smithsonian's sixteen-page Request for Qualifications, or RFQ, included a description of what was expected of the winning project. Most of the text was the sort of boilerplate that can be found in any competition brief: "The commission will demonstrate the value of a true integrated design that balances aesthetics, cost, constructability, and reliability; while simultaneously creating an environmentally responsible and superior place for staff and visitors." There was one requirement that caught my eye, however. "Detail in writing how you will infuse your participation and vision for this project with an appreciation of African American History and Culture." This suggested that the Smithsonian was looking for a special museum whose design in some way reflected its particular function.

Traditionally, museums on the Mall have striven merely to be good architecture. When the industrialist Charles Lang Freer commissioned Charles Adams Platt to design a museum for his magnificent Orientalist collection, all he wanted was a handsome building—which in 1918 meant an Italian Renaissance palazzo. When the Smithsonian engaged Gyo Obata to design the National Air and Space Museum, it instructed him to respect the other buildings on the Mall, and he designed four simple cubes connected by glass atria, and even matched the Tennessee marble of the cubes to the National Gallery across the Mall. The first building to radically depart from this respectful approach was the Hirshhorn Museum, which opened in the mid-1970s. Gordon Bunshaft of Skidmore, Owings & Merrill designed a striking windowless concrete drum that Ada Louise Huxtable compared to a bunker or an oil tank, "lacking only gun emplacements or an Exxon sign." When Douglas Cardinal was commissioned to design the National Museum of the American Indian, he, too, opted for novelty: "I wanted to make sure that the building was not just a continuation of the Greco-Roman style in Washington." There was little danger of that, since Cardinal's idiosyncratic style is wildly expressionistic. "I looked at the natural forms in the Americas and that was the basis for the building," he explained. The result is a curvy design that seeks—somewhat ham-handedly—to embody the spirit of the Great Plains and the continent's aboriginal peoples. No one would mistake it for a Greco-Roman building.

After Cardinal's self-consciously different museum, it was obvious that an African American museum had to express something unique, but what? The ancestors of many black Americans came from central and western Africa, but, after all, most Americans come from somewhere else. African Americans first settled in the South, but is Atlanta really more representative of black culture than Chicago or New York? Patterned kente cloth has become a popular symbol of African cultural heritage, but what does this product of Ghana and the Ivory Coast really have to do with black America? Moreover, although the particularities of black culture are highly visible in music, the arts, religion, and the civil rights movement, there is no identifiable black architecture.

Finding a compelling image for an African American museum would be a challenge.

Twenty-two architectural firms responded to the Smithsonian's RFQ, and the six teams selected to compete intentionally spanned the architectural gamut, from stars to up-and-comers. The international stars were Norman Foster and Moshe Safdie. Antoine Predock was less well-known, but had a proven reputation as an original designer. Pei Cobb Freed, founded by I. M. Pei, was the architectural equivalent of a white-shoe firm, solid and dependable. The two up-and-comers were the New York–based Diller Scofidio + Renfro, better known for theoretical writings and art installations than for buildings, and a largely African American team whose chief designer was a young British-Ghanaian architect, David Adjaye. The six finalists were each given a stipend of fifty thousand dollars, a detailed list of the museum's requirements, and two months to develop a design.

In April 2009, before the winner was announced, the six sets of drawings and models were exhibited in the Smithsonian's headquarters, the Castle. I was curious to see how the different competitors dealt with the challenging site, which is next to the country's greatest national memorial, the Washington Monument. And how they handled the problem of creating an African American icon—whatever that meant.

Foster + Partners' submission struck me as the most original, a coiled oval resembling a giant mollusk, with a spiraling ramp (shades of Wright's Guggenheim) that rose through the galleries and ended in a dramatic framed view of the Washington Monument. The glass-roofed space in the center of the oval contained a replica of a slave ship, a key part of the museum's exhibition program. Working with the celebrated French landscape architect Michel Desvigne, Foster covered the roof with terraces and gardens, and created a sunken entrance court that reduced the apparent bulk of the building. This was a classic competition entry: dramatic, easy to understand, and resolving several problems with a flourish. The mollusk-like drum was striking, and made an interesting bookend to Pei's triangular East Building of the National Gallery at the other end of the Mall. If there was a drawback to Foster's *parti* it was that the windowless form had a somewhat forbidding appearance, and bore a resemblance to the unfortunate Hirshhorn Museum.

Moshe Safdie's design was a large boxy building bisected by a gently curving, wood-lined atrium, likewise oriented to the Washington Monument. Safdie had successfully used a similar framing device in the remarkable Holocaust History Museum at Yad Vashem in Jerusalem, but in Washington he faltered. The view from the atrium was framed by two giant organic forms. But the abstract shapes were insufficient to enliven what was a rather pedestrian building. Moreover, the forms appeared whimsical and arbitrary, assertive but hard to decipher—the prow of a ship, a cracked urn, or giant bone fragments?

The Albuquerque-based Antoine Predock is an architectural maverick sometimes compared with Wright, and is known for designing striking buildings in a highly personal style.* For this competition he pulled out all the stops, creating an animated composition of jagged forms, sheets of water, dramatic interiors, and exotic materials (mica-schist quartzite, Mpingo wood). The building looked as if it had been forced out of the ground by a violent earthquake. I sensed that Predock was struggling to discover an architectural language suited to an African American museum, but while I could imagine his tectonic forms in a natural setting—a sandy desert or a rocky mesa—they seemed wrong for the National Mall.

Henry Cobb of Pei Cobb Freed designed the National Constitution Center in Philadelphia, a building that I admire. On the face of it, he would seem to have an inside track in the

---

*In 2006, Predock was awarded the American Institute of Architects Gold Medal, the AIA's highest honor; Foster was the only other competition entrant to have received this recognition.

competition; after all, his partners had designed two outstanding buildings nearby: I. M. Pei, the East Building of the National Gallery, and James Ingo Freed, the National Holocaust Memorial Museum.* But Cobb's design for the African American museum—a limestone-covered square box from which emerged a curvy free-form shape of glass—was disappointing. It was a banal statement about neoclassical Washington (the box) meeting the present day (the glass curves). Twenty years earlier, the Canadian architect Arthur Erickson had tried to combine classical and modernist motifs in the Canadian embassy on Pennsylvania Avenue; it hadn't worked for him, and it didn't work any better for Cobb.

Competitions can sometimes uncover new talent, as was the case with Utzon in Sydney and Revell in Toronto. Elizabeth Diller and her husband, Ricardo Scofidio (now joined by Charles Renfro), had a reputation for avant-garde projects, but at the time of the competition they had built only one major building, the recently completed Institute for Contemporary Art on the Boston waterfront, a forceful cantilevered form hovering over the water.† Their design for the African American museum was equally audacious. The architects are known for their intellectual approach to design, and their entry included a W.E.B. Du Bois quote on the "two warring souls, two thoughts, two unreconciled strivings" of blacks in America. The two warring souls were represented by a double-curved, cable-supported glass skin draped over a limestone-covered box that appeared to be melting. Such bulging organic forms are sometimes referred to as "blob architecture." Blobs look exciting in computer-generated drawings, but the rather crude model on display at the Smithsonian gave little assurance that such an eccentric building should—or indeed could—be built.

---

*Pei retired from Pei Cobb Freed in 1990; Freed died in 2005.
†For the African American museum competition, Diller Scofidio + Renfro teamed up with Philadelphia-based KlingStubbins, a very large architecture and engineering firm with several branches, including in Washington, D.C.

The least-well-known team in the competition was also the largest. It consisted of J. Max Bond Jr., who was often referred to as the dean of African American architects; the Durham, North Carolina–based Freelon Group, the largest minority-owned architectural firm in the country; and SmithGroup, a large architecture engineering firm with offices nationwide; as well as the London-based Adjaye Associates.* Although Freelon and Bond had developed the original museum program for the Smithsonian, giving them an inside track, and SmithGroup had been associated with the construction of the National Museum of the American Indian, neither they nor Freelon had as impressive a design track record as Foster, Safdie, and Predock. That was where David Adjaye came in. The forty-two-year-old architect had established his own firm in London only eight years earlier, but his minimalist modern designs and his glamorous clientele (he had designed homes for several movie stars) had already propelled him into the international limelight. He also brought proven competition-winning abilities to the team, having won several international competitions, including the Nobel Peace Center in Oslo and, most recently, the Museum of Contemporary Art in Denver, where he had bested several leading architects, including Predock.

Adjaye's design was the most conventional of the six: a box sitting on top of a rectangular podium. The limestone podium contained the lobby, while the main galleries were in the box. The box was really a building within a building, since the glass galleries were sheathed in a perforated bronze skin that would reflect different colors during the day, and act as a beacon at night. No curves, no contortions, no architectural gymnastics.

The reaction to the six designs was mixed. The critic of *The Washington Post* found Adjaye's design "too understated," and wrote that only the Diller Scofidio + Renfro submission "rises above the

---

*Bond died during the competition.

Freelon Adjaye Bond/SmithGroup, National Museum of African American History and Culture, Washington, D.C., 2015

rest." Bloggers had a field day, some picking one entry, some another, many grumpily dismissing all six. Meanwhile, the competition jury began its deliberations. There were ten members. Three were Smithsonian board members and four were associated with the museum in some capacity; one was the director of design at the National Endowment of the Arts; and only two were architects—Adèle Santos, dean of the school of architecture at MIT, and the *Boston Globe* architecture critic Robert Campbell.* The jury was notable for the absence of a big-name practitioner. "I've found that a strong personality greatly compromises the voice of the other jurors," says Don Stastny, an architect and the competition's

---

*Ten is a large jury. Paul Cret, who entered, and won, many competitions—and served on many juries—believed that the ideal jury was three persons; more than five he considered a "crowd." Preferably all, or at least a majority, should be architects, he wrote, "because they alone have the training required to balance the merits of various solutions of a problem."

professional adviser. He believes that a diverse, balanced jury is beneficial to the process and lends greater weight to the final decision. Evidently, there would be no Saarinen moment in this competition.

"I wanted all the judges to feel free to question and debate the options," Lonnie G. Bunch, director of the new museum, told me. Bunch chaired the jury, but he intentionally absented himself from the committee that had picked the six finalists. "I told the selection committee I wanted an array of architects, not simply variations on a theme, since I wanted to learn about the architectural alternatives," he said. It was Bunch who had inserted the statement about "an appreciation of African American History and Culture" into the RFQ. "I didn't know what the museum should look like," he said. "But I wanted to hear how the different architects would respond to that statement."

According to Bunch, four issues dominated the jury's discussion: the architects' vision for an African American museum; how the makeup of the team reflected this vision; how the building related to the Mall, especially the Washington Monument; and the chemistry between the architects and the museum. Bunch called three of the entries "stellar," though he declined to name them. The judges were drawn to the Freelon Adjaye Bond submission. "We liked the way this design related to the Washington Monument," said Bunch. "Although Adjaye had not done anything this big before, we were reassured by the presence of SmithGroup." It took three days to reach a decision, although Bunch waited a week before making the announcement. "I wanted to give the jury a chance to sleep on it. I didn't want anyone to be unsure, or on the fence." The vote for the Freelon Adjaye Bond project was unanimous.

At the beginning of the competition, the jury heard verbal presentations from each of the six teams, and when the designs were complete, each team had a further chance to explain its project in detail. "Adjaye was very good at articulating how his design captured our vision," said Bunch. "He talked about the angles on the building and showed a slide of Southern women in church, with their arms raised at a similar angle. I found that compelling." In other words, Adjaye directly addressed a key question of the competition: "What would make this particular building African American?"

Traditionally, buildings have conveyed meaning though figural decoration, as several federal buildings in Washington, D.C., demonstrate: the Pensions Building (today the National Building Museum), built after the Civil War to house the bureau that disbursed pensions to Union veterans, is circled by a frieze depicting soldiers and sailors; the pediments of the U.S. Post Office Department Building include allegorical sculpture referring to the mail system; and the Department of Agriculture occupies a building with bas-relief panels depicting animals native to the United States as well as a woman holding a peach and a bunch of grapes.

As a committed modernist, Adjaye eschewed figural decoration, but he found other ways to convey aspects of African American history and culture. On the Mall side, he placed a large portico, modern in design but recalling the porches of Southern houses; the perforated patterns in the bronze skin were inspired by New Orleans cast-iron fretwork; most strikingly, the box that enclosed the galleries was in the shape of a corona, or crown, a form that resembled superimposed beveled baskets and was based on Yoruba tribal art. At the same time, the abstract shapes remind me of Brancusi's *Endless Column*. In other words, the design manages to be both primal and modern, pictorial and abstract, and crafted as well as technological. These ideas resonated with Bunch. "I was looking for an architectural equivalent of spirituality and uplift, of understanding the heritage," he told me.

Over the next two years, the Freelon Adjaye Bond proposal underwent several modifications. Following numerous reviews by local and federal agencies, including the Commission of Fine Arts, the National Park Service, and the Advisory Council on Historic Preservation, the building took a simpler form—more than half of the functions moved underground, and the podium disappeared. But the porch remained, as well as the corona, which was enlarged and assumed added visual importance. This is common in a competition-winning design, when subsequent dialogue with the client—heretofore absent—can refine a design. Practical considerations also intrude: the exciting sketch has to be turned into reality—it has to be built. The important question is whether in the process the design is improved or merely diluted. In the case of the African American museum, the initial idea proved to have staying power.

HEDGEHOGS AND FOXES

The philosopher Isaiah Berlin wrote a famous essay based on a saying attributed to the ancient Greek poet Archilochus: "The fox knows many things, but the hedgehog knows one big thing." Berlin was referring to writers and thinkers—he characterized Plato, Nietzsche, and Proust as hedgehogs, Shakespeare, Goethe, and Pushkin as foxes—but the metaphor applies to architects, too.

Dominique Perrault is definitely a hedgehog. In 1989, he won an international competition to design the Bibliothèque Nationale de France, the last of President François Mitterand's Grands Projets. Among the almost 250 entrants were the Pritzker Prize winners James Stirling and Richard Meier, and the future Pritzker laureates Fumihiko Maki, Álvaro Siza, and Rem Koolhaas, as well as the relatively unknown Perrault. His striking design consisted of four twenty-five-story all-glass towers sitting on top of a large podium. Perrault was an admirer of Mies van der Rohe, and the idea had a Miesian simplicity: book stacks in the towers, public reading rooms and research facilities in the podium. The towers, L-shaped in plan, resembled four half-open books. Knowledge exposed for all to see, it was a compelling image.

Dominique Perrault, Bibliothèque Nationale, Paris, 1996

The problem is that Perrault's Big Idea is not so much simple as simplistic. The idea of vertical stacks has precedents in modern architecture: in the 1930s, the great Belgian architect Henry van de Velde designed a twenty-story library tower for the University of Ghent, and in America Paul Cret designed a thirty-one-story tower of books for the University of Texas at Austin. But both Cret's and Van de Velde's towers were largely solid, with occasional slotted windows. Perrault's all-glass book stacks raised the ire of librarians, who complained about exposing books to full sunlight. The solution was to add internal wooden shutters, which solved the light problem but severely compromised the transparency that constituted the core of Perrault's *parti*. Eventually, some of the books were located in the podium, and administrative offices took their place. The completed building received decidedly mixed reviews. Although the underground research reading rooms look into a landscaped court, many of the gloomy public spaces are basement-like. Just as the Toronto City Hall bureaucracy had to split itself into two, the French library's collection is divided into four. "The decision to reclassify all knowledge because of an architect's design caused a commotion in French educational and intellectual circles," observed one information specialist. The library—one of the largest in the world—was popularly known as TGB, *très grande bibliothèque*, a play on the acronym TGV (*train à grande vitesse*), but wags said the initials really stood for *très grande bêtise*, or Very Big Mistake.

If Perrault is a hedgehog, the architect of the new British Library, the late Colin St. John Wilson, was a fox. In 1962, he and Sir Leslie Martin had been commissioned to expand the British Museum Library. The project dragged on, and during subsequent changes of government the program was enlarged to become a full-fledged national library, and the site was moved from Bloomsbury to King's Cross. By the time that construction started in 1982, Martin had retired and Wilson was on his third design. His low-key architectural approach, influenced by the romantic modernism of Alvar Aalto, struck many as old-fashioned compared with the contemporary work of high-tech architects such as Richard Rogers and Norman Foster. The design was roundly criticized; modernists disliked the library, which was largely brick (to harmonize with a Victorian Gothic neighbor), because they found it too staid, and traditionalists like Prince Charles, who unfairly compared it to the "assembly hall of an academy for secret police," found it too modern. Wilson became so unpopular that his firm was obliged to go into liquidation for lack of work. These negative perceptions changed after the building opened.* The interior spaces, bright and airy, proved both functionally efficient and extremely popular with users. "The British Library works rather well," wrote Hugh Pearman, one of the few British critics

---

*The vindicated Wilson was knighted the year the building opened. He died in 2007.

Colin St. John Wilson, British Library, London, 1997

who had defended Wilson's design. "It's a congenial place to sit and study."

Wilson's hero Aalto was another fox. The Villa Mairea, for example, a large country house that he designed in the 1930s, is considered one of his greatest works, the Finnish equivalent in its own way of Fallingwater, although one would be hard put to find a view of the villa that is as iconic as the image of Wright's terraces hovering above a waterfall. From the exterior, the reticent Villa Mairea exhibits a blend of white-box modernism, handcrafted details, and a rambling casualness. The kidney-shaped entrance canopy is supported by a cluster of straight and angled wooden poles, some of them lashed together with cord. The white walls are lime-washed brick, rather than hard-edged plaster, which most European modernists used at that time.

The main living space demonstrates Aalto's quirky brand of modernism, which combines novelty with tradition. The living room, the dining room, and an art gallery—the clients collected modern paintings—are combined in a single multipurpose space, the library being defined by movable bookcases. All this is in the name of modernist flexibility. At the same time, the corner is occupied by a traditional Finnish raised-hearth fireplace, the ceiling is red pine, some of the tubular steel columns are wrapped with caning, and others are covered with beech slats. Although this is a rather large house, it has a bourgeois sense of unpretentious comfort, which sets it apart from Le Corbusier's dramatic villas, or Mies's luxurious minimalism. Aalto's aim is to create an environment that offers its occupants many small pleasures, rather than to impress the first-time visitor.

Louis I. Kahn was Aalto's almost exact contemporary, likewise born in a northern Baltic country—Estonia. Both men had been schooled in the techniques of the École des Beaux-Arts, and both rejected historical styles as their careers developed. Yet here the similarities end. Aalto's romantic modernism was rooted in the region where he lived, while Kahn's modernism aspired to be universal. Aalto was attracted to vivid colors, rich textures, and handcrafted details, while Kahn worked with a restricted and rather severe palette. Aalto designed everything; he was responsible for lamps, glassware, fabrics, and furniture—his easy chairs and stools are modern classics. Kahn designed no memorable furniture, and he tended to use generic pot lights and glass globes as lighting fixtures, for he was more interested in space and daylight than in the paraphernalia of everyday life.

The two architects' careers developed differently. Aalto was a prodigy, opening an office immediately after graduating from architecture school, and finding his own voice by the time he was thirty, while Kahn, a slow starter, bloomed as an architect only when he was in his fifties. Aalto was prolific, effortlessly churning out one design after another; Kahn worked slowly, almost painfully.* And while many of Aalto's designs are variations on similar themes, each of Kahn's buildings has its own unique character. Kahn did share one important quality with Aalto. He, too, was a fox, rarely designing buildings that depended on a single idea. His last project, the Yale Center for British Art in New Haven, is an unglamorous four-story box with two skylit interior courts. Kahn spent a year and a half designing the project and exploring several options, so the apparent simplicity was actually the result of a long development.

The Center for British Art is on Chapel Street. The eye is drawn first to a dramatic building designed by Paul Rudolph in the 1960s; big, rough, concrete, and monumental, it houses the school of architecture. It's possible to walk past the center without noticing it, for while Rudolph's operatic building is singing at the top of its voice, Kahn's architecture barely rises above a murmur. The exposed concrete frame is filled with a quilt of glass and matte stainless steel panels. Most architects use stainless steel in a way that suggests either mechanical perfection or luxury; in Kahn's hands the material appears almost homely, its surface variegated by acid-washing and the weather. "On a gray day, it will look like a moth; on a sunny day, a butterfly," Kahn told his skeptical client.

The lower floor of the center is taken up by shops, and the museum entrance is tucked unobtrusively into a corner. The entrance leads to the smaller of the two courts. Here, the same exposed concrete frame is filled with panels of creamy white oak; it's like being inside a beautifully built cabinet. The tall space is washed by natural light from a large skylight, and openings surrounding the court allow glimpses of the galleries. The building

*Aalto entered scores of architectural competitions—and won twenty-five. Kahn participated in only ten competitions, none of which he won.

Louis I. Kahn, Yale Center for British Art, Yale University, 1974

reveals itself gradually. The galleries, with linen-covered walls and strips of travertine on the floor, recall a residence rather than a conventional museum. The domestic scale is in keeping with the works in the collection, which were originally created for English country houses, and the paintings in the second court hang floor-to-ceiling, as in a traditional hall. This space is dominated by a monumental concrete silo that contains the main staircase. According to Kahn's biographer Carter Wiseman, the architect had been impressed by the large sculptural fireplaces in English manor houses, and the chimneylike form curiously adds to the domestic atmosphere of the court, which has comfortable sofas arranged on a large Oriental rug. The art critic Robert Hughes described the center as an ideal setting for experiencing art, "a building without gimmicks or stylistic narcissism, low-key but explicit, whose pale concrete, blond wood and natural linen wall coverings provide a strictly subordinate background to the paintings."

Every year since 1971, the American Institute of Architects honors "an American architectural landmark that has stood the test of time." Only one building is named each year, and it must be at least twenty-five years old. Unlike design awards, which are sometimes bestowed on buildings before they are even built, this prize recognizes that the best way to judge a building is in the fullness of time. Many a new building has made a splash, only to sink into well-deserved obscurity over the years, either because of functional drawbacks or because an idea that seemed compelling at the time turned out to be a dud. The 2005 AIA Twenty-Five Year Award went to the Yale Center for British Art, which the judges called "one of the quietest expressions of a great building ever seen." It was the fifth Kahn building so honored. The only other architect with five awards is Eero Saarinen.* The power of ideas lies at the heart of both men's work. For Saarinen, it was usually a single idea, which emerged from a detailed analysis of the building program, an examination of all the alternatives, and a distillation of the solutions into a single concept. "You have to put all your eggs in one basket," he once said. "Everything in the building has to really support that idea." Kahn's buildings, on the other hand, generally incorporated many ideas, arrived at after an introspective process that resembled a philosophical search rather than an architectural analysis. Characteristically, he explained himself in an oblique fashion. "You don't know what the building is, really, unless you have a belief behind the building, a belief in its identity in the way of life of man." Once he discovered that identity, the architecture would follow. If this sounds a little like a *parti*, well, Kahn attended a Beaux-Arts school in the 1920s, and in later life he often returned to its rigorous principles.

*The other Kahn buildings honored were: the Yale Art Gallery, the Salk Institute, Phillips Exeter Academy Library, and the Kimbell Art Museum. The Saarinen buildings were: Crow Island School, General Motors Technical Center, Dulles Airport, Gateway Arch, and the John Deere & Company headquarters.

2

THE SETTING

The first American exhibition on the Bauhaus was mounted by the Museum of Modern Art in 1938 in a temporary gallery in Rockefeller Center, and it attracted record-breaking crowds—a news photograph shows Frank Lloyd Wright at the opening, chatting with Walter Gropius, who organized the show. What they said to each other is not recorded. The exhibit included photographs, graphics, textiles, furniture, and lighting fixtures produced by teachers and students of the famous German design school. At the entrance was a model of that icon of modernism, the Bauhaus building in Dessau. The large-scale model included details such as balconies and windows, but provided no information about its setting, and gave the impression that the pinwheeling building had been conceived as a huge Constructivist sculpture. In fact, Gropius, who had been formally trained at the Königliche Technische Hochschule in Berlin, designed the building to fit into the Dessau street grid: the long workshop faced the town square, a vertical block anchored the street corner, while the bridge-like administrative wing formed a gateway for the street that led from the train station into the square. In other words, although the Bauhaus building had abstract sculptural qualities, it also responded to its setting. This essential difference is clouded when a building is presented as if it were a freestanding artwork, as it was in the MoMA show.*

Architectural photography also treats buildings as objects. Like a studio portrait, an architectural photograph includes only as much of the background as is needed to flatter its subject; anything offensive—a telephone pole, a stop sign, or an overhead wire—is cropped out. As a result, if your first encounter with a building is on the printed page, seeing the real thing can come as something of a surprise. The first architecture book I owned as a student was Frank Lloyd Wright's *A Testament*, a large album with a white cloth cover and the architect's trademark red square in the top left-hand corner. Wright's flowery prose didn't make much of an impression, but I admired his work, particularly the Robie House, a photograph of whose long brick façade stretched over two pages. When I finally had the opportunity to see the building, I was disappointed to discover that this "prairie house" was actually in Hyde Park, an urban neighborhood on Chicago's South Side. The house was on a shallow lot, very close to the sidewalk, with a walled service yard and virtually no garden, and it was surrounded by neighboring houses and apartment buildings, instead of by a natural landscape as in Richard Nickel's lyrical photograph.

FITTING IN

Paintings and sculptures can be autonomous works of art, but architecture is always part of a particular place. It is difficult to fully appreciate Kahn's design for the Yale Center for British Art, for example, without knowing that it stands across the street from the Yale University Art Gallery, a 1920s Gothic Revival building by Egerton Swartwout that includes a 1950s addition by Kahn

---

*A similarly abstract model was featured in MoMA's 2009 Bauhaus retrospective. *Plus ça change.*

himself. The Yale Center plays off Swartwout's richly ornamented stone façade, and is a metallic counterpart to the blank brick wall of Kahn's addition. Another important piece of information: Chapel Street forms a town/gown boundary, with the Yale campus on one side, and New Haven on the other. The center is part of the latter, which may explain why Kahn made the exterior so low-key (the ground floor contains shops). Or maybe he just chose to play David to Paul Rudolph's nearby Yale School of Architecture Goliath.

The setting that presented itself to Kahn consists of thoughtfully designed college buildings on an orderly street animated by the bustle of university life. This is very different from the surroundings facing Frank Gehry when he was making his reputation as an architectural maverick in the 1980s in Los Angeles. His residential commissions were small houses on cramped lots in Venice Beach, not villas in Bel Air. His settings were a scruffy mixture of popular styles, garish colors, and humdrum materials, hardly the ideal backdrop for conventional modernist buildings. But Gehry was an unconventional modernist. He saw what the leading American architects, mostly Easterners—Richard Meier, Michael Graves, Peter Eisenman—were doing and he was intent on going his own way. His surprising, but in hindsight perfectly sensible, response to his surroundings was to join the party. "Anything you put in Venice is absorbed in about thirty seconds," he said. "Nothing separates itself from that context. There's so much going on—so much chaos." Instead of elegant refinement and pristine design, Gehry's early projects explore rough materials, vivid colors, and unruly forms. A beach house has a pergola made out of what appear to be pieces of a telephone pole; a family house in the San Fernando Valley is finished in tar-paper shingles; a twin house in Venice has sections of exposed wood framing and walls of galvanized corrugated metal and unpainted plywood. This was a matter of limited budgets, but it was also a way for Gehry to deal with the brassy environment of Los Angeles.

Frank O. Gehry & Associates, Chiat\Day Advertising, Venice, California, 1991

Even when the commissions were larger, such as a three-story office building for the Chiat\Day advertising agency, the setting—Venice's Main Street—was a raucous mix of strip malls, garden apartments, and parking lots. Gehry responded to the small scale of the street by breaking his building into two parts, one almost banal, the other striking, with a projecting roof supported by a cluster of angled, copper-clad braces. The most unusual feature of the building came about by accident. As Gehry told the story, he was discussing a model of the project with his client, who said he wanted an art component in the building. Two years earlier, Gehry had worked with Claes Oldenburg and Coosje van Bruggen on a tower in the form of a giant pair of binoculars, and he still had the maquette on his desk. "I pushed it in front of the central shape as I was describing to Jay Chiat the sculptural qualities the center needed," Gehry said. "It worked."

Surroundings can also be an inspiration instead of a constraint. Alvar Aalto's Villa Mairea is one of several residences in a compound belonging to a prominent industrialist family, located in a dense pine forest in western Finland. The setting moved the architect to use wooden poles throughout the house. Poles support the entrance canopy, surround the staircase, and are used as balcony railings—at a time when modernist railings were always made out of steel pipes. Even the structural columns in the living room recall tree trunks in a forest. Rather than set the house in opposition to its natural setting, as Mies did with the Farnsworth House, Aalto used the surroundings to inform his architecture.

Another building that finds inspiration in its setting is the National Gallery of Canada in Ottawa, designed by Moshe Safdie. The site, a spit of land overlooking the Ottawa River, is dominated by nearby Parliament Hill and the federal parliament complex, a mid-nineteenth-century collection of Victorian High Gothic buildings with animated roofs, towers, and spires. The most striking structure on Parliament Hill that is visible from the National Gallery is the polygonal parliamentary library, which is modeled on a medieval chapter house, complete with flying

Moshe Safdie & Associates, National Gallery of Canada, Ottawa, 1988

buttresses, spiky finials, and a conical roof. Responding to this view, Safdie created a modern counterpart to the library, a tall, pinnacled steel-and-glass pavilion housing a combination lobby and gala space. This daring architectural gesture works on several levels. It provides a memorable image for the large, sprawling museum. It adds to the skyline of downtown Ottawa, which includes the parliament buildings, the nearby spires of Notre-Dame Basilica, the picturesque roofscape of the Château Laurier hotel, and the tall copper roof of Ernest Cormier's Supreme Court. Most important, it provides a visual link between two national institutions, one political, the other cultural.

The surroundings of the proposed African American museum in Washington, D.C., include no obvious architectural touchstone, for while the national capital is often characterized as a white classical city, the museums that line the National Mall are a remarkably motley group. There are several classical buildings: the somewhat pompous Museum of Natural History, the ponderous Department of Agriculture, John Russell Pope's magnificent National Gallery, and Charles Adams Platt's graceful Freer Gallery. On the other hand, James Renwick Jr.'s red-sandstone Smithsonian Castle is Gothic Revival, and Adolf Cluss's eccentric polychrome brick Arts and Industries Building defies easy classification. The modern buildings are no less varied: Pei's minimalist East Building stands opposite Cardinal's Gaudiesque American Indian museum; Bunshaft's drumlike Hirshhorn is next to the generic glass boxes of Obata's Air and Space Museum, and the neighbor of the future African American museum is the Museum of American History, one of the last projects of the venerable McKim, Mead & White firm, trying to be modern and not succeeding very well.

How did the architects in the competition for the African American museum deal with this variety? Antoine Predock obviously decided that the architectural potpourri gave him license to add his own voice to the mix, so did Diller Scofidio + Renfro.

Norman Foster opted for a distinctive circular form, echoing the Hirshhorn. Moshe Safdie and Henry Cobb related the general mass of their buildings to the boxy Museum of American History. David Adjaye described his design as a "hinge" between the informal grounds of the Washington Monument and the formal Mall landscape. He responded to his immediate surroundings by designing a square monumental form; at the same time he ensured a distinctive presence by making the corona bronze rather than marble or limestone. He also did something rather cunning; the angle of the beveled corona matches the angle of the capstone of the Washington Monument, establishing what architects call a "conversation" between the two structures.

Few buildings are as difficult to insert into an urban setting as a concert hall. Unlike a museum, which is a collection of rooms of various sizes that can be arranged in different ways, the shape of a concert hall is dictated by acoustics, sight lines, and, in the case of an opera house, extensive backstage facilities. Nevertheless, the architect must fit what is essentially a very large windowless box into its surroundings.

Gehry's 1988 competition-winning design for the Walt Disney Concert Hall created a memorable image of the building, which stood in a relatively nondescript part of downtown Los Angeles, by breaking down the hall into a series of giant alcove-like rooms focused on the orchestra. This neatly solved the problem of the exterior by creating an irregular form. At this point in his career, Gehry tended to design buildings that looked like jumbled collections of disparate volumes, and Disney Hall was no exception: the auditorium stood next to a domed greenhouse-like lobby and several smaller shapes. While the competition unfolded, the orchestra's building committee toured the world's leading concert halls. The committee, and the conductor Esa-Pekka Salonen, were particularly taken by Tokyo's Suntory Hall and its vineyard style of seating in which the audience occupies "terraces" that surround the orchestra. The acoustician who had worked on Suntory, Yasuhisa Toyota, was invited to join the Disney team. Gehry set aside his competition design and, working with Toyota, started over from scratch. They concluded that, for acoustical reasons, a vineyard-style hall should reside in a concrete box approximately 130 by 200 feet, with angled walls and roof. To soften the external visual impact of the ten-story-tall volume, Gehry wrapped it with sail-like shapes. Wrapping the building camouflaged the auditorium, and the space between the wrapping and the box accommodated the lobby, a café, an informal performance space, and outdoor terraces. The loose wrapping also left space for skylights, bringing natural light into the lobby as well as into the hall itself. The architect's early sketches show the wrapping as a flurry of wavy lines, lending credence to the story that he designed the hall by crumpling a piece of paper.* "That's mythology. I wish I could do that, but it's not true," he told an interviewer. "If only it were that easy. The Disney Hall was never a crumpled piece of paper. The fact is I'm an opportunist. I'll take materials around me, materials on my table, and work with them as I'm searching for an idea that works." Sometimes the opportunism backfires. The Experience Music Project museum in Seattle, which opened in 2000, is a motley collection of multicolored forms that are said by Gehry to have been inspired by the bodies of Stratocaster guitars. But when I saw the building twelve years later, the crowd streaming to visit the neighboring Space Needle hardly gave the idiosyncratic museum a second glance.

One of the stated purposes of Disney Hall was to galvanize the long-awaited development of downtown Los Angeles. Toronto already has a thriving downtown with dynamic street life, cultural institutions, and a large residential population. Thus, the

---

*The source of the crumpled-paper story was a guest appearance by Gehry on an episode of the television cartoon show *The Simpsons*.

Gehry Partners, Walt Disney Concert Hall, Los Angeles, 2003

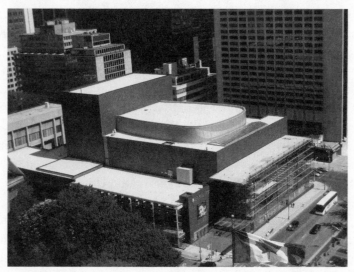

Diamond Schmitt, Four Seasons Centre for the Performing Arts, Toronto, 2006

challenge for the local architect Jack Diamond in designing a new ballet-opera house was to make sure that the building fit happily into the surrounding city rather than to create an urban magnet or a tourist attraction. Completed in 2006, the Four Seasons Centre for the Performing Arts occupies a full city block on University Avenue, the city's most prestigious thoroughfare. Diamond's design is basically a collection of boxes: the largest box contains the auditorium, a tall box houses the fly tower; lower boxes accommodate backstage functions; and a glazed box overlooking University Avenue contains the lobby. The interior of the building is warm: light-colored wood, Venetian plaster, ocher-colored tones. The auditorium has been highly praised for its acoustics, its excellent sight lines, and its intimacy—three-quarters of the two thousand seats are within a hundred feet of the stage.

Diamond studied under Louis Kahn, and while his style is different, he shares Kahn's belief that architectural form is the result of analyzing a building's essence. "You arrive at the sublime or poetic not by metaphor," Diamond has said, "but by making virtues out of necessity. That's the secret of design." The necessities of the Four Seasons Centre included a cramped site, the stringent requirements of the hall, and a restricted budget.* The building was designed from the inside out, just like Disney Hall, but Diamond wrapped the opera house in a distinctly less glamorous material than stainless steel: dark, chocolate-colored brick. Only the large front façade that looks out on University Avenue is glass.

"A touch of the spectacular on all four sides of the centre would have gone a long way to argue the noble cause of culture," wrote one dissatisfied Toronto critic. Another complained of the building's "earnest stolidity." The *Toronto Star* went further, listing the

---

*The budget for the Toronto hall was about $160 million, compared with $180 million (also in 2003 U.S. dollars) for Disney Hall, but an opera house includes extensive backstage facilities such as a fly tower and storage spaces for sets, which are not required in a concert hall.

Four Seasons Centre as "the fifth-worst building in Toronto." The reason for this dissatisfaction was the recent construction of several prominent new buildings in the city: an in-your-face university student residence by Thom Mayne, an art school raised on angled stilts by the British architect Will Alsop, and Daniel Libeskind's lopsided addition to the Royal Ontario Museum. By the inflated standard of these self-conscious signature buildings, the understated architecture of the Four Seasons Centre was a definite letdown.

The Toronto critics carped, but Valery Gergiev, artistic director of the Mariinsky Theatre in St. Petersburg, saw understatement as a good thing. Two successive high-profile international architectural competitions for a new opera house for his theater had produced no satisfactory result. The first competition had been won by the Los Angeles firebrand Eric Owen Moss, whose radical design resembled an iceberg. Moss's project, as well as his revision, were rejected by the Russian government (which was footing the bill), and a second competition was held, this one won by Dominique Perrault, architect of the ill-starred Bibliothèque Nationale. The Frenchman enclosed the opera house in a multifaceted dome of gold-tinted glass. Gergiev called the design "very flamboyant, very fractured and not easy to build"—St. Petersburgers called it "the golden potato." Costs spiraled, technical problems multiplied, and Perrault was fired. During a North American tour, Gergiev visited Toronto's Four Seasons Centre. He was struck, as he put it, "by its beauty, its practicality and friendliness with neighboring buildings, its superb acoustics," and he invited Diamond's firm, Diamond Schmitt, to St. Petersburg. A third competition followed, which the Canadians won.

The construction site of what is called Mariinsky II fills a city block across a canal from the original nineteenth-century Mariinsky Theater, designed by Alberto Cavos, a Russian architect of Italian descent. Italian and French architects had built the new city for Peter the Great in the eighteenth century, and over the years the center of St. Petersburg, then the capital, developed into a remarkably coherent architectural ensemble, a northern version of Venice. The Russian city is distinguished by canals and beautiful architecture in a variety of styles: colorful Baroque, sturdy neoclassical, delicate Empire, and romantic nineteenth-century eclecticism. The difficult but unavoidable question for an architect is how to add a new building to such surroundings: Should it stick out, fit in, or be something in between?

Moss and Perrault had opted to stick out. Their glassy designs were to be light beacons during the long, dark Russian winters, but they were also intended, in every way possible, to contrast with their surroundings—in material, form, and relation to the street. This worked for Gehry in Los Angeles but it seems wrong for St. Petersburg, a city where architects have been building for several hundred years, not necessarily in a consistent style, but in a manner that produced consistent results. Modernist architects argue that new architecture should contrast with old, although that is often merely an excuse for artistic license. That, at least, is

Diamond Schmitt, Mariinsky II, St. Petersburg, 2013

how it seemed to many people in St. Petersburg, where public opposition to "sticking out" accounted, in part, for the government's decision to abandon the two earlier projects.

Diamond took the middle road. He had experience building in historic cities, having designed a new city hall for Jerusalem, near the Jaffa Gate, a modern building that successfully fits into its ancient surroundings. His concept for the Mariinsky opera house, unlike Perrault's glass crystal, is exceedingly simple—a box housing a traditional horseshoe-shaped hall. Cities, as Diamond often points out, are composed of boxes. The St. Petersburg box—stone rather than brick, as in Toronto—is intended to harmonize with the surrounding nineteenth-century buildings, although the style of the architecture is modernist, with simple details and large expanses of glass. The opera house, which opened in 2013, also adds to the St. Petersburg skyline with a dramatic roof form and a roof terrace with curving glass canopies.

David M. Schwarz Architectural Services, Schermerhorn Symphony Hall, Nashville, 2006

All good concert halls are designed from the inside out. In a book written before Walt Disney Hall and the Four Seasons Centre were built, the eminent acoustician Leo Beranek ranked the world's best concert halls—seventy-six of them—according to a survey of conductors, musicians, and music critics. The top tier included only three halls: the Grosser Musikvereinssaal in Vienna, the Concertgebouw in Amsterdam, and Symphony Hall in Boston. All three, built in the late nineteenth century, are so-called shoeboxes: long, rectangular rooms with high ceilings and wraparound balconies. When the architect David M. Schwarz was commissioned to design a new concert hall for the Nashville Symphony Orchestra, he took the Musikvereinssaal as a model, added a balcony to increase the seating capacity, but preserved one of the old hall's attractive features, high windows in the two long sides.

The interior of Nashville's Schermerhorn Symphony Hall has less gilt than the Musikvereinssaal but it is designed in a similar neoclassical style. On the exterior, the entrance is identified by a portico in the shape of an ancient temple, although the Corinthian columns appear more Egyptian than Greek. The statues in the pediment of the temple front, sculpted by Raymond Kaskey, represent the musician Orpheus and his wife, Eurydice. Bernard Holland, the music critic of *The New York Times*, objected to the ancient symbolism, and found the building too tame. "It doesn't argue with the neighbors," he complained. "Originality, it has been decided, is not only bad policy but bad manners." But getting on with the neighbors is the whole point. Nashville has been long known as the "Athens of the South," and its downtown has many Greek Revival buildings, notably William Strickland's nineteenth-century Tennessee State Capitol, a 1920s replica of the Parthenon, McKim Mead & White's War Memorial Auditorium, and Robert A. M. Stern's recent Public Library. So Schwarz was merely adding another chapter to what was already a long classical story.

William Rawn Associates, Seiji Ozawa Hall, Tanglewood, 1994

Seiji Ozawa Hall in Tanglewood is another shoebox. Unlike most concert halls, the summer home of the Boston Symphony Orchestra in the Berkshires is in a rural setting, so how did the architect William Rawn design a largely windowless boxy structure in a grassy field? His solution was to give the box an industrial character, with heavy brick walls and a vaulted metal roof, which vaguely recall a New England textile mill. The somewhat stern effect is softened by barnlike wooden porches, and the hall fits very well into its bucolic surroundings. The interior is wood. In an updated version of his earlier study, Leo Beranek ranked Ozawa Hall the fourth-best American hall, after Boston's Symphony Hall, Carnegie Hall, and the Morton H. Meyerson Symphony Center in Dallas, designed by I. M. Pei.

Of course, concert halls are about more than acoustics, sight lines, and fitting a building into its setting. The German architect Erich Mendelsohn once wrote that architects are remembered best for their one-room buildings. In a one-room building like the

Pantheon, you are immediately *there*, at its heart, in its reason for being. Opera houses and concert halls have an added dimension: they are also places of public assembly. They encompass a shared experience and, like cathedrals, they are places whose architecture contributes to that experience. Once the curtain goes up, the hall belongs to the performers, but until then the architect is free to pull out all the stops.

ADDING ON

At thirty-six, Edwin Lutyens was already an experienced architect, having been in practice for sixteen years, and thanks to his talent, his satisfied clients, and the support of *Country Life* magazine, he had become the most fashionable country-house architect in Britain.* In 1905, he was commissioned to enlarge a seventeenth-century farmhouse at Folly Farm in Sulhamstead, Berkshire. He added a two-story hall, and a kitchen wing in the rear, and created a perfectly symmetrical garden façade. The new house combined delicate Queen Anne with simple Arts and Crafts details—silver-gray brick and red-brick trim—a style that Lutyens jokingly called "Wrennaissance." The pride of Folly Farm was an extraordinary garden, laid out by Gertrude Jeckyll, Lutyens's longtime collaborator and friend.

In 1912, Folly Farm was bought by Zachary Merton, an elderly industrialist whose new German bride was a friend of Lutyens's wife. The Mertons commissioned Lutyens to enlarge the house—they wanted a grander dining room, more bedrooms, and a larger kitchen. Even though the addition would more than double the size of the house, Lutyens chose neither to harmonize with his original design nor to upset its symmetry with an overpowering

---

*Lutyens once told a student audience, "I advise everyone to build a house at nineteen. It's such good practice."

extension. Instead, he reverted to the style of his earliest houses, which had been based on English rural architecture. The new red-brick addition, which he called a "cowshed," has an immense tiled roof that almost touches the ground, massive chimneys, and heavy brick buttresses that form a cloister beside a shallow fish-pond that Lutyens referred to as a "water tank." The overall effect is to make the original graceful house appear to be a later addition to a medieval barn, rather than the other way around.

The story of Folly Farm underlines another way in which architecture differs from the other arts—buildings are never really finished; new owners have new functional requirements, technology evolves, fashions change, life intervenes. In the past, the construction of a large building such as a cathedral or a palazzo could take many decades and it was assumed that the design would be modified by successive architects. King's College Chapel, for example, which was begun in 1446, was completed, three monarchs, one War of the Roses, and seventy years later. The work is generally attributed to four master masons, while an independent team of Flemish craftsmen is credited with the stained-glass windows. By the time that an oak rood screen was added to the chapel—in 1536—Gothic was out of fashion and the design of the celebrated screen is an example of early Renaissance classicism. Each builder observed the precedent set by the previous generation, but followed no strict predetermined plan.

Modern buildings take less time to construct, but they, too, are subject to change. When Fallingwater was completed, it must have seemed perfect, a finished work of art. Yet only three years after it was designed, with more visitors coming to the increasingly celebrated house, the Kaufmanns asked Wright to add a guesthouse, rooms for more servants, and a four-car carport. Wright, of course, obliged. He did not hide the uphill addition, which is linked to the main house by a striking curved canopy that steps down the slope.

Architects are rarely given the opportunity to enlarge a building

more than once. In the late 1950s, a pair of young Danish architects, Vilhelm Wohlert and Jørgen Bo, were approached by Knud
W. Jensen, a wealthy art collector who wanted to convert a
nineteenth-century country house into a private museum. The
site was a twenty-five-acre estate named Louisiana, overlooking
the Øresund strait, just north of Copenhagen. Wohlert and Bo
renovated the old house and added two freestanding galleries,
which were connected to the house—and each other—by glazed
corridors. The new wood-and-brick buildings were low-key, unpretentious, human in scale, and designed in the style that became
known as Danish Modern. Jensen's collection grew, and his museum expanded accordingly. On four separate occasions during
the next thirty-three years, the architects added more galleries, a
small concert hall, a café, a children's wing, a museum shop, and
a sculpture court. As a result, the Louisiana Museum has an unusual layout: a loose circle of connected pavilions in a spacious
old park beside the sea. While the architects' style developed over
the years, they stayed true to their understated modernist roots,
and their remarkably consistent meandering architecture has
produced a much-admired museum.

Consistency was not one of Philip Johnson's virtues. In 1961,
he was commissioned to design a memorial to Amon G. Carter, a
Fort Worth, Texas, newspaper publisher. The building, located in
a park, took the form of a small art gallery housing Carter's collection of Frederic Remingtons, and resembled a little temple with a
portico supported by delicate arches of smooth Texas shellstone.
This was Johnson's first building in a style that one critic called
"ballet classicism," referring to the tapered columns that resembled a dancer *en pointe*. The Carter Museum was hardly more
than a garden pavilion, and two years later Johnson was called
back to add a discreet addition in the rear. Fourteen years after
that, the museum undertook a major expansion, and Johnson,
who was no longer interested in classicism, added a large wing in
a heavy geometrical style. The result was hardly as felicitous as

Vilhelm Wohlert & Jørgen Bo, Louisiana Museum of Art, Humlebæk, 1958–91

Philip Johnson, Amon Carter Museum, Fort Worth, 1961

Folly Farm, however, and in 2009, when the museum needed to expand a third time, Johnson demolished both earlier additions and replaced them with a two-story granite-faced block that forms a sedate backdrop to his perfect little jewel box of a pavilion.

Neither Johnson nor Wohlert and Bo anticipated expansion, but buildings are sometimes designed with future growth in mind. When the Philadelphia architect Frank Furness designed the main library of the University of Pennsylvania at the end of the nineteenth century, he made it a "head-and-tail" building: the head housed a soaring reading room, while the iron-and-glass tail contained the book stacks. The stacks, which held a hundred thousand books, were designed to expand, bay by bay, from three bays to nine. But in 1915, the university thoughtlessly erected a building next to the library, effectively blocking any future expansion. Furness had died a few years earlier, so he had no say in the matter.

Furness's story is not unusual. A building may be designed to grow, but by the time that the need to expand occurs, several decades have passed and the original architect's intentions are often forgotten, or merely ignored. Moreover, it is likely that the new architect has his own ideas. That is what happened at Scarborough College, a suburban satellite of the University of Toronto, built in the early 1960s. The Australian architect John Andrews designed the entire campus as a linear concrete building, a so-called megastructure. Scarborough College was considered a cutting-edge design and a harbinger of the future; however, as the campus grew, later architects ignored Andrews's restrictive linear model. Instead, a library, student center, athletic facilities, and a school of management were each housed in separate freestanding buildings. Another Brutalist megastructure campus of the 1960s, this one in Britain, suffered a similar fate. Denys Lasdun designed the campus for the new University of East Anglia in Norwich as a linear megastructure incorporating raised pedestrian decks. Within a decade, the raised-deck concept was set aside, and soon even the contrived forty-five-degree diagonal geometry of the original plan was ignored. The first architect to detach himself from Lasdun's megastructure was Norman Foster when he built the Sainsbury Centre for Visual Arts. Fourteen years later, he was called back to extend the building. He knew exactly how to do it, since his linear plan could be extended at either end. However, his clients wanted the original building to remain unaltered. Accordingly, Foster designed an underground addition that left the shed intact.

No one can add to a Foster-designed building as confidently as Norman Foster, but at some future time, fifty years hence, say, the Sainsbury Centre may need to grow again, and some architect will have to decide how. In that case, he or she will have several options. Underground extensions are one alternative; another is to extend a building in the same way you lengthen a skirt or a pair of trousers—seamlessly. When Eero Saarinen planned Washington's Dulles International Airport in the early 1960s, he designed a building that could be extended at either end. Thirty-three years later, the airport needed to grow to accommodate more traffic, just as he had anticipated. The architect, Skidmore, Owings & Merrill, doubled the length of the terminal, replicating the original scheme of a draped concrete roof supported by catenary cables tensioned by outward-slanting piers. The building today looks much as before, except that instead of fifteen bays, there are now thirty.

When Romaldo Guirgola was commissioned to expand the Kimbell Art Museum in Fort Worth, Texas, he chose seamlessness. His longtime colleague and friend Louis Kahn had completed the building seventeen years earlier, but he was no longer alive. The museum consists of a series of parallel vaults, which Guirgola proposed to simply extend, increasing the building's length from three hundred to five hundred feet. His rationale was that Kahn had originally designed a longer building, but had been obliged to build a shorter version for budgetary reasons. However, most admirers of Kahn considered his building to be inviolable, and there was an international outcry. "Why ruin the masterwork of Kahn's life with such an ill-considered extension?" asked a letter to *The New York Times.* "To put it bluntly, we find this addition to be a mimicry of the most simple-minded character." The signatories included Philip Johnson, Richard Meier, Frank Gehry, and James Stirling. The museum balked, and Guirgola's reasonable attempt to add to a famous building by imitating its architecture was shelved.

One man's mimicry is another man's respect. In 2006, Allan Greenberg was commissioned to design an addition to Princeton's Aaron Burr Hall, a late work by one of America's most distinguished nineteenth-century architects, Richard Morris Hunt. Hunt built extravagant mansions in Newport, Rhode Island, as well as the Metropolitan Museum in New York and Biltmore House in North Carolina, but at Princeton he kept his usual flamboyance in check, perhaps because this was a workaday laboratory. He designed a straightforward brick box with carefully proportioned windows trimmed in sandstone; the only whimsical touches are a battered-stone base and crenellated battlements at the roofline. Greenberg dispensed with the battlements in his addition, but maintained the sturdy, almost military bearing of the building, matching the red Haverstraw brick, red mortar, Trenton sandstone trim, and battered-stone base. He carefully lined up the windows, cornice lines, and rooftop parapets with the original. At the same time he did not slavishly imitate his predecessor, and introduced contrasting bands of sandstone. He turned one corner with an octagonal tower containing a staircase, and added two decorative touches: rosettes with a bull's-eye pattern, and a discreet plaque with the university crest. In all, he managed to tease something original—albeit quite modest—out of Hunt's vocabulary. The addition, against all odds, is neither a pastiche nor a facsimile. It is more like a dialogue between two architects across the years.

Kevin Roche was even more circumspect at the Jewish Museum on New York's Fifth Avenue. The museum is housed in the former Warburg Mansion, designed in 1908 by Charles P. H.

Allan Greenberg Architect, Aaron Burr Hall, Princeton University, 2005

Kevin Roche John Dinkeloo & Associates, Jewish Museum, New York, 1993

Gilbert in the French Renaissance style. The museum moved into the mansion in 1947, and in 1963 added a bland annex on the Fifth Avenue side. In 1993, Roche was commissioned to further expand the building. He had been Saarinen's right-hand man and with John Dinkeloo had taken over the practice after Saarinen's death, and designed such modernist landmarks as the Oakland Museum of California and the Ford Foundation headquarters building. Roche might have been expected to design a contrasting addition to the Jewish Museum; instead, he hid the 1963 annex behind a new French Renaissance façade of Indiana limestone with pinnacled dormers and a mansard roof. The exquisitely detailed addition extends Gilbert's architecture in such a way that it is impossible to tell where the latter stops and the former begins. Instead of a conversation it is more like a séance—Roche channeling Gilbert from the grave.

Herbert Muschamp, the architecture critic of *The New York Times*, acknowledged that the new addition to the Jewish Museum respected the old architecture—which he mislabeled as "Gothic"—but he was uncomfortable with the contemporary use of a period style. "Though the expansion means to honor history, it ends up sacrificing history to taste," he wrote. "Mr. Roche has enlarged a chateau but not our view of its place in time." It is unclear how a different addition would have enlarged our view of the mansion's "place in time," but evidently Muschamp preferred the more conventional practice of contrasting the new with the old.

Contrast was the theme of the glass atrium designed by Bartholomew Voorsanger and Edward Mills in 1991 for the Morgan Library in New York. The original library, designed in 1906 by Charles Follen McKim, is a severe marble box, modeled on Baldassare Peruzzi's sixteenth-century Palazzo Pietro Massimi in Rome. There are only four rooms in the Morgan Library: two large chambers flanking a domed entrance hall, and a small office. The building shared the block with J. P. Morgan's pre–Civil War family mansion and a 1928 annex built by his son; Voorsanger & Mills's atrium linked all three. I recall eating in the atrium café and thinking that the curved glass roof was more suitable for a discotheque. Instead of a contrast, a clash.

When Renzo Piano was commissioned to extend the Morgan in 2006, he demolished the offensive addition and replaced it with a tall all-glass lobby, a handsome and exceptionally well-built space, so cool as to be almost diffident, carefully allowing McKim's palazzo to remain the star. The only loss in the new building— and it is a major one—is that the entrance to McKim's library is no longer the front door on Thirty-Sixth Street. Instead, one slinks ingloriously into the palazzo through an improvised corner entrance at the rear.

Piano is a master of the contrasting addition—he has to be, since it is impossible to blend his light, precisely detailed steel-and-glass architecture with older masonry buildings. His work is in evidence at the Los Angeles County Museum of Art, the Art Institute of Chicago, and the Isabella Stewart Gardner Museum in Boston, and he is designing a steel-and-glass pavilion for the Kimbell Art Museum, which is intended to contrast with Kahn's concrete-and-travertine building. It remains to be seen if this proves a superior solution to Guirgola's aborted extension.

Richard Rogers, too, is a master of contrast, as he demonstrates in 300 New Jersey Avenue, an addition to an office building in Washington, D.C. The older building, originally the headquarters of the venerable Acacia Life Insurance Company, was designed in 1935 by Shreve, Lamb & Harmon, the architects of the Empire State Building. Like the Empire State, the six-story Acacia Building is an example of early American modernism: a blend of Beaux-Arts planning, practical engineering, and an Art Deco sensibility. Rogers demolished a parking garage on the north edge of the site, replacing it with a new ten-story office wing, and turned the triangular courtyard between the new and old buildings into a roofed atrium. A similar strategy to Piano's at the Morgan, but

Rogers Stirk Harbour+Partners, 300 New Jersey Avenue, Washington, D.C., 2010

executed in a very different way. A jungle-gym tower stands in the center of the atrium. The tower contains glass elevators and supports the atrium roof, which looks like a giant glass umbrella. Glass-floored footbridges connect the tower to the new and old buildings. Precision is a hallmark of Rogers's architecture, but here precision is accompanied by a kind of rough-and-ready brashness that recalls the heroic architectural modernism of the 1920s. Painted steel, bare concrete, structural struts, and exposed plumbing are blended into one kinetic whole.

Such structural high jinks are light-years away from Shreve, Lamb & Harmon's orderly design. "That was then, this is now" is Rogers's message. Contrasting new and old is an architectural cliché that often leaves the old in its dust, but that's not the case here. One comes away admiring both buildings. Much has changed in seventy-five years, except the sense of conviction that is the accomplished architect's hallmark.

Rogers was a runner-up in a 1982 competition for an extension to the National Gallery in London. The unbuilt winning scheme, by Ahrends Burton & Koralek, occasioned the famous remark by Prince Charles, who described it as a "monstrous carbuncle on the face of a much-loved and elegant friend," and set off a firestorm of public debate about modern architecture. The result was a new competition, with six firms being invited to submit designs. The contestants were instructed that while the new wing should be "a building of outstanding architectural distinction," it should also fit into the setting of Trafalgar Square, and be a sympathetic neighbor to William Wilkins's neo-Grecian National Gallery, which, while not a great work of architecture, is an important feature of the Trafalgar Square setting.

Robert Venturi and Denise Scott Brown's winning scheme is an unusual combination of knowing seamlessness and gentle—and not-so-gentle—contrast; sometimes a reflection of its surroundings, sometimes a counterpoint to them. The façade on the square begins with what Venturi called a "crescendo of columns," an exact copy of Wilkins's giant Corinthian pilasters, blank attic windows, dentilated cornice, and rooftop balustrade. In Venturi's hands, these classical elements seem to fade—literally—into the new façade, until they disappear altogether. In contrast to this scenographic tour-de-force, the rest of the building contains no architectural allusions to the old building, except for maintaining the same roofline and using the same Portland stone. A single giant fluted Corinthian column stands at the corner, and seems to have wandered over from the gallery's portico. Or is it a reference to Nelson's Column in the square?

The critic Paul Goldberger observed about Venturi's design that "this is the late twentieth century trying not so much to abandon classicism as to make its own comment on it." Throughout, the new building alternates between respecting the architecture of its older neighbor and reminding us that it is, indeed, a modern building. The new wing is pulled away from the National Gallery, leaving a pedestrian passage and a glimpse of the interior grand staircase, visible through a steel-and-glass curtain wall that is harshly juxtaposed with the old building. The entrance to the new wing is through an aperture that appears to have been cut out of the façade with a sharp knife—Venturi has said that the size of the opening is based on the dimensions of a London double-decker bus. The rear wall of the wing is blank except for two large ventilating grilles and the name of the building carved into the stone in six-foot-high letters. Venturi explained how the setting influenced the design. "Each of the four façades is different—involving the Miesian glass curtain wall to the east, the severe brick-faced 'back' walls to the north and west, and the limestone façade to the south." He referred to the limestone façade as a "mannerist billboard."

Venturi, Scott Brown & Associates, Sainsbury Wing, National Gallery, London, 1991

Venturi, perhaps more than any architect of his generation, consciously founded his architecture on a theory. Most architectural ideas emerge from an architect's confrontation with a particular program, site, or client, and are refined in subsequent projects; Venturi's theory was presented first in a book. "In the medium of architecture, if you can't do it, you have to write about it," he observed, describing the situation of a neophyte exploring as-yet-unrealized architectural ideas through the medium of the written word. His 1966 manifesto, *Complexity and Contradiction in Architecture*, was a reaction to what Venturi considered the oversimplified sculptural and monumental forms of orthodox modernist architecture. He used historical examples to illustrate his thesis that great architecture had frequently been inconsistent, complex, and contradictory. In a later book, *Architecture as Signs and Systems*, written with Denise Scott Brown, he examined how buildings could communicate specific messages through iconographic decoration rather than through their form. This is what drove the design of the extension to the National Gallery.

The front façade as sign is independent of the other three façades of the wing, as it acknowledges its context: the original historical building, which it is a continuation of, and Trafalgar Square, which it faces.

This façade as billboard relates to the façade of the original building through analogy and contrast—that is, its Classical elements are exact replications of those of the original façade, but their positions relative to one another vary significantly to create compositional inflection of the new façade toward the old façade, while at the same time maintaining a unified monumental face toward the grand square.

Do we really need the architect's explanation to appreciate a building? The complicated visual games that architects such as

Venturi play often leave the viewer in a swamp of literary and historical allusions; I doubt that the casual passerby really perceives the façade of the Sainsbury Wing as a "billboard." If Venturi were a purely cerebral theoretician, his architecture would be stillborn, but he isn't and it isn't. Twenty years have passed since the Sainsbury Wing was built, and the weathered and stained Portland stone of the new building blends nicely with the old. The "crescendo of columns" is much less conspicuous than when the stone was new, and now appears merely amiably eccentric. From Trafalgar Square, the wing looks exactly right, a small addition to a large building, quietly asserting itself in quixotic and sometimes cheeky ways, but paying close attention to its larger neighbor.

3

SITE

A building may ignore its setting, but it cannot ignore its site. Disney Hall faces Grand Avenue, the main artery of downtown Los Angeles, and on this side, the building opens up to the sidewalk with a glass wall behind which are the lobby, a café, and shops. Around the corner, across First Street, is the Dorothy Chandler Pavilion. This huge hall, designed by Welton Becket in the ponderous monumental style that was popular in the 1960s, is one of the largest performing arts centers in the United States. Rather than try to compete with this behemoth, Gehry turns the other cheek and breaks down the scale of his building into smaller forms. On the opposite side of the site, across nondescript Second Street, Disney Hall faces a parking lot. Here, instead of sails, Gehry places a no-nonsense limestone box containing administrative offices. The box forms a hard edge against the street, and also provides a screen between the concert hall and whatever will eventually be built on the empty lot. Most Angelinos will arrive at Disney Hall by car, and the public entrance to the parking garage is here, too. Gehry deals with the two-story drop between Grand Avenue and the lowest point on the site by creating a limestone podium. The top of the podium is a public garden that provides a landscaped haven from the traffic on the surrounding streets, and includes a fountain, terraces, and an amphitheater for outdoor performances.

Every site has its own questions. What are the main views of the building, and what does one see *from* the building? Where do people arrive; that is, where is the entrance? What is the nature of the surrounding buildings: good, bad, or indifferent? Is the site flat or sloped? Where is the "back" of the building? Not least, from where does the sun shine? An architect must take all these factors into account, especially if one comes to the fore and affects the design in a major way.

LOOK AT ME

A prime consideration for a tall structure, whether it is a steeple, a minaret, or a pagoda, is how it looks from afar. The early skyscraper architects, such as Cass Gilbert and Raymond Hood, recognized this and drew their inspiration from cathedral spires. The results were such evocative towers as the Woolworth Building and the Chicago Tribune Tower. Eliel Saarinen's second-place design in the 1922 Chicago Tribune competition showed how abstract forms could also produce a memorable silhouette, which led to such stripped-down classics as the exuberant Chrysler Building, the stolid Empire State Building, and Rockefeller Center's soaring RCA Building. When Mies van der Rohe first arrived in the United States, he stayed at the University Club, close to the RCA Building. It was his first experience of a skyscraper. "I saw the main tower of the Rockefeller Center every morning from my breakfast table and it made a great impression on me," he recalled. "It has nothing to do with style. There you see that it is a mass. That is not an individual thing, thousands of windows, you know. Good or bad, that doesn't mean anything. That is like an army of soldiers or a meadow. You don't see the details anymore when you see the mass." For Mies, as for other modern architects in the fifties and sixties, the mass was inevitably a prism with a flat top. One of the first modern architects to break out of the rectangular mold was Mies's disciple Philip Johnson, whose thirty-six-story twin towers at Pennzoil Place in Houston resemble glass crystals. Today, the celebration of height has returned with distinctive skyscraper silhouettes such as Norman Foster's rocket ship–like Swiss Re building in London, Jean Nouvel's phallic Torre Agbar in Barcelona, and Renzo Piano's steel-and-glass stalagmite, the London Shard.

The skyline aside, urban buildings are viewed in one of two ways: those that face an open space may be seen head-on, but those on the street are seen only at an oblique angle. Mies was aware of the difference when he pulled the Seagram Building back from Park Avenue to create a plaza. "I set it back so you could see it," he said in a 1964 interview. "You know, if you go to New York you really have to look at these canopies to find where you are. You cannot even see the building. You see only the building in the distance."

Urban buildings without the benefit of a square or plaza are seen obliquely. The Guggenheim Museum in New York, for example, is usually photographed from across the street (with a wide-angle lens), but the first view for most pedestrians walking up Fifth Avenue is a tantalizing glimpse of a fragment of what appears to be a giant cream-colored Dixie cup. What on earth is it? As you get closer the mysterious shape turns out to be a dramatic upside-down bowl that looms over the sidewalk. By then you are under the overhanging base and about to enter the building. Wright has teased a powerful sequence out of what is a rather inauspicious site.

With the Yale Center for British Art, Louis Kahn adopted a different solution to the oblique approach. Instead of a sculptural façade along the street, he made the building as flat as it could be. Looking up at the building, there is nothing to catch your eye, and the difference between the glazing and the stainless-steel panels is so subtle, especially on a dull day, that the whole façade seems like a diaphanous gray skin—truly a moth. In an earlier

Gehry Partners, New World Center, Miami Beach, 2011

building that is likewise approached obliquely, Kahn took a more Wrightian approach. The site of the Richards Medical Research Laboratory at the University of Pennsylvania, beside Hamilton Walk, is so hemmed in that you don't see the building until you are almost upon it. Instead of designing a single horizontal block beside the walk—as his predecessor, Cope & Stewardson, had done in a medical laboratory building next door—Kahn broke his building down into an irregular row of seven-story laboratory towers and brick shafts containing stairs and exhaust ducts. The towers and shafts are not intended to be seen as a whole; instead they appear one by one as one proceeds down the walk.

The New World Center, an orchestral academy in Miami Beach, offered Frank Gehry both oblique and frontal conditions. The building is a white box wedged between two streets of the tight South Beach grid, so the two short sides come right up against the sidewalk and are seen only obliquely. On one side the building faces a narrow street, and the white façade with scattered windows is so mundane as to be unnoticeable. On the opposite side, the building abuts a four-lane thoroughfare. A shape that looks like a billowing canvas curtain, but is really a solid awning, projects over the sidewalk like a marquee. The awning shades a large glazed opening in the end wall of the concert hall, but its chief function is to announce the presence of the New World Symphony to the drivers who are speeding by on Seventh Street. The main façade of the center faces a public park. Behind the fully glazed wall is a jumble of Gehryesque forms that contain rehearsal rooms. The interior jumble notwithstanding, Gehry is uncharacteristically circumspect on the exterior. A large blank wall becomes an outdoor projection screen on which audiences in the park can watch live telecasts from the concert hall. The only whimsical touch is a delicate canopy of trees that is visible on the roof.

Jørn Utzon, the architect of the Sydney Opera House, referred to the roof as a building's "fifth façade." Roofs traditionally offered the architect an opportunity to create a memorable silhouette seen against the sky. Most modern buildings have unadorned flat roofs, which creates the impression that the architecture has been brutally truncated. The flat roofs are often littered with an assortment of ventilating stacks, elevator penthouses, air-conditioning chillers, antennas, and satellite dishes. At worst these are scattered indiscriminately across the expanse of the roof; at best they are camouflaged by ungainly screens. In either case, they lend the building a pathetic air, as if architecture were so unimportant that anything at all could be dumped on the roof. That is why good architects pay as much attention to the design of the roof as the rest of the building. On the roof of the New World Center, part of which is a garden, Gehry integrated the mechanical penthouses with sculptural forms that house a music library as well as various public rooms, and the ebullient roofscape turns a simple box into an animated composition.

ENTRANCE

The first question you ask yourself approaching a building is: Where is the front door? According to Christopher Alexander's *A Pattern Language*, always a useful guide, locating the entrance to a building is the single most important decision in the design process. "The entrance must be placed in such a way that people who approach the building see the entrance or some hint of where the entrance is, as soon as they see the building itself," he writes. There are several issues here. One is simply finding one's way. In a well-designed building you proceed to the entrance almost without thinking—you *know* which way to go, you should not have to look for signs or ask for directions. Furthermore, a building with a clearly identifiable entrance feels welcoming, whereas a building—especially a public building—whose entrance is obscured feels both annoying and forbidding. Equally bad are buildings like the renovated Morgan Library, whose front doors are permanently closed.

Historically, entrances were given pride of place simply by virtue of their location—in the center of the main façade. This is true whether the building is Buckingham Palace, a law school, or a country house. Such an entrance needs only minor additional architectural treatment—several steps or a prominent frame—to stand out. This remains an effective strategy. Mies van der Rohe experimented with asymmetrical entrances as a young man: the entry path into the Barcelona Pavilion is far from direct, and the front door of the Tugendhat House is completely hidden. But in his later buildings, he reverted to tradition. The entrance to the Seagram Building is in the center of the Park Avenue façade, and is emphasized by a canopy—another traditional device that signals "entrance."

The entrance to the Seagram Building is viewed head-on from a distance. What about a site where the entrance is approached obliquely and hence is less visible? The classic solution is to make

Ludwig Mies van der Rohe & Philip Johnson, Seagram Building, New York, 1958

the entrance more prominent by having it protrude, or by adding a porch or a canopy. The African American museum in Washington, D.C., will have a large freestanding porch facing the Mall, marking the entrance as unequivocally as Pope's Ionic portico and grand steps at the nearby National Gallery.

Michael Graves was faced with the problem of an oblique approach when he designed a municipal office building in downtown Portland, Oregon. He pushed out the main entrance to the edge of the sidewalk in the form of a portico, and made it the base for Raymond Kaskey's thirty-five-foot statue of a kneeling woman. As you walk down Fifth Avenue—despite the name a narrow street—you can see a giant copper hand emerging from the trees. Equally dramatic is the entrance to Frank Gehry's Chiat\Day Advertising building. The giant binoculars indicate the entrance to the building but, more important—since this is Southern California—they also form a portal to the basement parking garage. Like Kaskey's statue, the giant scale makes up for the fact that the binoculars are seen at an acute angle while driving down the street.

Nothing signals "important public building" as effectively as a

Michael Graves, Portland Building, Portland, Oregon, 1982

set of broad outdoor steps. Not only does the entrance gain in importance by being elevated, the act of climbing also lends processional gravity to the entry sequence. Think of the Lincoln Memorial, the National Gallery in London, or innumerable "courthouse steps." Critics of monumental steps consider them retrograde and vaguely undemocratic. Monumental they may be, but even a cursory glance at the people sitting or sprawling on the front steps of the New York Public Library or the Metropolitan Museum of Art dispels the notion that they are undemocratic. And, indeed, broad steps continue to be a feature of many modern buildings, including the Sydney Opera House, Disney Hall, the Bibliothèque Nationale, and Arthur Erickson's Law Courts building in Vancouver, whose steps ingeniously integrate a handicap ramp.

Another traditional position for an entrance, especially in an urban building, is at a street corner. This is less grand than a central location, but it has the advantage of being visible from two directions, which is why so many department stores are entered at street corners. Although the Four Seasons Performing Arts Centre in Toronto occupies an entire block, the main entrance is at the corner of two important streets. Disney Hall likewise has a street-corner entrance, as does the Yale Center for British Art.

The site of the National Gallery of Canada offered Moshe Safdie several challenges. Normally, a museum entrance leads directly into the most dramatic public space, as it does in Wright's Guggenheim Museum and in Pei's East Building. But in Ottawa the best location for the Great Hall was several hundred feet from the street corner where people arrived. According to Christopher Alexander, if people have to walk more than fifty feet to an entrance, they start to feel lost, wondering if they have taken a wrong turn. But if Safdie moved the Great Hall closer to the street corner, he would lose the dramatic view of the parliament buildings, and the crucial visual connection between the Hall and the Parliamentary Library. His solution was to place a smaller twin of the Great Hall at the street corner as an entrance lobby, and take people up to the Great Hall via a long ramped colonnade. Since the colonnade is on the exterior of the building it has views and natural light, and since it is tall and imposing, the ascent feels ceremonial rather than utililitarian. The long space also serves as an agreeable queuing area for blockbuster art shows.

Even good buildings can have poor entrances. The entrance to Saarinen's CBS Building in New York fails on two counts: it is so well integrated into the façade that it is almost invisible, and it is *down* several steps, and so feels lowly rather than welcoming. As Philip Johnson observed of CBS, "It can't be a very important building if you have to go down into it." Louis Kahn often had trouble with entrances, beginning with the Yale University Art Gallery, whose entrance doesn't face the street and requires climbing an awkward stair that is parallel to the sidewalk. The hidden entrance to the Richards Medical Research Laboratory is hinted at by two sets of steps, but these lead to a dark, unpleasant space—and you can't actually see the front door until you are in front of it. Wright often obscured the entrances to houses. The entrance to the Robie House, for example, is invisible from the street and is not in the main façade, as you might expect, but at one end of a narrow court on the north side of the building. The experience of entry is circuitous and slightly mysterious—like the man himself.

VIEW

The first real building that I designed, while I was still an architecture student, was a tiny shelter. My parents had bought a lot in North Hero, Vermont, and they needed somewhere to sleep and store camping equipment while they saved to build a summer cottage. I designed a triangular prism made out of six sheets of plywood and perched on four splayed legs. The two ends were closed with pine boards, and the roof was covered in asphalt shingles. It took me all of one weekend to build. A single window of corrugated fiberglass in the gable end cast a yellow glow inside. From the exterior, the pointed window looked vaguely Gothic and the shelter came to be known as the *kapliczka*—the little chapel.

That was 1964, the heyday of the A-frame vacation house, so my solution was hardly original. The popularity of A-frames was based on several advantages. They are relatively inexpensive to build—they are mostly roof—and they lend themselves to do-it-yourself construction. A-frames are durable—mine stood for thirty years—and there is something about the tentlike interiors that makes them particularly attractive as country retreats, whether they are in the mountains, on the beach, or by a lake, as in our case.

The A-frame fad blossomed in the 1950s, but the most interesting A-frame house is older than that. The architect was the California modernist Rudolf Schindler, who had trained in Vienna under Otto Wagner and Adolf Loos, immigrated to America, and ended up working for Frank Lloyd Wright. Eventually, Schindler established himself in Los Angeles, where he designed some very interesting concrete houses (notably, his own house in West Hollywood and the Lovell Beach House in Newport Beach), although he never achieved the public recognition of his friend and rival Richard Neutra. In the mid-1930s, Schindler was commissioned by an art teacher to design a modest summer cottage. The site, overlooking Lake Arrowhead, was in a planned community that mandated the Norman style. Schindler designed an A-frame house with a steeply sloping roof that almost touched the ground, and somehow convinced the local design committee that this was an authentic Norman form. In truth his design was anything but traditional. Most of the interior was finished in fir plywood, then a new industrial material; the kitchen was a compact workspace in the Wrightian manner; and the bedroom was in a loft overlooking the living room, whose end wall was entirely glass. Schindler was an ingenious designer, and he flattened out the steep roof of the A-frame on one side into a sort of dormer, to provide headroom for a dining nook and for glazed doors leading to a side terrace and a deck. As Esther McCoy, who knew the architect well, wrote, the house "had a spontaneity that made the later A-frames seem over-studied."

My wife and I once spent three months in a A-frame beach house in Alligator Point, Florida. Like Schindler's design it had a sleeping loft overlooking a tall living space, but it lacked his subtlety, being simply a triangular tube with a glazed wall facing the sea. The view of the Gulf of Mexico which so impressed us when we first saw the house soon lost its allure. The trouble was that wherever we were in the house, the view was always the same. We had lived in a waterside house before, an old stone farmhouse on Île Perrot in Quebec. The broad St. Lawrence River was across the road, but none of the windows focused on the view. Instead, it was only when one came out of the front door that the majestic, slowly moving river was visible. The view felt new every time.

Our experience underscores Christopher Alexander's wise observation that a good view may be spoiled by familiarity. "One wants to enjoy [the view] and drink it in every day," he writes. "But the more open it is, and the more obvious, the more it shouts, the sooner it will fade." He suggests that instead of building large windows oriented to the view, it is more effective if one catches only occasional, indirect glimpses. Alvar Aalto was a master of the indirect view. His own summer house on Muuratsalo Island in central Finland is a good example. Although situated close to the water's edge, the house, surrounded by forest, was designed around a central courtyard that functioned as a sort of outdoor living room, focused on a fire pit that was sometimes used for cooking. An opening in the courtyard wall provided a view of the lake through the trees, but most of the rooms looked onto the forest, or into the courtyard itself.

Louis Kahn handled the view indirectly when he designed the Salk Institute in La Jolla, California. The two laboratory build-

Louis I. Kahn, Salk Institute, La Jolla, California, 1966

ings on a dramatic site overlooking the Pacific Ocean are placed at right angles to the coastline, framing an open courtyard. The laboratories have no views. Four-story towers lining the courtyard contain individual offices that have angled windows offering a glimpse of the ocean. But it is only as you cross the paved courtyard, which is split down the center by a narrow channel of water, that you fully experience the spectacular view of the Pacific.

Where does this leave a glass house, which is all view, all the time? Philip Johnson's glass house had a desk in one corner, but it lacked bookshelves, and in 1980 he built himself a study-cum-library in a small one-room building some distance from the house. Johnson called the room his "monk's cell," and he liked to read beneath its tall conical skylight, sitting facing the room's only window. The small aperture looks out at a garden structure of chain-link fencing that Johnson built as an homage to Frank Gehry. Not quite the "Zen view" that Christopher Alexander advocated, but close.

TOPOGRAPHY

"With a small budget, the best kind of land to build on is flat land," Frank Lloyd Wright advised prospective house builders. "Of course, if you can get a gentle slope, the building will be more interesting, more satisfactory." Taliesin, the house that he built for himself at Spring Green, Wisconsin, is on such a slope; its several wings, built of roughly laid native limestone, girdle the brow of a hill. Walled gardens occupy the slopes above and below the house. Wright worked on Taliesin from 1911 until his death in 1959, rebuilding after two disastrous fires, enlarging, altering, and refining. In a choreographed sequence, the visitor drives up a winding road that circles the house, passes under a porte cochere, makes a sharp turn, and arrives in a courtyard between the building and the crown of the hill. This is not quite the end, however. Before entering the house, the visitor passes under a shaded loggia that—finally—offers a panoramic glimpse of the Jones Valley below.

In the 1920s, Wright established an office in Los Angeles, hoping to get work in the fast-growing city.* Despite his best attempts he was unsuccessful and several ambitious real estate proposals came to naught, but the short-lived venture did produce four memorable houses, the so-called textile-block houses, which were built out of patterned concrete blocks. Wright dealt imaginatively with the characteristically hilly topography of the Los Angeles area. Some of the houses are entered at an upper level, with sleeping quarters below; in the Storer House, the entrance level includes the dining room and bedrooms, while the living room is above; and the entrance of the exquisite Millard House, which is in a narrow ravine, is at mid-level, with the living room sandwiched between the dining room and the master bedroom. In all the houses, rooms open onto sheltered balconies, sleeping porches, roof decks, and courtyards and terraces carved out of the hillside.

The steep Southern California sites, so different from the flat Midwest, stimulated Wright to design differently—vertically rather than horizontally. The interlocking interior spaces are exciting; the results on the exterior are mixed, however. The small Millard House—which Wright named La Miniatura—is a little gem that Brendan Gill considered "assuredly among the most beautiful houses to be found anywhere in the world, regardless of size." But the larger Storer House overwhelms its hillside site on Hollywood Boulevard, and the templelike Ennis House would be at home in a Cecil B. DeMille epic. The monumental structure "threatens to crush the hilltop upon which it sprawls," wrote Gill, for whom the "bizarre vehemence with which it calls attention to itself" contradicted Wright's teaching about how a house should gently occupy its site.

Wright returned to the Midwest and the sort of houses that

---

*One of the apprentices who accompanied Wright to Los Angeles was Rudolf Schindler.

Frank Lloyd Wright, Ennis House, Los Angeles, 1924

he designed best: predominantly horizontal, on flat or gently sloping sites. The notable—and very successful—exception was Fallingwater. When Wright first visited the forested site, Edgar J.
Kaufmann showed him his favorite spot, a huge boulder on which
he sunned himself after swimming in a pool beneath a waterfall.
"Visit to the waterfall in the woods stays with me and a domicile
has taken vague shape in my mind to the music of the stream,"
Wright wrote Kaufmann. Instead of a house that overlooked the
waterfall, however, Wright designed a house on top of it. "E.J., I
want you to live with the waterfall, not just look at it," he told
his client. The dramatic result is the most daring example of an
integration of the man-made and the natural—building and
site—in Wright's oeuvre.

In the 1930s, before he built the Farnsworth House, Mies van
der Rohe designed several houses for rural sites. The first, sometimes referred to as the House for the Architect, was a house for
himself in the Tyrolean Alps. He was then unemployed—the
Bauhaus, of which he had been director, had closed and the Depression had halted all construction in Germany—so this was a

purely theoretical exercise. His charcoal sketch shows a long house spanning a valley depression. With stone walls and large areas of glass, it grows out of the landscape in a way that recalls Taliesin, which Mies would visit three years later. He was invited to the United States by Helen and Stanley Resor to design a summer house on their property in Jackson Hole, Wyoming, at the foot of the Grand Tetons. The site was unusual. The Resors had started work on a house with another architect, but had gotten only as far as four foundation piers. These were actually bridge piers, for the house was to straddle a mountain stream. Mies jumped at the opportunity to explore his earlier idea, and he proposed a long single-story box framed in steel. The two ends were clad in wood—teak—and contained the bedrooms at one end, and the kitchen and service rooms at the other. The central portion, spanning the stream, contained the living and dining area, and an immense fieldstone fireplace. The walls of this room were floor-to-ceiling glass, and provided movie-screen-size views of the imposing mountain scenery in two directions, a more subtle approach to the view than an all-glass house. The Resor House is a more compelling design than the Farnsworth House in other ways. The combination of teak, fieldstone, and glass is visually richer, and the arrangement of solid and glazed rooms is less precious and more practical. Unfortunately, the house was never built; a disastrous flood destroyed the foundation piers, and the discouraged Resors abandoned the project.

Difficult sites challenge the architect. It is not simply the technical difficulty of awkward topography but the responsibility of adding to what is already a beautiful natural setting. Yet the best buildings can actually enhance dramatic landscapes. This apparent paradox is explained by the relationship between the natural and the man-made. "The shape of architecture is the shape of the earth," wrote Vincent Scully, "as it is modified by the structures of mankind." A lighthouse standing on a headland beside the sea seems to complete the maritime scene, just as a chapel on a mountaintop can make its surroundings even more brooding and mysterious.

FRONT AND BACK

Our language and our way of seeing the world are influenced by our bodies, which have fronts and backs. Thus, we approach a person openly from the front, and sneak up on them from the back; we present a brave front to the world, or turn our backs on it; we tell someone to their face, or whisper behind their back. It is important to know which is which (that's why double-faced carnival masks are so disconcerting). Buildings likewise have identifiable faces (façades) and backs. Of course, this is also the result of practical considerations: houses need places where you take out the trash; museums need truck docks where works of art are unloaded; office buildings need delivery bays. The back is the place for mail rooms, temporary storage, garbage rooms, and access to parking, trash bins, and Dumpsters. Such messy impedimenta are ideally located away from the entrance, often screened from public view—at the back of the building.

The Seagram Building definitely has a front, which faces Park Avenue and whose entrance is reached by crossing a spacious plaza. From the vantage point of the plaza, the thirty-nine-story shaft looks like a perfect prism. In fact, the other side—the back—has a full-height spine, one bay deep, whose solid side walls brace the slender tower. These sheer walls are covered on the exterior by a grid of bronze mullions, just like the rest of the building, but filled with Tinian marble rather than glass. "I received a letter recently from an architect who asked, very sensibly, 'Why wasn't [the sheer wall] plain, like the U.N. building?'" recalled Philip Johnson, who worked with Mies on the design. "I must say it never crossed my mind. It seemed most logical to Mies and to me that the building all look the same."

One reason that Mies and Johnson didn't hesitate in making the different sides of the Seagram Building "all look the same" was that architects at the time—the late 1950s—took it for granted that while a building might have a functional back, it shouldn't *look* different from the front. That is why Johnson's glass house was so admired: its extreme perfection represented the early modernist ideal; if something was good enough for the front, it was good enough for the back. If, in the process, the back door was eliminated, well, too bad. "That we should have a front door to come in and a back door to carry the garbage out—pretty good," Johnson said in a famous Harvard lecture, "but in my house I noticed to my horror the other day that I carried the garbage out the front door."*

A decade after the Seagram Building, in the Garden Building at St. Hilda's College, Oxford, a women's residential college, Alison and Peter Smithson proposed a different solution to the front-and-back question. The husband-and-wife team were leaders in postwar British architecture, and their writings were at least as influential as their built work. They combined a particularly hard-nosed brand of modernism with an interest in offbeat subjects, Beatrix Potter as well as Le Corbusier. I visited the Smithsons' project in the mid-1970s. The Garden Building was tucked in among several nondescript Victorian buildings on the far side of the river Cherwell. At a time when British architects such as James Stirling and Denys Lasdun were building dramatic campus buildings, the Smithsons' little four-story block was decidedly humdrum. The modular exterior consisted of a precast concrete frame enclosing large plate-glass windows behind a Tudorish screen of crisscrossing wooden timbers that hung from the façade. "Absolutely it is unpretentious," wrote the architectural critic Robin Middleton, in a review titled "The Pursuit of the Ordinary." I was struck by one feature of the Garden Building. The

---

*Of course, Johnson didn't really take out the garbage himself—he had a staff.

Alison & Peter Smithson, Garden Building, St. Hilda's College, Oxford University, 1970

glass-and-concrete façade with the wood screen covered three sides of the square block, but the fourth side, which gave onto a service lane, was a blank wall of plain stock brick. The Smithsons had followed an age-old architectural practice: faced with a limited budget, they had put their money into the front of the building, and kept the back plain and simple.

The Harold Washington Library in downtown Chicago occupies a full block, bounded on three sides by major streets and on the fourth by a narrow alley. The architect, Thomas Beeby, put the public reading rooms and study carrels on the three sides facing the streets and placed all the service areas of the library—offices, staff rooms, book sorting, deliveries, elevators, and washrooms—against the alley. The difference is expressed on the exterior: while three façades of the nine-story building are elaborately decorated brick and stone, the back is a plain steel-and-glass curtain wall.

There are certain types of buildings that don't have backs. Airports terminals, for example, have two fronts—the land side and the air side; so where does one put the maintenance, delivery, and service areas? Norman Foster found the answer in Stansted Terminal, designed in 1991. The terminal, an enormous shed illuminated by skylights, functions on a single level that sits above a service floor, which Foster calls the "engine room." In addition to a station for the shuttle train that takes passengers to the departure gates, the lower level houses baggage handling and mechanical services. The precursor to Stansted was the Sainsbury Centre for Visual Arts. Like many university buildings, the centre is freestanding. Challenged by the need to provide service access to the building, Foster placed storage rooms and workshops in a basement, reached by a long external truck ramp. The National Museum of African American History and Culture in Washington, D.C., has a similar arrangement. Like all museums on the Mall, it is approached from two opposite sides: Constitution Avenue and the Mall itself. A long ramp takes trucks down to the basement, which contains the loading dock, mechanical rooms, and museum workshops and storage. Like the Sainsbury Centre and Stansted, the "back" of the building is underneath.

I am reminded of the importance of the proper relationship between front and back every day. I work at the University of Pennsylvania, in Meyerson Hall, an undistinguished brick-and-concrete building of the mid-1960s. The building has no real front and back, since all sides are given equal architectural importance, although the main entrance faces the campus, and a service entrance faces the street. The problem is that for people on foot, or arriving by car or bus, the service door—instead of the main entrance—provides the most convenient access. Over the years, this has become the de facto front door. The area immediately outside also houses food carts and Dumpsters, so, in addition to students queuing for lunch, and people entering and leaving the building, there are cars making drop-offs, delivery vans and service vehicles, and people taking out trash. It is an inelegant and uncomfortable mixture.

THE SUN

The first house I built was a summer cottage for my parents—after five years of camping in the *kapliczka* they were ready for something more comfortable. I based my floor plan on a house that Le Corbusier had designed for *his* parents. What appealed to me about his layout was that the bedroom was an extension of the main living space—a curtain provided privacy but could be left open when the couple was alone in the small house. The site of Le Corbusier's parents' house was on Lake Geneva, and to take maximum advantage of the view, the long, narrow house was parallel to the shore. My parents' house was beside a lake, too—Lake Champlain—but the lakeshore was bordered by a thick stand of trees, and since I wanted to remove as few of them as possible, I turned the building ninety degrees so that it was at right angles to the lake. In the narrow end wall that poked out of the trees, I placed a large window providing a view over the lake. The deck was at the other end of the house, separated from the water by the stand of trees. When the house was finished, it worked out as I had planned: in the mornings, my parents had a wonderful view through the open curtain, and the combined rooms made the tiny cottage—less than six hundred square feet—feel more spacious. However, the large window faced west, and in the late afternoon, the sun boomed straight into the room, making the glare off the water almost insupportable. Chagrined, I installed bamboo blinds.

Witold Rybczynski, Cottage, North Hero, Vermont, 1969

I learned an important lesson, and never again ignored the position of the sun. "South is the most important point on your compass," observes the experienced residential architect Jeremiah Eck in *The Distinctive House*. "I try to position the longest side of a house within thirty degrees of due south," he writes. "This means that most of the rooms of the house will get some direct sunlight during some portion of the day." The longest side of my current home is about twenty degrees off due south. Not only does this bring sunlight into most of the rooms, it also means that the front of the house is in the sun, and the sharp shadows make the façade appear cheerful—a sunless north façade always looks drab. On the other hand, the terrace of our house in

Philadelphia is on the north side and is shaded most of the day, which is an advantage in the hot summers. Our kitchen has an east window—as does our bedroom—so they are sunny in the mornings, whereas the porch, where we sometimes eat dinner in warm weather, is on the west side of the house, offering a view of the garden with trees casting long evening shadows on the lawn.

As Eck points out, few building sites are ideal, and orientation to the sun has to be balanced by other considerations such as views and topography. At Disney Hall, Grand Avenue runs northeast–southwest, so the corner entrance faces northeast and, except for a brief time in the morning, is in shadow most of the day. Hardly ideal, but Gehry mitigates the condition by lowering the building to allow sunlight onto the entrance plaza from the rear, and brings sunlight into the lobby through south-facing skylights. At the New World Center, the front of the building faces due east to the park. The east sun is low, but unlike the west sun it is less hot and glaring. On the other hand, this orientation means that the main façade of the center is in shadow most of the afternoon. By adding a large skylight over the interior of the building, Gehry ensures that the jumble of forms visible through the glazed east wall is brightly illuminated.

As a Nordic architect, Alvar Aalto was particularly aware of the sun. He rotated the plan of the Villa Mairea about thirty degrees from due south. As a result, the bedrooms get the morning sun, the courtyard and the swimming pool get afternoon and evening sun, and the living area, which has windows on three sides, is sunny all day long. The courtyard of his own summer cottage on Muuratsalo Island is sideways to the water but is oriented due south to capture the sun. Another of Aalto's buildings is almost entirely shaped by considerations of sunlight. In 1946, he designed Baker House, a student dormitory at MIT, where he was a visiting professor. The long, narrow site in Cambridge faces south to the Charles River and the Boston skyline. The conventional

Alvar Aalto, Baker House, Massachusetts Institute of Technology, 1948

solution would have been a long slab with a double-loaded corridor, but that would have meant that half the rooms would face north. Instead, Aalto decided that all rooms should have some direct sun. A long, single-loaded building wouldn't fit on the site, so he bent the plan into an S-curve, and as a result was able to place three-quarters of the rooms facing south (the balance face west).

A house designed to maximize the warming effects of the sun needs to be oriented very precisely in order to be effective. The winter sun in the northern hemisphere moves in a tightly constrained arc, rising in the southeast and setting in the southwest, and the sun's zenith (at noon) varies considerably with the seasons: low in winter and high in summer. This variation means that a roof overhang above a south-facing window will block the high summer sun, but will allow the low winter sun's rays to enter. If, in addition, the floor is masonry, preferably dark-colored, to absorb the sun's rays, passive solar heating is the result.

In 1980, I designed a house for a young couple, Jacqueline

Witold Rybczynski, Ferrero House, St. Marc, Quebec, 1980

and Jim Ferrero. They had two small children, and in addition to the usual rooms, they wanted a sunroom, a sauna, a mudroom, a study space, plenty of bookshelves, and a cold storage room in the basement. The budget was tight, and I had to fit all this into twelve hundred square feet. In addition, they wanted the house to be passively heated by the sun. The site, in southern Quebec, was in open farmland with no obstructing trees, and fortunately south coincided with an attractive view of distant hills. The problem was that due south was at a thirty-degree angle to the adjacent country road. All the neighboring houses faced the road—as rural houses generally do—and turning the house at an angle would look decidedly odd. The solution was a plan that resembled a dogleg: one wing facing the road, the other facing the sun.

I recently got an e-mail from the new owners of the house. They were satisfied with their new home, but with three growing children they wanted advice on how to add space. They sent me photographs. The cedar siding had turned silver, as planned, and the synthetic stucco had proved remarkably durable. The quilted blinds that insulated the large south-facing windows at night were still there; so was the wood-burning stove. Although the trees were now fully grown, the kitchen had been redone, and a patterned brick wall on the interior had been painted white. After almost thirty years the house looked remarkably unchanged. I sent them sketches with suggestions. I had not originally designed the house with expansion in mind, but it was easy enough to extend the southerly portion of the dogleg, enlarging the living room and adding a bedroom above. I also added a large window facing the sun.

4

PLAN

One of Le Corbusier's frequently quoted maxims is "The plan is the generator." What does that mean? In his Swiss Calvinist way, Le Corbusier saw planning as nothing less than the basis of civilization. "Without plan we have the sensation, so insupportable to man, of shapelessness, of poverty, of disorder, of willfulness," he wrote in his 1923 manifesto, *Towards a New Architecture*.

> The eye observes, in a large interior, the multiple surfaces of walls and vaults; the cupolas determine the large spaces; the vaults display their own surfaces; the pillars and the walls adjust themselves in accordance with comprehensible reason. The whole structure rises from its base and is developed in accordance with a rule which is written on the ground in the plan.

He included drawings of ancient buildings—the Temple at Thebes, the Acropolis, Hagia Sophia in Istanbul—to demonstrate how a three-dimensional form is the vertical projection of a floor plan, and that the plan is a timeless feature of architecture, irrespective of culture or epoch. He underlined its continued relevance by including his own plans for a so-called Radiant City, a city of geometrically laid-out towers.

Le Corbusier suggested that in designing a building, the most important thing was to decide on the plan—the rest would follow. Like many early modern architects, he had no formal training; nevertheless, his emphasis on planning followed accepted École des Beaux-Arts practice.* The École stressed three-dimensional design as well as details, but it was the plan that was considered the key to a good building. "You can put forty good façades on a good plan," Victor Laloux, a famous teacher, advised his students, "but without a good plan you can't have a good façade."

A Beaux-Arts drawing is a beautiful thing. I have a French friend whose grandfather, Léopold Bévière, attended the École in the 1880s, its glory days, and was accepted into the Atelier André, where Laloux had earlier studied. Several of his grandfather's student drawings hung in my friend's dining room, immense watercolor renderings showing in delicate detail a Class A (or final) project. I think it was a spa. I still have my first student watercolor rendering—a sculptors' camp in a forest—but it is a crude, coarse effort compared with these exquisite creations.

A Beaux-Arts plan may look like an exercise in accomplished draftsmanship, but its composition reflects careful study of the way that a building actually functions. In the late 1920s, Henry Clay Folger commissioned the French-born Philadelphia architect Paul Philippe Cret, a distinguished *ancien élève*, to design a building to house his remarkable collection of Shakespeareana. The prominent site in Washington, D.C., was on Capitol Hill, behind the Library of Congress. Cret had to accommodate a reading room, an exhibition gallery, and a lecture theater, as well as administrative offices. The theater and the exhibition gallery were for the general public, while the reading room was to be used exclusively by scholars. Since the library was both a museum and a place of study, Cret consciously—and inventively—broke

*Walter Gropius, Richard Neutra, and Alvar Aalto graduated from architecture schools, but such celebrated architects as Le Corbusier, Mies van der Rohe, and Frank Lloyd Wright learned on the job.

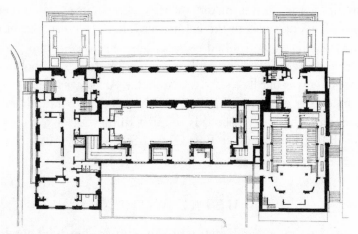

Paul Philippe Cret, Folger Shakespeare Library, Washington, D.C., 1932

with the Beaux-Arts convention that required plans to have a single central axis, and created a biaxial plan in the form of an elongated U. The central bar houses the gallery in the front, facing north, and the reading room behind it, while the shorter flanking wings contains the theater on one side and the administrative offices on the other. There are two identical entrances, one for the public and one for scholars.* Since the reading room was the symbolic heart of the building, Cret wanted to express this difference by making it taller, but Folger insisted on a uniform roof parapet. Cret's solution is better, but his client, who had been chairman of Standard Oil, was used to getting his own way.

The Folger Shakespeare Library abounds with symmetries, inside and out. The two entrances mirror each other on the long main façade. Although functionally different, the east wing

---

*Another notable exception to this rule are older schools, which likewise often had two entrances, one for girls and one for boys.

containing the theater mirrors the west wing in its overall dimensions. The entrances to the exhibition gallery face each other at
the two ends of the vaulted room. A large fireplace occupies the
precise center of the long wall in the reading room. At the same
time, Cret was hardly a slave to symmetry. At Folger's suggestion,
he made the elevation of the office wing more elaborate than its
function demanded, since it is the first thing you see as you approach the building down East Capitol Street.

SYMMETRY AND AXES

Beaux-Arts-trained architects took symmetry so much for granted
that John Harbeson, Cret's protégé and partner and the author of
a famous teaching handbook, felt obliged to add a chapter titled
"The 'Unsymmetrical' Plan." He pointed out that unbalanced pro-
grammatic requirements, or odd-shaped sites, sometimes called
for unsymmetrical plans, but observed that such plans were more
difficult to compose, and should not be undertaken lightly. It was
very clear from his description that the "unsymmetrical" plan—
the word always in quotation marks—was a rare bird.

The source of Beaux-Arts architects' interest in symmetry was
the architecture of the Renaissance, which they either visited in
person or studied in historical treatises. One of the most influential authors was Andrea Palladio, whose *Four Books on Architecture* was widely consulted by architects, since it was heavily
illustrated. An edition by the eighteenth-century British architect
Isaac Ware was for long the most authoritative English translation. To achieve maximum accuracy, Ware traced the original
woodcuts, which meant that his engravings were actually mirror
images of Palladio's drawings. The reader hardly notices, however, since the buildings illustrated are all strictly symmetrical.

"Rooms must be distributed at either side of the entrance
and the hall, and one must ensure that those on the right cor-

respond and are equal to those on the left so that the building will be the same on one side as on the other," wrote Palladio, although his stated logic for this arrangement—that "the walls will take the weight of the roof equally"—is dubious. An earlier architect, the Florentine Leon Battista Alberti, provided a more compelling rationale: "Look at Nature's own works . . . if someone had one huge foot, or one hand vast and the other tiny, he would look deformed."

My wife and I and two friends once spent eight days in a Palladio villa in Finale di Agugliaro in the Veneto. The sixteenth-century Villa Saraceno, designed relatively early in the architect's career, is one of his smallest houses, only five rooms. The grand courtyard shown in Palladio's drawing was never built, although a small portion on the east side was completed in the nineteenth century, giving the villa an endearingly lopsided appearance. Palladio would have disapproved, for his plan is perfectly symmetrical. The east side of the house mirrors the west, an imaginary line bisecting the wide entrance stair, the loggia, and the T-shaped *sala*, or reception room. Palladio's villas have only servants' stairs, never

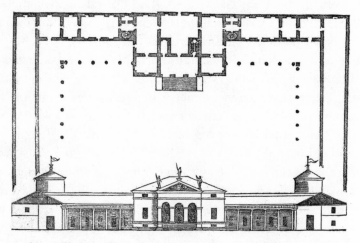

Andrea Palladio, Villa Saraceno, Finale de Agugliaro, c. 1550

grand staircases, and this one is no exception. The stair is carved out of the *sala*, balanced by a *camerino*, or small room, on the opposite side. Another line crosses the length of the *sala*, runs through the two side rooms, and extends into the two arms of the *barchesse*, or agricultural outbuildings. The two side rooms have smaller adjoining chambers, and each is lined up along a minor axis.

Palladio's axes were the lines of an idealized geometrical diagram, but they also governed the locations of the doors and windows. As a result, when we opened the large front and back doors, we could see straight through the house. Moving from room to room, we were always following one of Palladio's axes. Lining up the doors and windows creates long views through the house, and also brings the outside indoors in a way that is curiously modern. In addition to the many symmetries, small and large, inside and out, the villa has beautiful proportions, grand scale, and a sturdy simplicity. Together, these produce a palpable feeling of order and calm, pleasing to both the mind and the eye.

Palladio's strict adherence to axial geometry was based on ancient precedents such as the Pantheon, which he studied on several visits to Rome. The Romans derived the idea of symmetry—like the word itself—from the Greeks. The Oxford mathematician Marcus du Sautoy writes that the ancient Greek *symmetros* meant "with equal measure," and referred to the five Platonic solids—the tetrahedron, cube, icosahedron, octahedron, and dodedecahedron. To the Greeks, symmetry was a precise concept that could be demonstrated by geometry. But an interest in symmetry is hardly confined to the ancient Greeks, for symmetry is found in the plans of buildings of diverse civilizations: the Temple of Thebes at Luxor, the Dome of the Rock in Jerusalem, Angkor Wat in Cambodia, the Forbidden City in Beijing, and Shinto shrines in Ise. In all these examples, symmetry in plan is allied to ritual and ceremony, and also produces an aesthetic experience, a sense of harmony and balance reflecting beauty or perfection. Indeed, the desire for symmetry in our surroundings, whether it is placing a

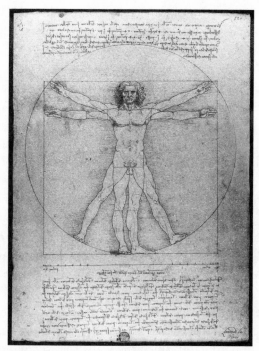

Leonardo da Vinci, Vitruvian Man, *c. 1487*

bowl of flowers in the center of a table or candlesticks on each side of a mantelpiece, appears to be universal.

Why is architectural symmetry so satisfying? As Leonardo da Vinci's famous drawing demonstrates, the human body incorporates many mirroring symmetries, it has a right side and a left, a back and a front, the navel in the center. Du Sautoy writes that the human mind seems constantly drawn to anything that embodies some aspect of symmetry: "Artwork, architecture and music from ancient times to the present day play on the idea of things which mirror each other in interesting ways." Architectural symmetry may involve geometrical patterns in floor tiles or panels on a door, but it can also be palpable. When we are inside a Gothic cathedral, for example, we experience many changing views, but when we walk down the main aisle—the line where the mirror images of the left and right sides meet—we know that we are in a special relationship to our surroundings. And when we reach the intersection of the transepts and the choir and stand below the crossing under the spire, we know we have arrived.

The architects whom Nikolaus Pevsner called the "pioneers of modern design"—Henry van de Velde, Otto Wagner, Josef Hoffmann, Peter Behrens, Adolf Loos—explored new, unhistorical shapes and forms but they did not reject symmetry. That fell to the succeeding generation, which thumbed its nose at tradition, especially Beaux-Arts tradition. "Modern life demands, and is waiting for, a new kind of plan both for the house and for the city," wrote Le Corbusier. To him "new" meant unsymmetrical; like historical ornament and old-fashioned craftsmanship, symmetry had to go. The plans of representative modern buildings of the 1920s and 1930s are all determinedly unsymmetrical. Although the eight columns supporting the roof of Mies van der Rohe's Barcelona Pavilion are arranged on a regular three-square grid, you can hardly tell, since the walls that surround them are so unevenly positioned. The wings of the Bauhaus building pinwheel in different directions and at different heights, and nothing in Fallingwater mirrors anything else. Le Corbusier's Villa Savoye, considered an exemplar of the International Style, looks symmetrical but isn't—it is not a perfect square, and while its grid of structural columns is more or less regular, the regularity is frequently undermined. "The house must not have a front," Le Corbusier wrote, so the front door is not on the arrival side but on the opposite side of the house. The door is in the center of the façade, but its location is intentionally compromised since there is a column directly in front of it. Classical buildings always have an even number of columns, to ensure that a space falls in the center opposite the entrance; the Villa Savoye, by contrast, has five columns a side.

Mies van der Rohe made the plan of the Farnsworth House

unsymmetrical, as we have seen, but this turned out to be one of the last buildings he so designed. At the Illinois Institute of Technology, which he planned, and where he was campus architect for twenty years, all the buildings that he designed are symmetrical in plan—the boiler plant as well as the chapel. Crown Hall, the school of architecture, is the most celebrated building at IIT, a clear-span, single-room design whose left and right sides mirror each other. The Seagram Building is likewise planned on an axis, which is emphasized by the flanking reflecting pools of the plaza and the four elevator cores of the lobby. Mies's biographer Franz Schulze has pointed out the similarity in axial planning between the Seagram Building and the building it faces across Park Avenue, the venerable Racquet and Tennis Club, designed by the Beaux-Arts graduate Charles McKim. The implication is that Mies planned his building to fit into its surroundings. This is true, but it is also true that by then he had rediscovered the power of symmetry, and used it in all his projects.

Eero Saarinen started his career as a follower of Mies, and his first major commission, the General Motors Technical Center, was inspired by the Illinois Institute of Technology. Although a few of Saarinen's later designs were unsymmetrical, like Morse and Stiles Colleges at Yale, which have been compared to an Italian hill town, symmetrical plans became his trademark. Symmetry came naturally to Saarinen, since he had studied architecture at Yale at a time when the curriculum was still organized along Beaux-Arts lines.

Louis Kahn was another second-generation modernist who rediscovered symmetry. The plans of early projects such as the Yale University Art Gallery and the Richards Medical Building are both resolutely unsymmetrical. But in later buildings, Kahn returned to the Beaux-Arts planning principles he had absorbed as a student under Paul Cret. Indeed, his most admired buildings— the Salk Institute, the Kimbell Museum of Art, the library at Phillips Exeter Academy—while modern in conception and design, gain much of their timeless quality precisely from their symmetrical plans.

READING THE PLAN

Architectural plans may puzzle the layman, but once mastered, they are a rich source of information. Plan drawings follow a few simple conventions. An architectural plan is conceived as a horizontal cut through the building at approximately waist height. Walls are indicated by two thick lines, sometimes filled in with a solid tone or cross-hatching, a technique that Beaux-Arts architects called *poché*; columns appear as circular or square black dots; windows are thin solid lines. Doors are sometimes shown and sometimes not; if they are drawn they are usually fully open, sometimes a quarter arc represents the swing. Dotted lines indicate something above the horizontal cut, such as a soffit, a beam, or a skylight. Plans may include flooring patterns, such as wooden decks or stone paving, and may use stylized patterns to denote special areas such as vestibules or lobbies; gridded tile patterns identify bathrooms, kitchens, and service rooms. Built-in furniture, such as bookshelves or window seats, is always shown. Sometimes movable furniture such as beds, desks, tables and chairs, and sitting arrangements is indicated, but more often rooms are empty. North is always up the page, unless otherwise indicated.

A floor plan represents the arrangement of walls in a building, but because it includes door openings it also describes movement. By tracing a line from the front door to the auditorium of a concert hall, for example, one can get an impression of the sequence of vestibules, lobbies, staircases, and twists and turns that form the processional experience. Since a plan also shows the location of windows, it is possible to see the sources of light, the views, and whether a room is sunny. "Reading" a plan involves imagining the space. Is the room a simple square, or is it lined with niches, say, or bookshelves, or surrounded by a colonnade? If the space is long and narrow, what does one see at the far end, and if it is circular, what is in the middle?

Most people are familiar with domestic plans, which are often reproduced in the real estate sections of newspapers and in magazine advertisements. The plan of the Ferrero House in rural Quebec, which was discussed at the end of the previous chapter, is skewed, since the lower portion of the dogleg is oriented due south, while the front of the house faces the angled road. The freestanding garage creates a partially enclosed court. The house is entered through a small porch with oversized steps, wide enough to sit on and hold flowerpots. The mudroom has a deep cupboard for umbrellas, walking sticks, and other outdoor paraphernalia.

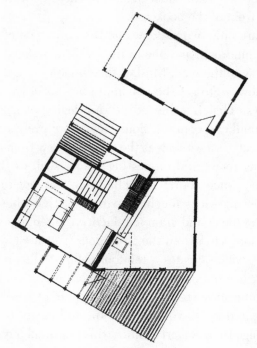

Witold Rybczynski, Ferrero House, St. Marc, Quebec, 1980

In this drawing, cupboards and closets are cross-hatched to distinguish them from habitable spaces. From the front door you get a long view—the longest in the house—through the hall, dining area, and sunroom to the exterior. The tiny hall is the heart of the house. From here you can take the stair to a sauna on the upper landing, and continue to the bedroom floor; you can go down to a powder room on the lower landing, and continue to the basement; or you can go straight through to the dining area. Dining and kitchen are in one room, separated by a low wall; sliding doors lead into the sunroom, which connects to a deck outside. Three steps lead down to the living room. The steps are necessary, since the concrete living room floor (which provides the thermal mass of this passively heated solar house) rests directly on the ground. The steps are wider here, too, and one of them extends across the front of the bookcase.

There are only two windows on the north side of the house: one in the mudroom and one in the kitchen, giving a view down the driveway to the road. Most of the windows face due south or south-southwest, to get the maximum benefit of the sun during winter days. That is achieved by the dogleg plan, which also makes a small and compact house feel more lively, creating odd and unexpected views such as the diagonal view from the kitchen to the living room, and interesting spaces such as the partially enclosed entrance court. The challenge was not to make the house imposing—it is much too small for that—but to keep it from feeling mean and cramped. Hence the ten-foot-wide porch steps, the long vista from the front door, and the lowered living room floor, which creates a ten-foot ceiling. The dotted line in the living room indicates an opening up to the second floor; the wood-burning stove stands against a thick brick wall (more thermal mass), and a tall window rises the full height of the house. Taking a page from Robert Venturi, this is a small building with a large scale.

The plan of the Ferrero House is solid and compressed, the

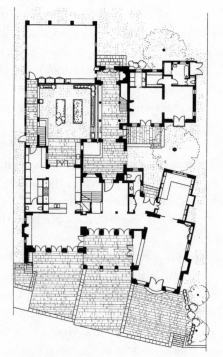

*Appleton & Associates, Villa Pacifica,
California, 1996*

compactness reflecting its windblown site in a northern climate.
The plan of the Villa Pacifica in sunny Southern California, on
the other hand, is expansive. The architect, Marc Appleton, was
approached by a television and Broadway producer who owned a
beautiful site overlooking the Pacific, and wanted a house that
would remind him of his native Greece. The result is a house that
resembles a Greek village with thick walls, small windows, outdoor staircases, and vaulted roofs; even the view is eerily Cycladic,
with the blue Pacific standing in for the Aegean.

The house encloses several shaded courtyards and some of
the movement between rooms takes place out of doors. The plan
looks like a casual arrangement of volumes, but it incorporates a

strong axis. This axis begins at the entrance gate to the compound, moves along an outdoor walk under a trellis beside the kitchen courtyard, arrives at the front door, and continues into the hall, terminating in a loggia, an outdoor room that overlooks a terrace high above the Pacific. All the spaces fall on one side or the other of this imaginary north–south line: the garage, kitchen courtyard, kitchen, and dining room on the west; a guest cottage, the garden courtyard, and the living room and study on the east. Obviously, one is drawn to the terrace with its spectacular view, but in some ways the key space of the house is the loggia, which also serves as an outdoor eating area. With its central position at the head of the axis it firmly anchors the rest of the rooms.

The plan of the Villa Pacifica minimizes western exposure and opens the courtyards up to the morning sun. Most of the house is orthogonally planned, to make the best use of the narrow lot, with the exception of the living room, which is cranked slightly to the west, to give a better view of the sunset and a distant landfall on the coast. As in the Ferrero House, the angle creates some unexpected views and interesting spaces, and it also undermines what might have been a staidly symmetrical plan—the loggia too neatly sandwiched between the dining and living rooms. "If the geometry had all been orthogonally organized, it would have looked overly planned, like an architect did it, rather than slightly accidental," explains Appleton. "We were at self-conscious pains to create spaces and details that did not in the end look self-conscious." Appleton's approach to the design of the villa is unusual in that he largely removes himself from the end result. "I've always admired Billy Wilder's movie direction, because you're not aware of it, only of the story he's telling," he observes.

MOVEMENT

Plans reveal a lot about an architect's intentions. At first glance, Robert Venturi and Denise Scott Brown's plan of the Sainsbury Wing's main gallery floor appears unremarkable. The wing was specifically intended to hold the National Gallery's early Renaissance collection of paintings, and the curators requested a variety of rooms of different sizes to provide an intimate setting for the collection. The challenge for the architects was to lay out the rooms without creating a labyrinth—or odd-shaped galleries that would distract from the art.

Venturi made one decision early on that had an important effect on the plan. The site of the Sainsbury Wing is an irregular shape, thanks to surrounding angled streets. Instead of squaring off the building to create an orthogonal plan—as most architects would have done—Venturi exploited the irregularity. He explained his reasoning:

> When it came to the plans, I thought a lot about the way Lutyens in London had fitted his great Midlands Bank building onto an awkwardly shaped City site. Look, too, at the way Wren's classical churches were made to fit old medieval sites. In Rome, the great palaces are placed into a much older city plan and sometimes they are not as regular as they appear, in fact their regular rectangular grids are often quite distorted.

In the Sainsbury Wing, the rooms are arranged in three rows, running north–south the length of the building. The four enfiladed rooms of the central row form a kind of spine. They are the largest and tallest galleries, and are given additional importance by their architectural treatment. The rooms in the east row are slightly smaller and lower, and have windows that look down into the staircase; the rooms in the west row are the smallest and

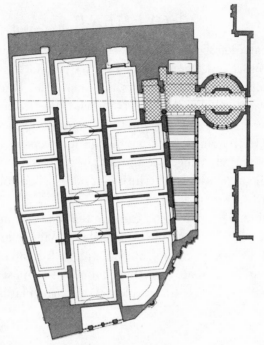

*Venturi, Scott Brown & Associates, Sainsbury
Wing, National Gallery, London, 1991*

lowest—and the least rectangular, since they absorb the irregular angle of Whitcomb Street. The dotted lines indicate clerestories that introduce daylight from above.

The galleries are reached by climbing the wedge-shaped stair from the entrance lobby; the glass wall on the right overlooks Jubilee Walk and Wilkins's National Gallery. The stair ends at a landing opposite a bank of elevators; on the right, a bridge in the form of a circular room connects to the old building, on the left is the entrance to the new galleries. From here, through four door openings, the visitor has a view of Cima's *Incredulity of St. Thomas* on the far wall. The distance appears greater than it is, since the openings are made progressively narrower, an example of so-called forced perspective. The visitor is pulled in this direction to the central gallery, where another visual axis, down the central spine of rooms, terminates in the *Demidoff Altarpiece*, a fifteenth-century polyptych. The two axes—and the varying heights of the rooms—create a hierarchy within the space and give a subtle sense of organization to the sixteen galleries. Once the visitor enters the rooms, there are only walls with paintings, no architectural distractions.

Axes on plans are imaginary, yet they are among the architect's most powerful tools. A good example of how axes can help to organize a large and complicated program is the George W. Bush Presidential Center, designed by Robert A. M. Stern. The site is at the edge of the campus of Southern Methodist University in Dallas. Like all presidential libraries, the center contains a museum and presidential archives, but it also houses a policy institute, which will be used by students and faculty as well as visiting scholars. To distinguish the different functions, Stern created two separate entrances, one on the north (facing the arrival road) for the presidential library, and one on the west (facing the campus) for the policy institute. The entrance to the library follows a north–south axis that begins in the parking lot, arrives in a colonnaded entrance court, and continues through a vestibule until it terminates in a tall square space—Freedom Hall. The hall ends the entry sequence and provides access to the museum, and to a large space for temporary exhibitions; directly ahead is an outdoor terrace. A second axis, east–west, aligns with the entrance portico of the institute, which faces the end of Binkley Avenue, an important campus thoroughfare. The two axes cross in Freedom Hall, a tall space topped by a limestone lantern that functions as a sort of beacon. The lantern is visible as one approaches the library from the parking lot, and also terminates the vista down Binkley Avenue. According to Stern's partner, Graham S. Wyatt, "Axiality and symmetry are formative principles that everyday people understand as they experience them in three dimensions,

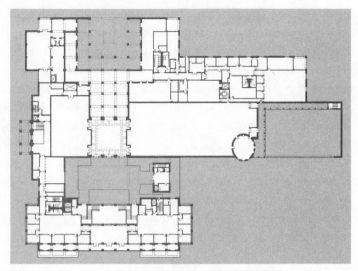

Robert A. M. Stern Architects, George W. Bush Presidential Center, Dallas, 2013

and for a lot of people they imply formality, maybe even a degree of gravitas." Wyatt points out that secondary uses such as the security screening area and the gift shop were intentionally located "off axis" so as not to compromise the sense of occasion as one enters and leaves the building.

The presidential library, which was designed with the landscape architect Michael van Valkenburgh, includes several memorable outdoor spaces, which further structure the plan—two anchoring the north–south axis, and two anchoring the east–west. A colonnaded entrance court with a fountain is balanced by the outdoor terrace—an important amenity in Texas, which has mild springs and autumns. The terrace is accessible both from the library and from the institute. On the west side, a circular drive creates a formal arrival space in front of the institute entrance, while at the other end of the east–west axis is a reproduction of the White House Rose Garden. The Rose Garden is immediately adjacent to a replica of the Oval Office, a staple of presidential libraries, but here oriented in the southeast corner of the building, exactly as it is in the White House.

Although portions of the Bush Library, such as the entry court, and the west and south façades of the institute, rely on symmetry, this is not really an unsymmetrical Beaux-Arts plan in John Harbeson's sense. Rather, it recalls the plans of a first-generation modernist such as Eliel Saarinen, who loosened up Beaux-Arts planning without altogether giving up its principles. While the Bush Library relies on axiality, the Stern office has elsewhere explored combining axiality with informal planning. "The residential colleges we are currently designing for Yale are a good example," says Wyatt. "The main axis of the plan is a walkway that ends in a square where a new axis re-centers and redirects the movement in a way that is picturesque rather than formal."

ORIENTATION AND DISORIENTATION

Two recent museums face each other in San Francisco's Golden Gate Park: the California Academy of Sciences, designed by Renzo Piano, and the de Young Museum, designed by Jacques Herzog and Pierre de Meuron. Both plans generate the architecture—in Le Corbusier's sense—but they do so in different ways. The California Academy, a museum of natural history, is a large rectangular building. The public entrance is on the north side, precisely in the center; the staff entrance is opposite, on the south. A line between the entrances divides the plan in two equal halves. The two symmetrical rectangles flanking the main entrance on the north side are slightly different: one contains a replica of the African Hall that had been part of the neoclassical building that once stood on this site but was irreparably damaged in a 1989 earthquake; the other houses a café and museum shop. The two blocks on the south side contain offices, research spaces, and classrooms. The space in the center contains exhibits and two ninety-foot-diameter spheres, one opaque and enclosing a planetarium, the other transparent and containing a rain forest exhibit. The darkly shaded areas on the drawing are a saltwater tidal pool and an artificial coral reef. The coral reef is deep enough to be visible from the museum's basement, which also houses aquariums. The rectangle in the precise center of the plan, where the two axes cross, is what Piano calls the Piazza, a glass-roofed atrium that is used for receptions and social events.

Traditional science museums are rabbit warrens of dark rooms, one for insects, one for fish, another for rocks, and so on. The chief impression of the California Academy is of a large exhibition hall that, thanks to the glazed end walls and many skylights, is brightly lit. Although Piano's axial plan demonstrates Beaux-Arts planning rigor, his architecture is the antithesis of the Beaux-Arts—steel and glass rather than masonry, lightweight rather than heavy, inspired by technology rather than history. Yet the axial symmetry and the mirroring of forms—the two spheres—provide a clear and simple sense of orientation. This is important, for the huge hangarlike space is filled with an array of exhibits and displays crowding in upon one another. The discipline of the plan binds the whole thing together.

Facing the California Academy of Sciences across a wide landscaped concourse is the de Young Museum, which likewise replaced a predecessor damaged in the same earthquake. The art museum's plan is rectangular and roughly the same overall dimensions as the Academy, but the interior is organized differently. Architects have sometimes used triangular modules to structure a plan—I. M. Pei often used isosceles triangles (notably in the plan of the East Building of the National Gallery)—but there is nothing modular about Herzog and de Meuron's triangulated plan. Irregular wedges are cut out of the building to create

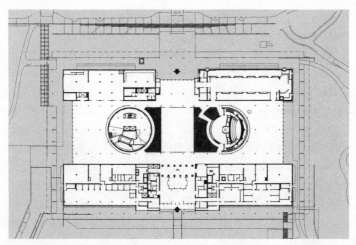

Renzo Piano Building Workshop, California Academy of Sciences, San Francisco, 2008

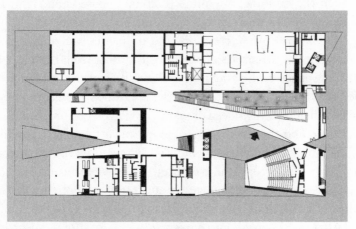

Jacques Herzog & Pierre de Meuron, de Young Museum, San Francisco, 2005

penetrating spaces and trapezoidal courtyards, walls do not line up, nothing mirrors anything else, there are no axes.

The entrance is through a pinched tunnel that leads into a polygonal-shaped open-air courtyard. The unmarked, uncanopied front door is located almost haphazardly on one side. The backdrop to the odd-shaped lobby is a glass wall looking into a fern garden. To get to the museum you turn left and walk through another bottle-necked space until you reach a trapezoidal two-story atrium, dominated by a large painting by Gerhard Richter. On the left is a wide stair going up to the second floor, on the right is a long—extremely long—stair that descends to the lower level. A diagonal path, next to another court, leads to the galleries; another diagonal takes you to the café.

What are Herzog and de Meuron up to? Nothing in their plan takes precedence, there is no right way or wrong way to move through the building, any route that you choose is all right. For example, you can enter through the distinctly ungrand front door, or else via the café terrace, under a dramatic overhanging roof. Herzog and de Meuron's approach is different from the clear hierarchy suggested by traditional plans. It is also different from the idealized universal space of Renzo Piano's Academy of Sciences. The de Young doesn't have an obvious structure, but it has character, and the fractured spaces evoke earthquakes and shifting tectonic plates. Was this allusion intended by the architects? Maybe. "Architecture is like nature—it tells you something about yourself," Jacques Herzog said in an interview. "Nature is very empty—it confronts you with yourself and your experience of it and what you know about yourself in the context of a landscape, river, a rock, a forest, a shadow, the rain." In other words, their architecture is something of a blank slate.

The lack of visual axes and hierarchy in the de Young is only slightly disorienting; this is not a maze. The one place where the architecture quiets down is in the galleries themselves. The rooms in the northwest corner of the ground floor, for example, contain

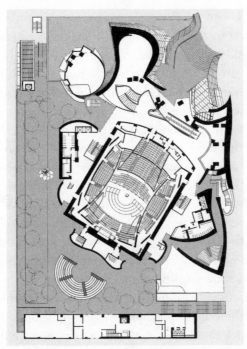

Gehry Partners, Walt Disney Concert Hall, Los Angeles, 2003

twentieth-century art. The visitor slides in at an angle, but from then on continues in a conventional fashion from one rectangular room to the next. Upstairs, a series of enfiladed top-lit rooms provides an appropriate setting for the museum's collection of nineteenth-century American art. In the galleries, the old rules prevail.

The plan of the de Young is consistent in its use of trapezoidal spaces and diagonal movement. But what is one to make of the plan of Walt Disney Concert Hall in Los Angeles? The walls gyrate and swivel according to mysterious hidden rhythms, the shapes defy logic, the forms seem to lack rhyme or reason. Yet Disney Hall is the result of a simple idea. "You have to have a nice

room," Gehry said in an onstage interview at an Aspen confer-
ence, referring to the concert hall. "Forget the exterior. It starts
with that inside. That inside was the key issue." The architect
and acoustician Yasuhisa Toyota explored many shapes for the
auditorium—some of them highly irregular—building large-scale
models before settling on an arrangement with curving tiers of
seats facing each other on all sides of the orchestra. For acoustical reasons, the auditorium was surrounded by a concrete enclosure. "That's a box," Gehry explained. "And on either side of the
box are toilets and stairs. And you've got to join those toilets and
stairs on either side with a foyer. That's the plan." When he said
this, the Aspen audience laughed. He made it sound so simple,
while the built result is obviously so complicated. Yet the underly-
ing principle of Gehry's plan *is* as simple as he described: box,
toilets, stairs, a foyer, a front door.

How is it possible for five distinguished architectural firms to
have such different approaches to planning a building?* Asked
whether he took the de Young Museum, which was built first, into
account when he designed the California Academy of Sciences,
Renzo Piano's tactful response was that he didn't think much
about it. "This is what you get when you are yourself and they are
themselves," he said. A good answer. The differences between the
California Academy and the de Young Museum, like those among
the Sainsbury Wing, the Bush Library, and Disney Hall, are less
the result of different functions, settings, or sites than of different architects being themselves. Robert Venturi and Denise Scott
Brown are interested in adapting history to modern needs, but
they also delight in exploiting the quirky and even awkward dis-
junctions that sometimes arise in the process. Theirs is a modern
reinterpretation of old ideas, often keeping those old ideas at arm's
length. Robert A. M. Stern, on the other hand, embraces history.

*Venturi, Piano, Herzog & de Meuron, and Gehry have all received the Pritzker Archi-
tecture Prize; Stern was recently awarded the Driehaus Prize for Classical Architecture.

"Our firm welcomes new ideas, and we cherish ideas from the past," he has written. "We believe that everything is possible, but that not everything is right." A concern for continuity is evident in the plan of the Bush Library, which does not strive for novelty but is satisfied with the old architectural verities: clarity, order, balance.

The plan of the California Academy, on the other hand, suggests that Renzo Piano is only slightly interested in the past. The plan has a neoclassical simplicity, but it is merely a starting point for his real passion, which is building. This plan is less a generator than a sort of armature. It is as if he said, "We have to have a plan, so let's keep it very simple, and let's focus on how the building is constructed." Not for nothing does he call his office the Renzo Piano Building Workshop.

Herzog and de Meuron's plan for the de Young Museum is the most conventionally modernist of the group—that is, it rejects tradition and history and is designed without recourse to axes, symmetry, lines of movement, vistas, or any perceived geometrical order. The result can be appreciated in purely graphic terms, as if it were a sculpture or a large woodcut. It is no coincidence that in the early years of his architectural practice, Jacques Herzog pursued a parallel career as a conceptual artist.

While Herzog and de Meuron seem interested in pushing the plan in a new, aesthetic direction, the plan drawing of Disney Hall seems almost like an afterthought. Modern architecture's greatest iconoclast (after Le Corbusier), Gehry has upended one of its long-standing tenets; for him, the plan is *not* the generator. His preliminary sketches are never plans; instead the squiggly ink lines portray a three-dimensional image of the building. Then come the crude paper study models, more elaborate wooden models, the shapes mapped by computer software, and only at the end the floor plan.

So, is the plan the generator? In many cases, it remains primary. An ordered plan provides an image in the mind's eye that

guides us through a building. It helps us find our way. In that regard, symmetry, especially axial symmetry, remains a useful tool.
At the same time, having broken free of the conventions of symmetrical planning, there is no easy return. Architects no longer
feel obliged to present the public with a simple diagram. Sometimes, as in the de Young, a sense of adventure is required to learn
what is around the corner. The master of this approach is Gehry.
In Disney Hall, the sense of excitement in the chaotic lobby
spaces heightens the experience of concertgoing. Yet, in the hall
itself, Gehry reverts to tradition and designs a serene space for
listening to music, axially planned and perfectly symmetrical.

5

STRUCTURE

The most prominent features of ancient Greek temples are the columns. Made out of massive superimposed stone drums, their surface carved with shallow grooves, or flutes, the columns resemble soldiers at attention, the sharp vertical shadows suggesting the folds of a Greek chiton, or tunic. A classical column has a gentle swelling, an unevenly tapered profile called entasis, which means "stretching tightly" in Greek, as if the column was straining to support its load—another human reference. The entablature that spans between the columns is composed of elaborately carved parts, each with its distinctive form and name. A Doric frieze, for example, is made up of alternating triglyphs—stylized beam ends—and metopes, square panels that are sometimes adorned with bas-reliefs. The cornice above the frieze contains brackets decorated with guttae, or "drops," an architectural trope for the blood that ran from the sacrificial altar. Except for their wooden rafters and clay-tile roofs, Greek temples were built entirely of white Pentelic marble. Assembled without mortar, and with only occasional bronze centering pins and lead clamps, these monolithic buildings have long been considered the purest expression of structure transformed into architecture.

When the twenty-four-year-old Charles-Édouard Jeanneret, not yet renamed Le Corbusier, visited Athens in September 1911,

Witold Rybczynski, Propylaea seen from Parthenon, July 11, 1964

he spent three weeks on the Acropolis, sketching the ruins. The Parthenon overwhelmed him. "Never in my life have I experienced the subtleties of such monochromy," he wrote in his travel diary.* "The body, the mind, the heart gasp, suddenly overpowered." While there, Charles-Édouard experienced a sort of epiphany: "The hours spent in those silent sanctuaries inspired in me a youthful courage and the true desire to become an honorable builder."

The walls of Le Corbusier's early villas are uniformly painted white, and the columns are always round, although lacking flutes and entasis. He worked hard to achieve the monolithic simplicity of ancient Greek architecture and the "subtleties of monochromy," and like temple ruins his buildings appear to be constructed of

---

*We now know that Greek temples were originally painted in many colors.

one solid material. This illusion required considerable effort. Modernist architects used ribbon windows in lieu of openings punched into the wall, and since in the Villa Savoye these windows stretch across the entire façade, the reinforced concrete lintels are so long that they are actually suspended from the roof slab above. None of this complicated structure is visible, however, since the concrete and masonry are plastered over and painted to create the smooth, uniform surface that the architect desired.

Le Corbusier remained highly selective about revealing what made his buildings stand up. His famous apartment building in Marseilles, the Unité d'Habitation, was raised off the ground on massive piers that Lewis Mumford described as "cyclopean" when he visited the building. "[Le Corbusier] has used concrete for all it is worth as a sculptural form," Mumford wrote, "emphasizing and even exaggerating its plastic qualities, to the extent of leaving untouched the evidences of crude, sometimes inept workmanship." Although the hollow piers are structural, most of the visible concrete is not, and the largely hidden structure of the building is a mixture of cast-in-place concrete, precast concrete, and steel framing. Thus, while the Unité d'Habitation popularized the use of rough concrete, or *béton brut*, giving rise to the term Brutalism, its construction is actually a hybrid.

Two examples from the 1940s show how, contrary to Le Corbusier, some architects went to great lengths to make known the structure of their buildings. At the Illinois Institute of Technology, Mies van der Rohe designed a series of low buildings consisting of steel frames with brick and glass infill. The actual structural steel was encased in concrete to meet fire codes, so Mies added nonstructural I-beams and channels on the exterior to "express" the hidden columns and beams. In the Equitable Savings and Loan Association Building in Portland, Oregon, Pietro Belluschi—another European immigrant—likewise expressed the structure, in this case a reinforced-concrete frame. He filled the space between the floor slabs with sea-green tinted glass and dark cast-aluminum panels, and covered the grid of concrete columns and beams with contrasting silver aluminum. Like Mies, Belluschi wanted the structure to—as much as possible—*be* the architecture.

Architects have always had to decide how to deal with structure: express it or ignore it, display it or hide it, play it up or play it down. The decision depends on the materials and techniques available, and on the engineering know-how of the time, but the choice also depends on the architect's intentions. Some architects care deeply about an "honest" representation of how a building is built and reveal the structure, which complicates life for

Pietro Belluschi, Equitable Building, Portland, Oregon, 1948

the builder, since what *looks* simple is often difficult to construct. When columns and beams cannot be revealed, architects like Mies and Belluschi resort to a sort of faux structure. Others choose to conceal structural members altogether, for the sake of dramatic visual effects. I once saw a stair whose treads magically cantilevered out of a wall; the architect, Moshe Safdie, explained that hidden inside the wall was a framework of heavy steel members to which the treads were welded. Another architect might have revealed how the treads were supported, as Aalto did in the Villa Mairea, where exposed steel I-beams carry the treads, or he might make the stair entirely self-supporting, as Jack Diamond did in a dramatic all-glass stair in the Four Seasons Centre for the Performing Arts.

THEORIES OF CONSTRUCTION

"An architect cannot construct a building without a theory of construction, however simple-minded that theory might be," writes the architectural historian Edward R. Ford.

> Construction is not mathematics; architectural construction is just as subjective a process as is architectural design. Construction involves a more complex set of concerns, the application of scientific laws, and a tradition (or perhaps a conventional wisdom) as to how things ought to be built, but that tradition and that wisdom are no more or less valid than the tradition or conventional wisdom as to how buildings should appear.

In other words, there are many ways of building, ways that are more or less beautiful, more or less dramatic, more or less evident, and, of course, more or less expensive. I once designed a house

*Ludwig Mies van der Rohe, Farnsworth
House, Plano, Illinois, 1951*

using conventional wood-frame construction. Since the spans
were short, it was easy to calculate the size of the floor joists, but
there was one large space that required a special beam, and I
turned to an engineer friend for advice. "Do you want it cheap, or
architectural?" Emmanuel Leon asked me. Since this tall room
was the main living space of the house, I chose the latter, and he
designed a striking upside-down king-post truss, with cables as
tension members.

Mies's solutions were always architectural. Although fire regulations prevented him from exposing steel in large buildings, he
was able to do so in a private residence such as the Farnsworth
House. The external columns are eight-inch-deep steel I-beams

carrying fifteen-inch steel channels that support the floor and roof.* Although the columns and channels are exposed, the way they are attached—by a plug weld on the back of the column flange—is concealed from view. The I-beams that span the width of the house and support precast concrete roof planks are likewise hidden behind a suspended plaster ceiling. As Ford writes, Mies "preferred, in later life, to expose the steel, but he would accept concealment if required," a theory of construction that is nothing if not pragmatic.

In the late 1920s, Frank Lloyd Wright wrote a famous series of essays, "The Meaning of Materials," arguing that "each material has its own message and, to the creative artist, its own song." It's a compelling metaphor, but in practice Wright was as pragmatic as Mies, sometimes revealing the "song," often muting it. The most striking feature of the Robie House in Chicago, for example, is a dramatic twenty-foot roof cantilever—an unprecedented dimension for wood construction. What makes this cantilever possible is that the wooden rafters rest on concealed steel beams. As for the "floating" balconies and roofs that appear to be carried by heavy brick piers, they are also supported by a hidden steel frame. In this house, steel is not allowed to sing.

Wright often exposed concrete, although he recognized that it is not a particularly attractive material. "As an artificial stone, concrete has no great, certainly no independent, aesthetic value whatsoever," he wrote. "As a plastic material—eventually becoming stone-like in character—there lives in it great aesthetic property, as yet inadequately expressed." At the time that he wrote this, he had already used exposed concrete in the Unity Temple in Oak Park, and in the four Los Angeles textile-block houses. But none of these projects exploits the unique properties of reinforced concrete as dramatically as Fallingwater. The terraces,

---

*The large size of the columns and channels is the result of visual rather than structural requirements.

Frank Lloyd Wright, Robie House, Chicago, 1909

parapets, eaves, and balustrades form one continuous, monolithic piece of poured-in-place concrete. Wright is not interested in revealing the structure, however. All the concrete is uniformly plastered over and painted. The four large girders that support the terrace over the stream are concealed behind a flat soffit. The girders are supported by three exposed concrete brackets, but these are seen only from the stair that descends to the water; the fourth bracket, which is visible from the exterior, is made out of stone rather than concrete. Elsewhere, the supports of the upper terrace are disguised as window mullions to further the illusion of weightlessness.

Fallingwater is a combination of concrete, steel, and stone, while the Guggenheim Museum is built entirely of reinforced concrete. As in Fallingwater, the plastered and painted concrete surfaces are continuous, so it is impossible to distinguish what is structural and what is merely infill. The balustrade, for example, stiffens the spiraling ramp; the twelve ribs from which the ramp cantilevers look like walls and at the top turn into supports for the glass dome that covers the atrium. The curved ramp has a bulging bay on each floor—does it help to support the ramp? Impossible to tell. "As an object by itself, the Guggenheim Museum interior is, like the exterior, a remarkable example of abstract sculpture," wrote Lewis Mumford in a *New Yorker* review. "Without ornament, without texture, without positive color, in a design as smoothly cylindrical as a figure by Fernand Léger—this is how Wright shows himself here a master of the abstract resources of modern form." That was written in 1959, when the idea that a building could be a work of sculpture rather than a work of construction was still a novelty. Thirty years later, as we shall see, that would no longer be the case.

EXPOSING THE BONES

The great pioneer of concrete, the French architect Auguste Perret, once observed that "architecture is what makes beautiful ruins." Louis Kahn took this dictum to heart, and more than any other modern architect he was obsessed by the idea of revealing the main supporting elements of a building, as if what remained when a building fell into ruin was architecture's true soul. This attitude was undoubtedly influenced by his visits to ancient sites such as the Parthenon, which he saw when he was forty-nine, just before he designed the Yale Art Gallery and embarked on the most creative phase of his illustrious but short career.

Kahn believed that how a building was constructed should be clearly visible, without subterfuge or artifice. For this reason, he favored walls that were monolithic—that is, solid concrete or solid brick. However, modern construction is layered—what looks like a solid brick wall consists of a thin brick veneer, an air space, a vapor barrier, insulation, a backup wall, and the interior finish. This reality made Kahn's preference for "honest" construction hard to achieve. The exposed concrete space-frame ceiling of the Yale Art Gallery is visually striking but has no structural logic. "Kahn's structure uses a massive quantity of concrete in a complex arrangement to achieve what is ultimately not a particularly impressive span," writes Edward Ford. The precast concrete beams of the Richards Medical Building effectively reveal how the floors are supported but are needlessly complicated and expensive to build. When Kahn's friend Eero Saarinen saw the Richards Building, he asked, "Lou, do you consider this building an architectural or a structural success?" Saarinen, who had designed research laboratories for General Motors, IBM, and Bell Telephone, was implying that the structure compromised the function—which it did. Although the exposed structural system is visually striking, the large areas of

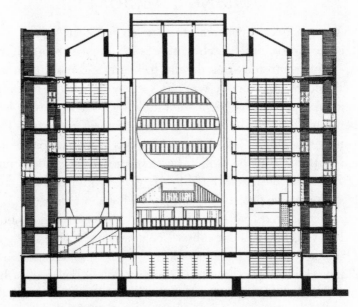

Louis I. Kahn, Section, Phillips Exeter Academy Library, Exeter, New Hampshire, 1972

glass create glare, and the dust from the exposed concrete compromises the laboratories.

In a library for Phillips Exeter Academy, Kahn came close to designing a building that straightforwardly expresses its construction. The eight-story library resembles a square doughnut. The architectural concept is extremely simple: the doughnut consists of two rings, the outer ring contains study carrels, while the inner ring houses the book stacks; the "hole" is an atrium lit by a large skylight. Initially the building was to be all brick, but to save money Kahn built the stacks of reinforced concrete, and the hybrid result is an evocative example of his approach to structure. "I felt the striving not for severity but for the purity that I sense in a Greek temple," Kahn said of the library. That purity is visible in the two construction systems: reinforced concrete columns, beams, and slabs for the heavy book stacks, and brick piers and arches for the carrels.

The plasticity of poured-in-place concrete, which Kahn called "molten stone," is expressed by huge circles cut out of the four walls that enclose the library atrium. The joints of the formwork are everywhere clearly visible, since the concrete is exposed. The surface is marked by a regular pattern of small circular recesses, a detail that Kahn developed at the Salk Institute. Cast-in-place concrete requires wire ties to keep the forms from being pushed apart when the heavy mix is poured in; after the concrete has set, the ends of the ties are snipped off and the concrete is patched to prevent the wire from rusting. Kahn designed a neat recessed lead plug to replace the unsightly patch. The regular pattern of plugs was a kind of decoration, and, equally important to Kahn, the plug revealed how the wall was made.

Ford calls the Exeter library "the purest of Kahn's brick structures." The openings in the brick façade are spanned by traditional jack arches, flat arches made out of radially sawn bricks. However, the exterior walls are less solid than they appear. Kahn was sometimes able to use solid brick walls—in India and

*Louis I. Kahn, Phillips Exeter Academy Library,
Exeter, New Hampshire, 1972*

Bangladesh—but in America, labor costs and the need to accommodate insulation mandated a cavity wall. The library wall is actually two layers (with a cavity and insulation between them): a twelve-inch structural bearing wall made out of brick and cement block, and an inner veneer of brick that is only four inches thick. There is a small detail that few will notice. The exterior wall includes a line of header bricks every eight courses to bind the bricks and blocks together, while the inner wall, being a veneer, has no headers. This attitude differentiates the architect from the stage designer; the former works to satisfy his own constructional logic, while the latter is concerned only with the view from the seats.

Renzo Piano worked briefly in Kahn's office. While Kahn

Renzo Piano & Richard Rogers, Centre Pompidou, Paris, 1977

used mainly masonry and concrete, and Piano's structures are generally steel, Kahn's attitude to construction clearly had an influence on the young Italian. Piano's first high-profile commission, the Centre Pompidou, the result of a competition he entered with Richard Rogers, revels in its construction. The main columns are thirty-four-inch-diameter steel masts; steel trusses span one hundred and fifty feet, the entire width of the building; tension rods provide lateral bracing; and escalators and services are suspended from cast steel gerberettes—cantilevered brackets that recall Victorian cast ironwork. The steel in the building is exposed throughout, and fireproofed either by water cooling (in the case of the water-filled masts) or by mineral-wool heat shields covered by stainless steel (in the case of the trusses). A third fire-protection technique involves coating the steel with an intumescent material that expands during a fire to produce a light char that retards the transfer of heat. Since this coating is as thin as paint, it allows the connection details to be plainly visible. And there is much to reveal. "Everything in the structure is articulated," wrote Ted Happold, an engineer who was a member of the

Foster + Partners, Hongkong and Shanghai Bank,
Hong Kong, 1986

design team. "Every detail shows how the building has been looked upon as a framed mechanism."

A decade after the Centre Pompidou opened, Norman Foster completed the Hongkong and Shanghai Bank, whose planning likewise stresses flexibility and adaptability by providing large column-free spaces. Large spans inevitably provide an opportunity to dramatize the structures. Foster and Rogers had been partners, and Foster treated the structure of the bank with equal daring. Most high-rise office buildings are supported by columns that carry loads down to the ground, but Foster opted for a different solution, suspending the floors from intermittent bridge-like trusses. The trusses and columns on the exterior of the building are exposed and are a visual explanation of how the forty-seven-story tower is built.

The Centre Pompidou and the Hongkong Bank dramatically reveal their long-span structure. Did these two buildings herald a new approach to construction? Not exactly. For one thing, many architects are uninterested in featuring structure. For another, exposing columns and trusses on the exterior of a building is expensive, in terms of both construction and maintenance. Moreover, few buildings require the high degree of flexibility achieved by extremely long spans. Where long-span structures really shine is in airport terminals, which require large spaces that can accommodate the ever-changing mix of ticketing counters, screening areas, and shops. Foster, Rogers, and Piano have designed striking terminals in Britain, Spain, China, and Japan, whose chief architectural feature is dramatic structure, and which achieve the modernist dream of revealing—not simply expressing—the bones of a building.

LAYERS

While generations of architects have admired the Acropolis, its structural purity is atypical; most ancient buildings were more complicated, especially after the Romans invented hydraulic cement. This material used volcanic dust (pozzolana) or gypsum and lime as binders, and enabled builders to make a crude sort of concrete that could be cast into vaults and domes. Since the surface of concrete is unattractive, it was generally covered by a layer of marble or brick, making the "honest" expression of structure difficult.* The Coliseum, for example, is cast-in-place concrete faced in brick on the interior and travertine marble on the exterior. The prominent attached half-columns carry no loads, nor are

---

*Roman concrete was unreinforced, acting only in compression like brick and stone.

they even an expression of the structure, since the floors of the amphitheater are supported by arches and vaults, rather than by columns and beams.

The Coliseum was completed in A.D. 80, and fifty years later the Romans built another impressive concrete building: the Pantheon. The dome is more than 140 feet in diameter, a tapered shell that is 21 feet thick at the base and 4 feet thick at the top. The exposed concrete coffers of the interior reduce the weight of the dome. The thick concrete wall that carries the dome on brick relieving arches is sheathed in marble on the inside and brick on the outside. The forty-foot columns that support the portico represent an older technology, being made out of single pieces of granite five feet in diameter. Monoliths, indeed.

*Thomas Ustick Walter, dome of U.S.
Capitol, Washington, D.C., 1859*

Nowhere is the discrepancy between appearance and reality more pronounced than in the construction of domes. The horizontal thrust of Brunelleschi's octagonal brick dome of the cathedral of Florence is taken by concealed reinforcement—four rings of sandstone and iron, and one of wood. The dome itself consists of two independent shells; an external nonstructural shell that supports the roofing tiles, and an internal shell that does all the structural work. The dome of Christopher Wren's St. Paul's Cathedral has no fewer than three shells: an inner plastered-brick dome, a timber-framed outer dome, and between them a brick cone that supports both the outer dome and the heavy stone lantern.

Like Brunelleschi, Wren was a pragmatist—for him construction was merely a means to an end. His particular architectural problem was to create a landmark that would be visible throughout the city, a replacement for the tall Gothic spire of the old St. Paul's Cathedral, which had been destroyed in the Great Fire. As a classicist, he wanted a dome, and for additional height he added the seventy-five-foot lantern. The inner dome is hemispherical and much lower, and like the Pantheon has an oculus to light the interior. Wren's assistant Robert Hooke, likewise a philosopher, architect, and polymath, devised the method of counteracting the outward thrust of the dome, which Wren described: "Altho' the Dome wants no Butment, yet, for greater Caution, it is hooped with Iron in this Manner; a Chanel is cut in the Bandage of Portland-stone, in which is laid a double Chain of Iron strongly linked together at every ten Feet, and the whole Chanel filled up with Lead." The vital chain, like the arched buttresses that brace the masonry cone, was invisible—it was required "for greater Caution," but not required to be seen. Thomas Ustick Walter's dome of the U.S. Capitol likewise consists of three shells, with an inner dome made of cast iron, although you would hardly know this looking at the classical exterior, a reminder that there is no rule that construction must take precedence.

THE PILASTER IS A LIE

At the end of the Renaissance, architects such as Michelangelo and Giulio Romano consciously distorted classical motifs, making what had ossified into a canon once more fresh—that is, making what was familiar unfamiliar. The distortions included irregular column spacing, "dropped" keystones, "broken" pediments, columns with alternating "uncut" drums, and artificially "rusticated" stonework. What was later christened mannerism broke the rules, but it also depended on them, for, as Venturi writes in his classic *Complexity and Contradiction in Architecture*, "convention, system, order, genericness, *manners*, must be there in the first place before they can be broken."

Venturi's mannerist leanings are evident in the hybrid construction of the Sainsbury Wing of the National Gallery. The floors are cast-in-place concrete supported by irregularly spaced columns that carry beams aligned with the gallery walls. The exterior wall is concrete faced with Portland stone, Cornish granite, or Ibstock brick; the roof with its clerestory lanterns, on the other hand, is carried on a steel frame. This steel structure is hidden, and with few exceptions concrete columns are concealed inside walls. While some of the visible columns in the Sainsbury Wing carry loads, there are several that are what Venturi called "symbolically structural"—that is, fake. A row of columns in the entrance foyer, for example, and the Tuscan columns in the archways of the galleries, are in the latter category; so is a series of arched trusses above the main staircase. Deliberately using structural elements in nonstructural ways has a long history. The most obvious ancient example is the pilaster, which looks like a flattened column but carries no load. "The pilaster is a lie," observed Goethe disapprovingly.

Venturi is the leading modern mannerist. The colonnade of the entry porch of the Vagelos Laboratories at the University of Pennsylvania consists of irregularly spaced single and double col-

Venturi, Scott Brown & Associates, Roy and Diana Vagelos Laboratories, University of Pennsylvania, Philadelphia, 1997

umns. Some carry loads, some don't; some line up with the structural grid of the reinforced concrete frame that supports the five-story building, some don't; some line up with the brick piers of the façade—only some of which are structural—some don't. What is the reason for this intricacy? In part, it reflects the complex program of the building, which houses offices and laboratories for bioengineering, chemistry, chemical engineering, and medicine. In part, Venturi is grappling with an architectural problem of the site: how to create a main entrance façade on the short end of a building. His solution is to make the façade complicated, contradictory, and paradoxical. He hints that the columns should not be taken altogether seriously by giving them stylized, flattened, almost cartoonish capitals, and by separating the capital from the wall above. The games that Venturi plays with structure are also an *hommage* to his Victorian predecessor Frank Furness, whose highly mannered university library stands across the street.

The Los Angeles architect Thom Mayne favors materials that are industrial-looking but he is likewise a mannerist. The U.S. Federal Building in San Francisco is a narrow eighteen-story office slab with a façade shrouded in a perforated-stainless-steel skin that is mysteriously sliced and peeled away, apparently at random. At the entrance, a column leans perilously aslant. The leaning column is real, but what about the beam that forces its way out of the wall and stops short of the column? Like a dropped keystone in a Renaissance building, it suggests instability—hardly what we expect in a government building. The Federal Building abounds in such contradictions. Alongside a walkway is a giant garden pergola with a steel structure as heavy—and as un-garden-

Thom Mayne/Morphosis, U.S. Federal Building, San Francisco, 2007

like—as the underside of stadium bleachers. The most striking feature of the entry façade is a mundane fire escape, casually draped over the building. Comparing harmony and dissonance in architecture, Venturi wrote that wearing a gray tie with a gray suit was an example of harmony, wearing a red tie with a gray suit was "contrasting harmony," while wearing a gray tie with red polka dots was "dissonant harmony." Mayne's unruly building goes a step further, dispensing with the tie altogether, and leaving the shirt-tail hanging out, in what might be called "dissonant *dis*harmony."

Some architects play with structure, others simply ignore it. In the chapel at Ronchamp, Le Corbusier created a pillow-like roof that looks like solid concrete but is really a diaphragm made up of two thin skins separated—and supported—by hidden internal girders. The roof rests on roughly plastered walls that appear massive but are actually hollow—cement sprayed onto a metal mesh—and conceal a concrete frame. At Ronchamp, Le Corbusier

Gehry Partners, Jay Pritzker Pavilion, Millennium Park, Chicago,
2004

hides what holds the building up and even creates make-believe structure.

Ronchamp was built in the 1950s. Today, buildings that resemble large sculptures are commonplace. There are columns here and there at the de Young Museum, but the steel structure is concealed, even in the fifty-five-foot roof cantilever that mysteriously hovers over the café terrace. The cantilever, like the outlines of the building, is dictated by formal considerations. The structure of Disney Hall is a steel frame, and is likewise inconsequential to the animated exterior, which is purely sculptural. Gehry's casual attitude to construction is even more evident in the outdoor band shell that he designed for Millennium Park in Chicago. A band shell is required to be a sound reflector, and Gehry creates a wooden backdrop for the stage, framed by wavy, stainless-steel, sail-like forms. These forms are supported by a utilitarian framework of steel props and braces that cannot be seen from the grassy seating area, but is completely visible from the sides and rear and is as prosaic as the back of a billboard. This seemingly makeshift solution is light-years away from the ordered solidity of the Parthenon. Perhaps it reflects Gehry's view of our improvised and unruly modern condition.

6

SKIN

Le Corbusier defined architecture as "the masterly, correct and magnificent play of volumes brought together in light," but what we actually see when we look at a building is its skin. Whether it is the painted stucco of the Villa Savoye, the veined white marble of the Folger Library, the bronze and glass of the Seagram Building, or the matte-gray stainless steel of the Yale Center for British Art, it is the skin that makes the first impression.

Building skins are a modern concept. Although the Romans built concrete buildings with brick or stone veneers, most traditional construction was monolithic: a single material such as brick, stone, adobe, or timber (in the case of log cabins) served as both structure and skin. The eighteen-inch-thick stone walls of my house are Wissahickon schist, a locally quarried stone that is silvery-brown with glistening flecks of mica and quartzite. The undressed stones are laid randomly with rough mortar joints, a technique chosen for economy, and to give the house a rustic appearance in keeping with its countrified French style.

By the early 1900s, when my house was built, monolithic construction was on the way out. It was less expensive to build load-bearing walls out of brick, adding a thin layer of stone as an external finish. This was true even in McKim, Mead & White's fabulous Morgan Library in New York, which cost more than a million dollars in 1906. The milky Tennessee marble exterior with its paper-thin joints is a veneer—albeit a hefty eight inches thick; the actual structural walls are twelve-inch-thick brick. Charles McKim left an air space between the marble and the brick to retard the transmission of moisture and safeguard the books. Several decades later, cavity walls became standard practice for all buildings.

Most large buildings today are supported by structural frames—columns and beams—made of steel or reinforced concrete. In a frame building, the external skin is supported by—or hangs from—the frame. The modern architectural expression of the steel-and-glass skin appeared in the late 1940s in Chicago, when Mies van der Rohe designed a pair of apartment towers on Lake Shore Drive facing Lake Michigan. The twenty-six-story buildings are wrapped in lightweight skins that hang from the steel skeletons—like curtains. While Belluschi's curtain wall at the Equitable Savings and Loan Association Building mimicked its structure, Mies's wall was almost entirely glass, with regularly spaced steel mullions and spandrels covering the edges of the floor. Since the mullions, which stiffen the glass, are shaped like small I-beams, the muscular skin looks purposefully structural.

Mies considered the I-beam mullion a modern version of the classical pilaster, and he designed it that way. When he was questioned about why he felt it necessary to add mullions to the surfaces of the corner columns, where they were functionally superfluous, he answered:

> It was very important to preserve and extend the rhythm which the mullions set up on the rest of the building. We looked at it on the model without the steel section attached to the corner columns and it did not look right. That is the real reason. Now the other reason is that the steel section was needed to stiffen the plate which covers the corner

column so this plate would not ripple, and also we needed it for strength when the sections were hoisted into place. Now, of course, that's a very good reason—but the other one is the real reason.

Mies used this type of curtain wall for the rest of his career, whether he was building in New York, Mexico City, or Montreal. The mullions and spandrels, usually black, could be a variety of materials, depending on the budget: bronze in the Seagram Building, painted steel in the Bacardi office building in Mexico City, or anodized aluminum in Montreal's Westmount Square. Westmount Square consists of two apartment towers, an office tower, and a low pavilion. Mies saw no reason to vary the curtain wall, and the skin is similar throughout, except that in the apartment towers the lower portion of the window is openable, whereas in the office tower and the pavilion the glazing is fixed.

Ludwig Mies van der Rohe, Westmount Square, Montreal, 1967

HEAVY AND LIGHT SKINS

The Miesian steel-and-glass curtain wall was widely imitated and became, as Robert Hughes put it, "the lingua franca of the modern age." That was one reason that the fiercely competitive Eero Saarinen, designing his first high-rise building, wanted to try something different. His design for the thirty-eight-story CBS Building in New York is concrete rather than steel, a perimeter bearing wall of closely spaced V-shaped concrete piers, each pier alternating with a sheet of glass. There are no columns inside the building. The exterior faces of the triangular piers, which are hollow and contain air-conditioning ducts, are covered in two-inch-thick slabs of matte, dark gray granite, mitered at the corner,

Philip Johnson & John Burgee, AT&T Building, New York, 1984

more like armor than skin. The architectural effect is the antithesis of the Miesian glass curtain wall, and seen at an oblique angle the CBS Building looks implacably solid—if somewhat gloomy—giving rise to the nickname Black Rock.

Saarinen used a traditional stone skin, but he used it in an abstract and distinctly untraditional manner. On the other hand, the stone skin of the AT&T Building, designed by Philip Johnson and John Burgee, mimics traditional masonry. The steel-frame skyscraper is clad in rose-gray granite slabs, whose joints—some real, some false—give the impression of stone courses. The building is crowned with a split pediment modeled on a Chippendale highboy. The grand entrance and outdoor arcade at the foot of the building are based on the 1908 Municipal Building in downtown Manhattan. Johnson explained: "I did a classical skyscraper, because it seems to me the most viable history, if there is any, in New York City is McKim, Mead & White."

The architectural critic Ada Louise Huxtable considered the AT&T Building "a pictorial pastiche that was flat and one-dimensional . . . a shallow send-up of the past." Whether the building is a send-up is debatable, but the skin is hardly shallow: the columns are clad in six inches of stone, and some of the ornate moldings and profiles are ten inches thick. In all, thirteen thousand tons of granite carapace hang from the steel frame. But Huxtable is correct that the skin is aesthetically one-dimensional, for there was nothing witty or inventive about the way that Johnson and Burgee used the stone. Perhaps they chose the wrong historical example. Both Stanford White and Charles McKim were dead by the time that the Municipal Building was built—the design is credited to McKim's protégé, William M. Kendall—and it lacks McKim's sure touch. The taut marble skin of the Morgan Library, with its hairline joints and spare details, might have made a better model.

The Canadian Centre for Architecture in Montreal, designed by Peter Rose, is a poured-in-place concrete structure with a

Peter Rose, Canadian Centre for Architecture, Montreal, 1989

masonry skin, built a decade after the AT&T Building. At first glance, the masonry looks similarly traditional. The basement courses are rusticated with raked-out horizontal joints, while the upper courses are ashlar, or smooth-cut. The basement windows have large, keystone-shaped lintels surmounted by a bulging to-rus molding. The façade is topped by a frieze of vertical stone panels attached with exposed steel pins, and a projecting alumi-num cornice that resembles a catwalk. The pins and the cornice recall the Viennese architect Otto Wagner's 1907 Austrian Post Office Savings Bank, whose design heralded a shift from neoclas-sicism and Art Nouveau to an ahistorical simplicity. Like the AT&T Building, the CCA refers to the early twentieth century, but instead of late Beaux-Arts, Rose chose a more interesting mo-ment, when nineteenth-century architecture was being trans-formed into something new. "There's a lot of elaboration to make the building less sober, a little bit more abstract and more modern," he explained.

The skin of the Montreal building is unusual in several respects. Like the Morgan Library, the thick limestone skin supports itself, rather than being hung from the structure. "We sought to make the CCA well built and respectful of the best construction traditions," Phyllis Lambert, the founding director of the Centre, has written.

The stone facing, four and six inches thick, is self-supporting, bearing its own weight up to the topmost stones, which are pinned in place. The cut and bedding of the stone is symbolic of the forces. In the areas of greatest stress, on the lintels and along the string courses, the stone is laid in its bed. The rest of the stone—whether the rusticated base courses, or the ashlar of the body of the building—is cut against the grain, minimizing weathering and at the same time emphasizing the figure of the stone.

The decision to make the heavy masonry skin self-supporting gives the CCA a weightiness and solidity that recall the early houses of Mies van der Rohe, when he was still designing in a traditional style. Lambert was instrumental in securing the Seagram Building commission for Mies, and later studied under him at the Illinois Institute of Technology. Mies's approach to teaching was influenced by his early training as a stonemason, which left him with an abiding respect for building materials. "When I was young, we hated the word *architecture*," he once told an interviewer. "We use in German the word *Baukunst*, that are two words, the 'building' and the 'art.' The art is the refinement of building." It is said that when he started teaching at IIT, noting that the students were spending all their time at their drawing tables, he had a load of bricks delivered to the drafting studio so they could experience the material firsthand.

While stone and brick make a weather-resistant, durable, and attractive building skin, not all architects like its traditional imag-

*James Stirling & Michael Wilford, Neue
Staatsgalerie, Stuttgart, 1984*

ery. In their museum addition to the Staatsgalerie in Stuttgart, James Stirling and Michael Wilford use a stone veneer in such a way that it is obvious that it *is* a veneer. Alternating bands of one-and-a-half-inch-thick travertine and sandstone are attached to a structural concrete wall with stainless steel clips. Although the stone appears to be laid in a running bond (like the skins of the CCA and AT&T), the joints are open rather than mortared. This is a rain-screen wall, in which a cavity behind the skin equalizes the extreme drop in air pressure between the outside and the inside of a building, and rain is deflected by the skin rather than being drawn into the building (as it is in a conventional wall). An added advantage, from Stirling's point of view, was that, on closer inspection, what appeared to be traditional stonework turned out to be a thin skin suspended in front of the structural wall.

He delighted in such apparent contradictions—at one spot in the museum, a solid sandstone block on the ground appears to have "fallen out" of the wall, even though the void in the cladding clearly exposes the veneered nature of the masonry. The jokey gesture highlights Stirling's intention to undermine modern building techniques, even as he used them. "The structural content in architecture is likely to increase as traditional methods of construction decline, and new buildings get larger and more complicated," he told a lecture audience. "However, I think it will be ever more necessary for architects not to rely merely on the expression of techniques for the architectural solution. Humanistic considerations must remain the primary logic from which a design evolves." Stirling's solution was to turn to history, including recent history, as a way of counterbalancing the impersonal technical demands of modern, industrialized building techniques.

Louis I. Kahn, Kimbell Art Museum, Fort Worth, 1972

Although he was not above using prefabrication in his projects, he never embraced a purely technical aesthetic as a later generation of so-called high-tech architects would do.

Louis Kahn dealt with the skin by clearly differentiating it from the structure. The Kimbell Art Museum in Fort Worth is a low, spreading building consisting of a series of parallel cast-in-place concrete vaults supported by beams and columns. Since the galleries are lit from above, there are no windows, and Kahn fills in the space beneath the beams with Italian travertine. To emphasize that this material is not structural, he leaves a gap of several inches between the top of the travertine and the concrete beams, and fills the space with a strip of glass. However, the travertine is laid in a traditional running bond, which gives the impression that this is a heavy wall, even though the marble is only one inch thick and is supported by a concrete backup wall.

Kahn's theory of construction had little to do with actual building methods, which may be why he had so much trouble

Renzo Piano Building Workshop, Menil Collection, Houston, 1986

reconciling his demanding philosophy with modern building techniques. In the Yale Center for British Art, he finally resolved the structure-skin relationship to his satisfaction. Here the stainless-steel skin is obviously lighter than the exposed concrete frame, and he did not have to resort to tricky details. The difference between skin and structure is beautifully and obviously clear: *this* holds the building up, *that* is merely infill.

Renzo Piano follows in Kahn's footsteps when it comes to expressing the difference between structure and skin. For example, the structure of the Menil Collection in Houston, a long, low, predominantly one-story building, is an exposed steel frame, and the space between is filled with cypress tongue-and-groove boards. The museum is in a residential neighborhood, and the wooden skin harmonizes with the surrounding houses. Indeed, the overall effect of the museum is so low-key that Reyner Banham described it as "an upscale UPS warehouse." But a very beautiful warehouse, Piano might reply.

Renzo Piano Building Workshop, Central St. Giles, London, 2010

Piano used a nonstructural masonry skin in three urban projects, two in Paris and one in London. The IRCAM addition to the Centre Pompidou, a musical research center founded by Pierre Boulez, is located between two historic brick buildings, and Parisian regulations mandate a brick façade. Piano's solution is unusual. The specially made Roman bricks are stacked inside aluminum frames with mortarless joints, which both enable the skin to function as a rain screen and demonstrate that this wall is not solid. A six-story low-income apartment complex on the rue de Meaux is clad with terra-cotta tiles that are clipped to extremely thin prefabricated panels of concrete reinforced by glass fibers. Since the tiles are framed by exposed steel brackets, the result blends the warmth and texture of fired clay with the precision of steel. Central St. Giles, a residential and commercial project in London, has a terra-cotta skin consisting of glazed extrusions. The nonstructural nature of the skin is expressed by its design: the ten-story sections of curtain wall hang from the building like giant screens. Terra-cotta, a clay-based ceramic, is an ancient material that was produced industrially in the nineteenth century and is associated with architects such as Louis Sullivan, who designed terra-cotta facings with molded plantlike patterns. Piano takes advantage of the material's moldability to fashion a richly modulated skin, and he varies the colors of the glazing on the different sides of the building: bright orange, lime green, lemon yellow, and red, as well as white.

MANUFACTURED SKINS

When it opened in 1978, Norman Foster's Sainsbury Centre for Visual Arts at the University of East Anglia was often described as a "silver shed" because of its aluminum skin. The most unusual feature of this skin is that it covers the roof as well as the walls. A Boeing 747 has a metal top, Foster said; why not a building? The four-by-six-foot aluminum panels come in different configurations—solid, glazed, and louvered—with curved panels forming the junction between walls and roof, and glazed panels serving as both windows and skylights. The panels are bolted to the structural frame and sit in a continuous grid of neoprene gaskets, which seal the joints and function as gutters, leading rainwater across the roof and down the walls to a collection trough at the base of the building. Unlike Kahn and Piano, Foster seems unconcerned about the nonstructural character of the skin, and unlike Johnson, whose granite cladding mimics the details of traditional masonry, Foster treats the skin of the Sainsbury Centre as an industrial product—which is precisely what it is. He has referred to the body panels of mass-produced automobiles as an inspiration.* "The building is essentially a series of machine-made components," he told a lecture audience at the university, "and that relates to the realities of cost control, to the manner in which buildings are assembled, and the materials from which they are made."

Just because the skin of a building is manufactured does not mean it has to look industrial. Like the early modernists he admires, Richard Meier is more interested in conveying the impression of an abstract, ethereal skin than in expressing how a building is actually built. The white skins of many of his buildings are porcelain-enameled aluminum panels. While the technology is similar to that of the Sainsbury Centre, the architectural expression is very different. In Foster's building, the joint grid of the skin is simply the result of connecting the panels; in Meier's hands, the grid is an aesthetic device. He organizes the joint lines between the panels into a square grid, and uses the same grid to dimension windows, openings, and piers. In the Getty Center, this effect is only slightly lessened by the use of travertine as well

---

*The original ribbed panels recalled the body panels of a Citroën 2CV van. In a 1988 renovation, these panels were replaced by smooth white panels, which make the skin resemble that of a jumbo jet.

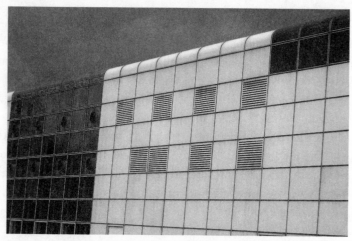

Foster Associates, Sainsbury Centre for Visual Arts, University of East Anglia, Norwich, 1978

Richard Meier & Partners, Getty Center, Los Angeles, California, 1997

as metal, since the stone slabs are exactly the same size as the metal panels. The result is that the buildings look as if they are wrapped in giant graph paper.

Jacques Herzog and Pierre de Meuron are well-known for experimenting with building skins, and the de Young Museum in San Francisco is no exception—the steel-framed building is entirely sheathed in copper. Copper is a common roofing material, since it can be easily shaped and acquires an attractive green patina as it ages, but it is rarely used on walls, especially on this scale. The joints of the thirty-nine-inch-wide copper sheets are invisible, and the surface is embossed and perforated with bottle-cap-size circles, concave and convex dimples as well as holes. The circles are designed to form treelike patterns, like dots in a half-tone illustration, although these images are only indistinctly perceived from a distance. The mottled effect heightens the overall impression of an organic skin, like a giant lizard. Or perhaps a chameleon. Most copper roofs are artificially treated to rapidly

Jacques Herzog & Pierre de Meuron, de Young Museum, San Francisco, 2005

Gehry Partners, Walt Disney Concert Hall, Los Angeles, 2003

achieve an even green patina, but the de Young skin will be left to age naturally, and over a decade it will change from reddish brown to gold, blue, black, and eventually green, forming a sort of mutating camouflage.

The skin of the de Young is not articulated, nor is its method of manufacture revealed; instead Herzog and de Meuron treat it like a wrapper, a part of—yet disassociated from—the building. In the 1980s, Frank Gehry experimented with different sorts of wrappers. The most extreme example was a small guesthouse designed for the Winton family in Wayzata, Minnesota. The tiny building was broken down into a collection of six sculptural forms, each a different shape and each covered with a distinctive skin: Finnish plywood, brick, Kasota stone, lead-coated copper, and galvanized metal. Gehry likened his composition to a Morandi still life. "So it is hoped that this building will have a certain amount of humor and mystery and fantasy, so that visiting children will remember their trip to grandma's house," he said.

Gehry's first designs for Disney Hall continued this theme, a boxy auditorium surrounded by several smaller volumes of differ-

Gehry Partners, IAC Building, New York, 2007

ent shapes and materials. In the final building, however, many of the curved forms had become curved *planes*, more like a billowing cape than a skin. The original material was limestone, which was later changed to stainless steel when making a masonry skin that was earthquake-resistant proved too costly.* Gehry, an avid yachts-man, has compared the shapes to sails. Just as he had liberated building form from a literal translation of structure, Gehry frees the building skin from the mundane function of simply enclosing space and turns it into an expressive medium in its own right.

This freedom is evident in Gehry's IAC building in New York's Chelsea district. Although this is a straightforward ten-story office building, the scalloped shape creates a sculptural ex-terior that also recalls sails, which is fitting, since the building faces the Hudson River. But what is most unusual is the skin

---

*The billowing skin at Disney Hall actually predates Gehry's famous titanium skin at the Bilbao Guggenheim, although the latter building opened in 1997, and Disney Hall was not completed until 2003.

itself. At first glance, the all-glass wall looks like a distilled Miesian curtain wall, without mullions or spandrels, only a smooth glass surface. On closer inspection, however, the skin turns out to be unusual. The glass is fritted—that is, it is covered with a fused screen of ceramic glazed dots or squares. Frits can be different colors and densities, and are used either decoratively or to reduce the amount of sunlight that enters a building. Gehry uses a white frit and varies the density, from highly transparent in the viewing portion of the skin, to milky opaque where the glass skin covers the edges of the floor slabs. Because the change from transparent to opaque is finely graduated, the façade appears blurred, like an out-of-focus photograph. Thus Gehry accomplishes the not inconsiderable feat of making a modern glass curtain wall that appears, if not exactly warm, certainly fuzzy.

SCRIMS

Across West Nineteenth Street from the IAC Building is an example of a very different sort of skin. The back and sides of 100 Eleventh Avenue, a twenty-three-story residential tower designed by Jean Nouvel, are nothing special: somber black glazed brick with punched-out windows of different sizes. The curved façade facing the river, on the other hand, consists of a metal grid divided into a variety of different-sized windows. Some of the windows are quite small, less than two feet square; some are large; and the individual panes are set at different angles, producing no fewer than sixteen hundred different configurations. In addition, there are subtle variations in the colors of the glass. "When the whole thing is put together, it looks like a vast, reflective Mondrian, or like huge glass shingles, randomly assembled," wrote Paul Goldberger in *The New Yorker*. Or like a steel-and-glass crazy quilt.

Nouvel sometimes extends the gridded skin beyond the edges

Ateliers Jean Nouvel, 100 Eleventh Avenue, New York, 2010

of the building, and, as if one crazy quilt were not more than enough, he adds a second, overlapping metal grid on the lower five floors, like a layered screen. Building screens have a long tradition in Islamic architecture in the form of latticework *mashrabiyas*, which mask the exteriors of windows and balconies like wooden veils. Perforated screens were introduced to modern architecture by Edward Durell Stone in the 1950s in several buildings, notably the U.S. embassy in New Delhi, a large building entirely sheathed in a delicate two-story grille of glazed terra-cotta and concrete. Although his buildings were well received by the general public, Stone was much criticized for the ornamental nature of such screens. Nouvel reintroduced the *mashrabiya* concept in his first high-profile commission, the Arab World Institute in Paris. The all-glass south façade is shaded by a perforated metal screen whose geometrical pattern resembles an Islamic mosaic. The high-tech screen consists of hundreds of camera-lens-like apertures that are photosensitive and motor-driven to open and close in response to the amount of sunlight. Although Nouvel's complicated sunshade ran into predictable mechanical difficulties, the idea of protecting glass buildings with a permeable skin caught on.* It was a way of environmentally taming the Miesian glass skin, and—equally important—it was *architecturally* more interesting, creating façades with a greater sense of depth.

An external sunscreen shades the glass façade of the New York Times Building. Renzo Piano makes the screen a major design element, wrapping the building on four sides (including the north!), and also extending the screen a full six stories above the top of the building to create a filigree crown. The screen itself is made of horizontal ceramic rods resembling fluorescent tubes. Unfortunately, the rods have a dull gray finish, which affects the appearance of the tower: "As gray and dour as a rain-soaked copy of the Sunday Styles section," complained the *Daily News*. In a recent competition-winning design for a new U.S. embassy in London, Steven Kieran and James Timberlake propose to cover an all-glass building on three sides with a partially transparent polymer skin that acts as a sunscreen and also incorporates embedded photovoltaic cells. Since the flexible polymer is crystal-like, the effect should be sparkling rather than dour.

Kieran and Timberlake refer to the polymer wrapper of the London embassy as a "scrim." In theater lingo, a scrim is a drop made of gauze that appears opaque when lit from the front, and turns transparent when illuminated from behind. Some productions of *Les Misérables* used a scrim as a stage curtain, so that at the beginning of every act, as the houselights dimmed, the actors and the set appeared as if magically, "bleeding through" the scrim. Scrims entered modern architecture in the late 1990s, when architects introduced translucent screens as a way of adding a more ambiguous dimension to their designs. One of the first to do so was the Swiss architect Peter Zumthor. The Kunsthaus on Lake

---

*As Robert Hughes foretold, the lenses soon broke down and are no longer operable.

Constance in Bregenz, Austria, is a four-story cube with two glass skins. The inner skin of insulated glass is the actual wall of the art gallery; the outer skin, separated by a three-foot gap, is a glass scrim. The translucent panes of etched glass, which diffuse light into the interiors, are suspended on a metal frame like loosely overlapping shingles, with gaps between the panes. The scrim is particularly effective at night, when the ghostly shadows of stairs and moving people are visible through the milky glass. According to Zumthor, "From the outside, the building looks like a lamp. It absorbs the changing light of the sky, the haze of the lake, it reflects light and colour and gives an intimation of its inner life according to the angle of vision, the daylight and the weather."

About the same time as the Kunsthaus opened, the Mexican architect Enrique Norten was designing a scrim in Mexico City. Norten's task was to transform an existing and decrepit apartment building into a boutique hotel. After rehabilitating the interior, he clad the five-story block with a glass skin, and then wrapped it in a freestanding scrim of frosted glass. The space between the two walls was wide enough for narrow balconies. During the day, the scrim appears milky white, with a random pattern of patches of clear glass that serve as windows. At night, drawn and undrawn curtains and varied backlighting animate the façade, a theatrical effect that is in sharp contrast to the coolly functionalist architecture.

Both Norten and Zumthor are minimalists, and they dispense with window mullions, supporting the scrim on metal clips, which gives the impression that the glass sheets are floating in front of the façade. This method of attachment also emphasizes the gauzy, nonstructural nature of the scrim. It is hard to say what propelled two different architects on two continents toward a similar solution. Certainly not function, for these are two dissimilar buildings. When Mies van der Rohe was designing the Seagram Building, in order to avoid a disordered appearance on the façade, he installed window blinds that had only three positions: open, half-open, and

Peter Zumthor, Kunsthaus, Bregenz, Austria, 1997

closed. Zumthor and Norten are no less disciplined than Mies, but a scrim, which both reveals and conceals, allows them to enliven their architecture by embracing life rather than constraining it.*

Norten and Zumthor stretch the scrim tightly across the face of the building, creating a second skin that mimics the form beneath. Thom Mayne, on the other hand, uses scrims to create building forms. In the U.S. Federal Building in San Francisco, a perforated stainless-steel scrim runs up the façade and folds to

---

*Coincidentally, Norten received the Mies van der Rohe Award in 1998 and Zumthor in 1999.

*Enrique Norten/TEN Arquitectos, Hotel Habita,
Mexico City, 2000*

make what looks like a distorted mansard roof, but is no more
substantial than a billboard; at the bottom of the building the
scrim appears to crumple like folded paper. In an academic building for Cooper Union in New York, Mayne shapes and gouges a
similar perforated stainless-steel scrim and peels away gashes to
reveal the simple glass-faced building beneath. None of these ag-
gressive shapes is "real," in terms of conventional architecture, yet
part of Mayne's mannered aesthetic is to make us aware of their
unreality. His explanation is somewhat obscure: "It starts in a
more generic sense, and it moves into something that has broader
formal properties, that is more interpretive—the capabilities of
the second skin."

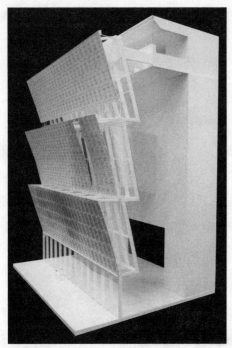

*Freelon Adjaye Bond/SmithGroup, National
Museum of African American History and
Culture, Washington, D.C., 2015*

The theatrical origin of the scrim is a part of its appeal, and since it is independent of the building, the second skin can be manipulated at will while the actual building, often a generic box, sits primly underneath. This is David Adjaye's strategy at the National Museum of African American History and Culture in Washington, D.C., where the scrim creates a striking corona form. The scrim is perforated with decorative geometrical patterns that are based, according to the designers, on historic iron grilles from Charleston and New Orleans. The density of the perforations varies, depending on the degree of sun shading required. In selected cases, "windows" are cut out of the scrim, framing key views such as the Washington Monument and the Lincoln Memorial. Adjaye's scrim is a veil that both is—and isn't—a building skin. The decorative scrim preserves modernism's injunction against ornament by being detached from the building proper. The skin is sculptural, but its form does not compromise the functional and structural integrity of the building behind it. The result is the architectural equivalent of the layered look in fashion: something on top of—or underneath—something else. Now you see it, now you don't.

The evolution of the design of the African American museum highlights the importance of the skin to the architectural impact of a building. The material of the scrim was originally to be bronze, which would have set the building apart from all the other structures on the National Mall, which are either marble or limestone. Yet because bronze is traditionally associated with commemorative statues and memorials, the contrast would not be inappropriate. However, during the September 2012 meeting of the Commission of Fine Arts, Adjaye revealed that (presumably to save money) the bronze scrim would be replaced by aluminum sprayed with bronze-colored paint. What was presented as a small technical modification drastically alters the project, for, as one commissioner observed, while the architect's renderings showed a building that glimmered and sparkled in the light, the sample of the painted aluminum did not appear to have these qualities. The appeal of bronze is its warm golden sheen and the rich patina that it acquires over time, but uniformly painted surfaces lack these attributes, and over time they don't age, they merely flake. When Frank Gehry was obliged to abandon limestone as the skin of Disney Hall, he did not shift to limestone-colored concrete or artificial stone, but to an entirely different material—stainless steel. At the time of writing, the African American museum risks compromising its original intention. In architecture, beauty sometimes really is only skin-deep.

7

DETAILS

What sets the tone in a building are the details. There are scores of them: doors and doorframes, windows and window frames, cabinetwork, baseboards, lighting fixtures, and door handles. Details occur whenever a floor meets a wall, when a wall meets a roof overhang, or where hardware is required. There is always more than one way to design a detail: the concrete may be smooth or rough, the brick joints flush or raked, the wood paneling book-matched or random, the attachments exposed or hidden. In some buildings details act as a visual adornment, like the bronze mullions on the façade of the Seagram Building, or the perforations and dimples on the copper wall of the de Young Museum. In others, such as Wright's Guggenheim Museum, details seem to disappear. Details—or their lack—reveal a great deal about the architect's intentions. As Roger Scruton has observed, while much about the design of a building is dictated by the context and the site, the client's demands, building codes, and functional and structural requirements, the design of details is one thing over which the architect exercises almost complete control. That is why details are important: they express architectural ideas— and ideals.

Consider a simple balustrade. The dictionary defines a balustrade as "a railing at the side of a staircase or balcony to prevent people from falling," and as a safety device a balustrade is strictly regulated: the height of the guardrail is prescribed; the balusters, or spindles, must be close enough to prevent a child's head from passing through; and the banister, or handrail, must provide a continuous support and be small enough to be easily grasped. All balustrades must meet these relatively inflexible parameters, but do all balustrades look the same? Far from it. While identical in function and similar in general dimensions, balustrades vary wildly in detail. They can be made from different materials—wood, metal, or glass—and these materials may be combined in a variety of ways. Balustrades can be simple or complicated, plain or elaborate, demure or theatrical. It all depends on the architect.

The choice of how to design a detail such as a balustrade is not arbitrary, however, as the following examples will show. Accomplished architects develop their own method of detailing, and these methods fall into one of five general categories: details that are consistent with a historical style; details that complement the architect's personal vision; details that represent or explain how a thing is made; odd details that appear out of step with the building; and last, details that are designed to fade into the background.

STYLISTIC CONSISTENCY

"The Georgian house is loved as much for the moldings of its sash windows, for its brickwork and doorframe, for its iron railings and area steps, as for the grace of its proportions," observes Scruton. Getting the details right is obviously important for an architect working in a historic style. A monograph on the work of Robert A. M. Stern describes the Baron House in Dallas as "English Regency sifted through American Federal," adding, "inside and outside, the detailing is classical, building upon the work of Sir John Soane to be sure, but with more than a nod to the twentieth-century work of John Russell Pope." The Regency style grew out of Georgian, but was visually lighter and more lively. The great eighteenth-century English architect John Soane designed severe brick country houses, and his stylized classicism obviously influenced Stern. The reference to Pope is to the 1915 Ogden L. Mills House (since demolished) in Woodbury, Long Island, whose H-shaped plan Stern adapted to his own design. Pope's entrance portico, with its stylized Adamesque Corinthian columns, also reappears almost intact, as does a limestone band that binds the extensive brick façades together. The Baron entrance hall, like that of the Woodbury mansion, is dominated by a semicircular black-and-white cantilevered stair; the treads are marble, the balustrade iron. The balusters are a series of overlapping circles linked by gold medallions, and joined to the banister and the curving skirt board by small gold spheres. The sparkling details resonate with the exuberant spirit of this rather theatrical house.

John Russell Pope is best known as the architect of austere classical buildings such as the National Archives, the National Gallery of Art, and the Jefferson Memorial, but his architectural range was broad. He designed country houses not only in the Regency style but also in picturesque Tudor, prim Colonial Revival, rambling Shingle Style, and grandly monumental Georgian, deploying the appropriate details as required. Like Pope, Stern is an eclectic who tailors his buildings to their clients and their sites. "I don't see architecture as being about autobiography," he once told an interviewer. "I see it more as an art of portrait painting. Portraits of places and institutions."

In his residential work, Stern looks to durable American domestic styles such as the Shingle Style, Federal, Arts and Crafts, and Spanish Colonial. A house in California is inspired by a 1930s Los Angeles style known as Hollywood Regency, a glamorous

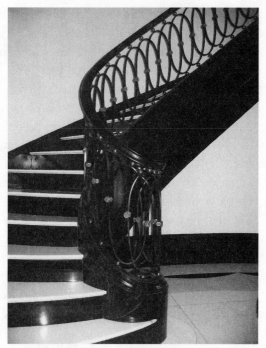

Robert A. M. Stern Architects, Baron House,
Dallas, 2000

blend of Regency, nineteenth-century French neoclassicism, and
Art Deco. The exterior is white-painted brick with limestone
trim and modern-looking black-painted steel windows. The
entrance hall has a circular stair similar in general configuration
to that of the Baron House and likewise ending in a tight curl.
But the details are different. The balusters are more sinuous, almost wavelike, the banister is brass, and the treads and risers are
black stone. The effect is lighter and, in a way hard to define,
more modern.

For a large house in Montecito, California, Stern adopts the
local Mediterranean style that dates from the early 1900s, when

Robert A. M. Stern Architects, Residence, California, 2005

George Washington Smith introduced the Spanish Colonial style to Santa Barbara. Smith's rambling, casual houses, with patios, loggias, and deep roof overhangs, suited—and still suit—the mild climate and relaxed way of life of Southern California. Stern's Montecito house is distinctly less formal than the two previous examples—pale yellow stucco rather than brick and limestone, wood rather than stone floors, casual outdoor spaces. The informality is reflected in the design of the curving main stair, which is constructed of wood. The traditional solution for a wood staircase is to support the banister on closely spaced vertical balusters countersunk into the treads. Heavier posts—newels—at the

*Robert A. M. Stern Architects, Residence, Monte-
cito, California, 1999*

landings typically act as reinforcement. Stern refines this classic
configuration, making the balusters extremely slender and terminating the banister in a tight spiral that forms a sort of clustered
newel. Simple and elegant.

CREATING A WORLD

Richard Meier is a different sort of architect than Robert A. M.
Stern. The two face off, so to speak, in the Preston Hollow neighborhood of Dallas, where Meier's Rachofsky House sits across a
small pond from the Baron House: white enamel-coated alumi-

num opposite red brick and limestone. The façade of the Rachofsky House is defined by flat, abstract planes whose surfaces are
inscribed by a square grid. Originally designed for a single occupant, the house is an extreme example of the minimalism for
which Meier has become famous. "The Rachofsky House is an
ideal," he observed, "an investigation into all of the possibilities of
house as a building type without many of the usual compromises."
Meier's uncompromising world is one in which every piece of furniture, every object, every flower vase, has its prescribed place. All
the surfaces except the polished black granite floor and the black-
leather-covered Mies van der Rohe furniture are white. There are
no baseboards, no cornices, no moldings, no visual distractions of
any kind. Where joints cannot be hidden, they are barely visible
hairlines. But even a purist cannot avoid some details. The two-
story living area is overlooked by galleries with all-steel railings.
The white banister is a square steel tube, the newel post consists
of two steel angles, and traditional balusters are replaced by steel
bars. The steel pieces are precisely welded, with no hint of construction, nothing extra, nothing added. Since the horizontal balusters are continuous, and since there are five of them, the abstract
composition reminds me of a musical staff.

Nothing could be further from Meier's sober and rather precious minimalism than Marc Appleton's picturesque Villa Pacifica.
The house, designed to recall the vernacular architecture of its
owner's native Greece, has vaults, domes, roughly plastered walls,
and irregular stone paving. Appleton treads a fine line between
image and reality—after all, the house is in Southern California,
not Greece, and its designer is a Yale-trained architect, not a village mason. He does not artificially age the materials but lets
rustic simplicity emerge from the building details. The outdoor
pergolas are made of trimmed branches with the bark left on; the
stone stair treads are dressed on only one side and lack a nosing.
The wooden balustrade is reduced to its basics: a shaped banister, simple vertical balusters, and slightly bulkier newel posts,

Richard Meier & Partners, Rachofsky House, Dallas, 1996

Appleton & Associates, Villa Pacifica, California, 1994

enlivened with just the hint of chamfers. The balusters are carried by a lower rail, which is a less sophisticated detail than balusters recessed in the treads. The all-white balustrade is as minimal as Meier's, but with its heavier proportions it is intentionally unaffected, almost homely. And it's practical: since the wood banister is shaped to fit the hand, it is more functional than a square steel bar.

Appleton reminds me of a musical composer like Smetana, say, or Dvořák, who turned folk melodies into studied compositions. The same could be said of many Arts and Crafts architects, who admired medieval workmanship and adapted old details to new situations. For example, medieval builders sometimes constructed rustic balustrades of single boards set on edge with the handrail acting as a stiffener, and Arts and Crafts architects likewise used this detail. In some houses, the boards are elaborated with cutouts or fretwork, and in the hands of a master like Bernard Maybeck, the cutouts assume organic shapes, the two-dimensional equivalent of traditional ornamental balusters.

Jeremiah Eck uses a variation of the board-baluster detail in the stair of a small cottage on Isleboro Island, Maine. The low-key cottage looks like a converted fisherman's boatshed that has had lots of windows added, as well as a screened porch and a very large stone fireplace. The interior, constructed of a variety of inexpensive woods, is unified by being painted entirely white, but the effect is very different from the Rachofsky House, since the crisscrossing wooden roof trusses, posts, and planked walls are all exposed. It is hard to characterize Eck's design, which blends tradition (a gable roof, a porch) with modernity (exposed structure, an all-white color scheme) and extremely simple details. He calls the style a combination of Shaker and Adirondack. The board balusters of the stair are extended to make a screen wall, and the banister is a hand-size strip of wood, grooved to receive the boards. According to Eck, "Stairs can take on great prominence as transitional spaces filled with expressive details." Here the expressive detail is a repetitive geometrical pattern cut out of the boards. The positive and negative forms recall an Amish quilt, and are a unique ornamental exclamation point in the otherwise austere interior.

The stair in the Isleboro Island cottage leads to a loft that contains the children's bedroom. A screen wall dividing the space repeats the same cut-out board detail as the balustrade. Since this is a wall rather than a balustrade, the detail here takes on the role of a motif. Perhaps the most familiar examples of motif details occur in Gothic churches, where pointed arches were used at different scales and in different materials: in wooden screens and paneling, stone altarpieces, brass light fixtures, even

Eck MacNeely, Temple Residence, Isleboro, Maine, 2004

Steven Holl Architects, Department of Philosophy, New York University, New York, 2007

the carved adornment of pews. The modern architect who excelled at motifs was Frank Lloyd Wright. His models were either plant forms or geometric shapes, and the stylized patterns appear in door handles, light fixtures, stained glass, and furniture. "The differentiation of a single, certain, simple form characterizes the expression of one building," he explained. "Quite a different form may serve for another . . . but in every case the motif is adhered to throughout."

Contemporary modern architects tend to eschew the kind of rich visual expression that Wright practiced, but the use of architectural motifs persists. In the ambassador's residence of the Swiss embassy in Washington, D.C., Steven Holl uses sandblasted structural glass planks as an exterior cladding, and repeats the detail in a stair balustrade. In a renovation of a six-story nineteenth-century building for New York University, Holl introduces a new stair shaft, lit from above by a skylight. Treating the stairwell as a giant light fixture, he perforates the ash-veneer plywood wall with a random pattern of holes that resemble paint spatters. Inside the stairwell, the same motif reappears on the balustrade, which is made out of thick steel sheets, laser-cut with similar perforations.

HOW THINGS ARE MADE

"My details are about how things are made," says Peter Bohlin. This is evident in the glass cube that he designed for the Apple Store on Fifth Avenue in New York. The structure of the thirty-two-foot cube is a series of portal frames supporting a roof and walls, all made of glass.* This is the ultimate glass building; there is no steel structure at all—the sheets of tempered glass support themselves and are joined by titanium and stainless-steel fittings. In the center of the cube is a glass cylinder containing an elevator, around which is wrapped a circular stair. In public buildings, the building code requires a forty-two-inch-high safety guardrail in addition to a traditional thirty-six-inch-high banister. In the Apple Store, a spiraling glass sheet acts as the guardrail, and also as a helical beam supporting the laminated glass treads; the handrail is a stainless-steel pipe attached to the glass. The metal fittings are similar to those of the walls, though they hardly qualify as a motif, since they are merely the same hardware per-forming a similar function. What one sees is only the minimum necessary to hold things together.

---

*The original cube, finished in 2006, was sheathed in ninety sheets of glass; five years later these were replaced by fifteen larger sheets.

Bohlin Cywinski Jackson, Apple Store Fifth Avenue, New York, 2006

Renzo Piano Building Workshop, Nasher Sculpture Center, Dallas, 2003

Renzo Piano also likes details that show how things are made. The Nasher Sculpture Center in Dallas is a one-story pavilion that consists of six parallel walls enclosing five spaces facing a garden. Each bay is spanned by a glass-covered vault surmounted by a cast-aluminum perforated sunscreen. The filtered light washes the interior to create an exceptional setting for sculpture. To enable the arches of the vault to be as thin as possible, each arch is suspended at the center by stainless-steel rods that are attached to the walls on either side. As in other Piano buildings, some of the construction is revealed, some isn't. The thick travertine-covered walls, for example, look solid but are actually hollow and contain steel columns that support the arches, as well as mechanical services.

Piano does not articulate every joint, which would simply create visual confusion; instead, he picks certain details and gives them a star turn. One of the highlighted details is a tempered-glass balustrade. Glass balustrades have been a staple of modernist architecture since I. M. Pei used them in the East Building of the National Gallery, but Piano's design is subtly different. He dispenses with the usual metallic top cap, spaces the individual glass sheets slightly apart, and rounds their corners. Instead of disappearing into a slot in the floor, the glass is clamped to the stair stringer by plainly visible bolts. The handrail itself is attached to the glass by prominent metal brackets; unlike the Apple stair, the handrail is wood rather than stainless steel. Wood is warm to the touch, and it lends a sense of traditional craft to this otherwise coolly mechanical assembly.

Bing Thom, like Bohlin and Piano, is a builder. In a satellite campus of Simon Fraser University in Surrey, British Columbia, he was given the unusual task of placing a new academic facility for five thousand students on top of an existing shopping mall. To give identity to the academic portion and set it apart from the mall, he used unusual structural systems: laminated wood beams, timber trusses, and a space frame fabricated from so-called

Bing Thom Architects, Simon Fraser University, Surrey, British Columbia, 2004

peeler cores, the wood cylinders left over when plywood layers are stripped from a log. The tall structural columns are Parallam, an engineered product made from parallel strands of wood bonded with adhesive. These timber elements are combined with articulated construction details: cast-aluminum joints, tension cables, and cast-iron pin joints where the columns meet the floor.

Like Piano, Thom uses tempered glass balustrades with wooden banisters, but he combines them differently. The glass does not support the banister. Instead, the glass guardrail and the wooden handrail are both supported by metal stanchions. The stanchions, at five-foot intervals, consist of two metal bars clamped to a floor anchor. Glass, wood, and metal each perform separate functions, and the details of their construction are clearly expressed. Well, almost clearly: the maple handrail is actually reinforced by an internal steel bar.

QUIRKS

Details follow a historical style, contribute to the general atmosphere of a building, or express the way things are made. In *The Architectural Detail*, the historian and architect Edward R. Ford describes a fourth category—the incompatible detail, "unrelated to an all-encompassing composition, following its own rules, and seeking its own configuration." An example of such a detail occurs in the Villa Mairea. The columns in the living room are steel tubes wrapped with cane or covered in wood strips. Despite having treated these columns in a craftsmanlike manner, Alvar Aalto switches to an industrial vocabulary in a single column in the library. The column is bare concrete—the marks of the wooden formwork are plainly visible—and it is painted white. There is no exposed concrete elsewhere in the house, so why this discrepancy? I once heard an anecdote about Aalto. When he was teaching at MIT, he gave his class the problem of designing a grade school. After one student had finished explaining his project, Aalto's first question was: "But where does the tiger come in?" He meant, where is the element of fantasy that should be part of a building intended for young children. The Villa Mairea is not a grade school, but a degree of fantasy is present in all of Aalto's designs, and it often appears as an idiosyncratic detail—a lamp, a door handle, or a solitary concrete column. Such details make his architecture, which otherwise adheres to the strict tenets of Modernism, more approachable, more human. "Certain flaws are necessary for the whole," wrote Goethe. "It would seem strange if old friends lacked certain quirks."

Louis I. Kahn, Kimbell Art Museum, Fort Worth,
1972

Quirky is not a word one associates with Louis Kahn's laboriously studied designs. The interior of the Kimbell Art Museum is defined by concrete vaults, white oak floors, and Belgian linen display panels. The details are generally simple and call no attention to themselves. A notable exception is the perforated aluminum reflectors hanging below the skylights, which Kahn called "natural-light fixtures." These striking metallic forms, designed with the lighting consultant Richard Kelly, are an unexpected presence. Their delicacy—and their sense of being a functional device—emphasizes the brooding power of the monumental vaults. Another odd detail is the handrail of a stair that leads up to the galleries from the lower level, which is how most people enter the museum. The handrail, attached to the wall, is made out of a strip of stainless steel bent into a profile that resembles a question mark. Kahn could have used a simple metal bar or a wooden rail, but he opted for this original solution. The choice of curved sheet metal may have been suggested by the aluminum reflectors, for it creates a similarly striking contrast between paper-thin metal and the travertine wall of the staircase. Whatever the inspiration, the curved handrail—a little impulsive aside— emphatically signals one's arrival to the museum's galleries.

Tadao Ando is a great admirer of Kahn, and designs simi-larly understated buildings. The galleries of the Modern Art Museum of Fort Worth, which stands opposite the Kimbell, are

Tadao Ando, Modern Art Museum of Fort Worth, Fort Worth, 2002

concrete enclosures within glass boxes. The glass is shaded by overhanging roof slabs carried by striking Y-shaped supports. The details are extremely simple. The impossibly thin concrete roof slab has no fascia and no soffit; the glass walls are supported by unprepossessing aluminum frames. Light switches, electrical plugs, and even exit signs are recessed into the concrete walls (which seems simple but is very complicated to do). For the balustrade of a bridge that crosses the two-story lobby, Ando uses sheets of tempered glass set in a slot in the floor and capped by a stainless-steel tube. There is something slightly mysterious about a glass balustrade—it's hard to believe that normally fragile, handle-with-care glass is really strong enough to support our weight—and Ando elaborates on that mystery. When the balustrade reaches the stair, the sheets of tempered glass appear to slice through the stone treads like a knife through butter, leaving several inches of the stair treads outside the railing and unusable. Ando emphasizes the "leftover" portion of the tread by making it bare concrete instead of granite. It is an odd, mannered detail for a minimalist like Ando, and while it draws attention to itself, it reveals nothing about its construction. Sometimes a quirk is just a quirk.

Glass balustrades are so commonplace, they have become a cliché. Another cliché is the cable railing. Cable railings are balustrades in which stretched horizontal cables replace balusters. Cable railings originated in racing yachts, whose safety railings are made out of wires to reduce weight. This makes little sense in buildings, but I suspect that many architects simply like the technical-looking hardware: the turnbuckles, clamps, swaging studs, tie bars, and other fittings. Interior cable railings have always struck me as an affectation, but on the exterior they have two great advantages: they don't obstruct the view, and unlike glass, they don't have to be regularly cleaned. That is why Jeremiah Eck used cables in a railing on the deck of a house that is perched high above Flanders Bay in Maine. This is an unconventional

Eck MacNeely, Louis Residence, Treasure Island, Maine, 2004

cable railing, however. The cables are at the eye level of a person sitting in an Adirondack chair, but the lower portion of the balustrade is made of closely spaced horizontal wood slats that, given the steep drop, provide a sense of security as well as an added measure of safety for small children. The banister consists of a flat board on edge, offering the least visual obstruction and wide enough to set a glass on. Eck plays down the technical details of the cables, for this railing is part of a house that is rather traditional in appearance, with a shingled roof, gables, dormers, and a corner bay window. The nautical-looking balustrade stands somewhat apart, appropriately drawing attention to the view, which is the chief attribute of this dramatic site.

MUTE DETAILS

While a Renzo Piano building sometimes looks as if the detail came first and the rest of the building followed, in a Frank Gehry building it is the big idea, expressed in his first rough sketches, that drives the design. In order to create no distractions to his main idea, Gehry often makes details that appear quite ordinary. Of course, it takes a lot of work to resolve the joints when colliding surfaces meet at odd angles, but the results rarely call attention to themselves. One looks in vain for intricate balustrades or cable railings in a Gehry building. The railings of the main entry stairs of Walt Disney Hall are simply stainless-steel pipes. Nothing fancy.

Pipe railings first appeared as an architectural detail in the 1920s. Always painted white, they were inspired by the ocean liners that modernist architects so admired. Pipe railings, which were intentionally plain and a self-conscious rebuke to bourgeois notions of domestic décor, had another advantage: they were unobtrusive. Architects such as Le Corbusier, who considered architecture to be the "play of volumes brought together in light," didn't want the distraction of finicky details.

Gehry Partners, Walt Disney Concert Hall, Los Angeles, 2003

Jacques Herzog & Pierre de Meuron, de Young Museum, San Francisco, 2005

When Jacques Herzog and Pierre de Meuron were awarded the Pritzker Prize, Carlos Jimenez, a member of the jury, observed, "Much has been written about the architects' proficiency with materials, to the extent that their work might at times be perceived as an obsession with tactile properties, surface, or textural potential." Indeed, the skin of a Herzog and de Meuron building is often its most memorable feature, whether it is the gabion walls of the Dominus Winery, the photolithographic concrete façade of the Eberswalde Library, or the perforated copper skin of the de Young Museum. Using copper in a wall—an unorthodox application— might have resulted in unusual details, but like Gehry, Herzog and de Meuron keep them in the background. The balustrade of the main interior stair of the museum consists simply of stanchions and a handrail made of steel pipe painted black. In less capable hands, this throwaway detail might appear crude, but one can only assume that, like their fellow Swiss, Le Corbusier, Herzog and de Meuron simply don't want any distractions.

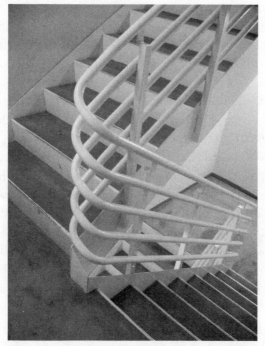

Rem Koolhaas & Joshua Prince-Ramus/OMA,
Seattle Public Library, Seattle, 2004

Sometimes Herzog and de Meuron make the details disappear completely. When the copper skin of the de Young meets the ground or the roof, for example, nothing special happens—the skin simply stops. According to Ford, many contemporary architects consider details unnecessary, even undesirable. He quotes Rem Koolhaas: "For years we have concentrated on NO-detail. Sometimes we succeed—it's gone, abstracted; sometimes we fail—it's still there. Details should disappear—they are old architecture." This statement is calculated to provoke, but Koolhaas definitely often pushes details into deep background—that is, there are details in his buildings but they don't play a role in the design. In the Seattle Public Library, the columns and diagonal braces that crisscross the main level are encased in plasterboard up to a height of about eight feet, above which the I-beams, covered with sprayed-on fireproofing and painted matte black, are simply left exposed. The underside of the ceiling, as well as ducts and pipes, is likewise painted black—as glamorous as a discount warehouse. On the other hand, the floor is covered in two-foot-square stainless-steel tiles. This unconventional flooring is screwed rather than glued, and a recessed screw is plainly visible at the corner of each tile. This straightforward detail says a lot about Koolhaas's pragmatic philosophy of construction. The balustrades in the library are simple galvanized steel grilles; lacking a handrail and stanchions, they have all the poetry of floor gratings tilted up on edge. At the same time, there are some quirky details. The sides of the escalators are made out of canary-yellow plastic, illuminated from behind. The steel balustrades of the emergency stairs are likewise visually striking, being painted bright orange. The pipe railing follows the stair in a fluid twist, the pieces simply welded together without any concern for expressing the connections. No details.

WORDS

Whenever I walk past the Law School on the University of Pennsylvania campus, I enjoy looking at the details. The building was designed by Walter Cope and John Stewardson in 1901, and like all good academic buildings it has a touch of the domestic. The grand brick-and-limestone mansion is in the seventeenth-century Stuart style, to commemorate the period when British common law originated. The swags over the entrance, the tall paneled doors, even the wrought-iron fence, are a visual delight. A circular motif graces the façade: round windows, finials above window frames, stone spheres that cap the columns of the surrounding fence, and a series of stone roundels. Each roundel is carved with the name of a historical jurist, Supreme Court justice, or celebrated legal scholar.

The tradition of adorning buildings with writing dates back to the Roman Pantheon, whose pediment carries the inscription M.AGRIPPA. L. F. COS.TERTIUM. FECIT, meaning "Marcus Agrippa, son of Lucius, three times consul, built this." The most famous inscription on an American building is probably the one that appears on McKim, Mead & White's façade of the main New York post office: NEITHER SNOW NOR RAIN NOR HEAT NOR GLOOM OF NIGHT STAYS THESE COURIERS FROM THE SWIFT COMPLETION OF THEIR APPOINTED ROUNDS, adapted from Herodotus. Robert Venturi often uses writing to enliven his buildings. The first instance is a 1960s design for a home for the elderly in Philadelphia that has its name—GUILD HOUSE—in four-foot letters over the entrance. His Seattle Art Museum displays its name in eight-foot letters carved into the stone façade in shallow relief. THE NATIONAL GALLERY appears on the rear wall of the Sainsbury Wing, the size of a billboard, while inside the museum, along the grand staircase that leads to the galleries, a two-foot frieze carved into the limestone commemorates Renaissance artists: DUCCIO · MASACCIO · VAN EYCK · PIERO · MANTEGNA · BELLINI · LEONARDO · RAPHAEL.

Words on buildings are evocative as well as decorative. I recently saw another charming example of architectural writing. I was in downtown Little Rock, Arkansas, looking for the main library. I had been told it was housed in a converted five-story warehouse, which wasn't much to go on. As I approached a plain-looking building, I glanced up and saw a frieze of names just below the cornice: SHAKESPEARE · DR. SEUSS · PLATO · WHITMAN. This must be the place.

FIGURES

Another of my favorites on the Penn campus is the Quadrangle, a dormitory complex, also designed by Cope & Stewardson.

Although the firm pioneered the use of Collegiate Gothic on campuses such as Princeton, for Penn it used an eclectic blend of Jacobean Revival and Elizabethan Tudor; more Hampton Court than medieval Oxford. Stone swags and armorial crests abound, the keystones are in the shape of grotesque masks, and the gargoyles, some said to be modeled on professors and students, include a scholar holding a book, and a crouched football player. Figural details have historically performed two functions: being a part of the building and representing something. A Corinthian capital joins the column shaft to the entablature, but is also a bunch of acanthus leaves; a wrought-iron railing is a fence, but it is also a row of spears; a gargoyle is a water spout, but also a goblin—or a football player.

Figural details are ornamental, but they can also suggest the function of the building. This is the case with another building at Penn, designed by Paul Cret in the 1940s. The building, which houses chemical laboratories, is a composition of large simple volumes, bereft of ornament, with a streamlined rounded corner and ribbon windows—Cret's take on the International Style. These features are visible from a distance; closer up, the brickwork and the austere limestone moldings become apparent. It is only when one approaches the entrance that one becomes aware of a carved stone plaque set into the wall over the door. The work, by the sculptor Donald De Lue, is titled *The Alchemist*, and depicts in high relief a gnarled old man in medieval garb holding a sphere and sitting at a workbench with a retort in the background. It is charming, funny, and informative, all at the same time.*

De Lue's bas-relief is a reminder that architectural details are generally experienced close up, and that this intimacy is an important part of the experience of buildings. "It is a disheartening feature of much modern architecture, that it lacks this flair for

---

*The Boston-born De Lue would go on to become a leading American sculptor of figural monuments in the post–World War II period, responsible for the Omaha Beach Memorial in Normandy and the Boy Scout Memorial in Washington, D.C.

Paul Philippe Cret, Chemistry Building, University of Pennsylvania, Philadelphia, 1940

detail," wrote Roger Scruton. Modern architects' attitudes toward figural details were influenced by Adolf Loos's famous 1908 essay, "Ornament and Crime," which advocated the banishment of all ornamental motifs from buildings. It was a Faustian bargain, for it produced buildings that lacked intimacy and the deeper level of experience—intellectual as well as tactile—that had been an integral part of architecture since Greek sculptors carved bas-relief metopes on the Parthenon. There were attempts to bring intimacy to modernist details. Mies used natural materials with rich surfaces such as travertine, onyx, and tropical woods; Le Corbusier integrated art into Ronchamp in the form of hand-painted motifs in the main door and the windows; Aalto designed handcrafted door handles. Interesting, although less fun than gargoyles and alchemists.

Contemporary buildings by architects such as Meier, Gehry, and Koolhaas provide a wealth of experiences, but at the most intimate scale they tend to keep the user at arm's length. The pristine exterior of the Rachofsky House, for example, says all it has to say from a distance; on closer inspection, the grid lines that organize the façade are simply narrow joints, the aluminum panels themselves are just white surfaces. The swirling metallic skin of Disney Hall seen up close has nothing further to reveal, any more than the Seattle Public Library's glazed lattice. Look closer and all you see is caulking.

A rare modernist example of evoking the function of a building through figural details occurs in the Yale School of Art and Architecture building, where Paul Rudolph scattered historical fragments throughout the interior: Greco-Roman friezes built into the wall of the fire stair, Egyptian bas-reliefs in the penthouse guest apartment, a medieval figure in the lobby, and a replica of the Greek goddess Athena in the fourth-floor studio. These plaster casts were a leftover from Yale's Beaux-Arts days, but Rudolph incorporated other architectural fragments, such as column capitals rescued from New Haven demolition sites, a new concrete relief depicting Le Corbusier's Modulor Man, an ironwork elevator grille from Louis Sullivan's Chicago Stock Exchange, and, above the door to his own office, friezes from Sullivan's recently demolished Schiller Building. At the time, many critics assumed that Rudolph, a confirmed modernist, was poking fun at the past. Robert A. M. Stern, the current dean, disagrees: "Rudolph brought them out and showed them because he always wanted to have students recognize that modern architecture did not come from nowhere."

The Art and Architecture Building was built in 1963, and it would be more than two decades before an architect again used figural ornament to enrich the experience of a building. Thomas

Hammond, Beeby & Babka, Harold Washington Library, Chicago, 1991

Beeby, who studied under Rudolph at Yale, won a competition to design the Harold Washington Library in Chicago. Beeby was interested in the architectural traditions of his hometown, and he decorated the exterior of the library's massive brick walls with figural cast-stone ornaments: an interlaced ribbonlike frieze, called a *guilloche*, at the base; keystones bearing images of the Roman goddess of agriculture, Ceres, and Chicago's motto, URBS IN HORTO; and, near the top of the building, medallions adorned with the face of a puffed-cheek blowing man, recalling Chicago's nickname, the "Windy City." Beneath the medallions, which are joined by leafy swags, is a ribbon of corncobs that cascades down the full height of the building. "All that was an attempt to make clear that this was a public building," Beeby explained.

The Chicago building contains oversized acroteria, or roof ornaments, in the shape of owls, the ancient Roman symbol of wisdom. Architects since antiquity have used a variety of devices to enliven the skyline of buildings: statues, obelisks, finials, spheres, urns, pineapples, and pinecones. The desire to place objects on the roof also has something to do with humanizing the building; that's why Baroque buildings often have rooftop balustrades even when they are not functionally required. Sometimes these features are symbolic—the pineapple represents welcoming hospitality, the pinecone is an ancient symbol of regeneration; sometimes they are merely decorative. The contemporary British architect Robert Adam has written, "The opportunity to vary the level of decoration of the orders to suit the size, significance or cost of a building gives classical design great flexibility and can be applied to individual features or details." Adam is not talking about simply adding classical fragments to a modernist building, however, as Rudolph did—or as some postmodern architects do; he is advocating an across-the-board revival of the classical vocabulary. Which brings us to the thorny question of style.

8

STYLE

Lester Walker's *American Shelter*, a handbook of house styles, lists one hundred categories, from Log Cabin and Saltbox to Italianate and California Ranch. In some ways the book resembles a birdwatcher's field guide: the reader is directed to look for certain features—cupolas, shingles, skinny columns, picture windows—*et voilà*, the style. But that is being a little unfair to the author, a practicing architect whose genial catalog is not intended to be either scholarly or polemical. "I wanted to treat each style equally," Walker writes. "The Shacks and Shanties Style was as interesting to me as the Greek Revival Style." He presents American housing styles as a series of independent ventures, undertaken by different individuals with vastly different resources and in greatly different circumstances. The catholic result is a chronological compilation in which architects and do-it-yourselfers, commercial homebuilders and carpenters, Gilded Age financiers and Nebraska sodbusters, follow one another in sometimes bewildering succession.

The challenge for art historians is to make sense of the past, and styles are a useful tool in this task. As James S. Ackerman put it: "For history to be written at all, we must find in what we study factors that at once are consistent enough to be distinguishable and changeable enough to have a 'story.'" The search for a stylistic story originated with the Renaissance painter and architect

Giorgio Vasari, whose *The Lives of the Artists* is considered the foundation text of art history. Vasari believed that the evolution of an artistic style mirrored the cycle of life—that is, a style was born, it matured, it aged, and it died, to be replaced by a new and vigorous successor. Although this view dominated the field for centuries, not everyone agreed with the metaphor. Geoffrey Scott, the author of *The Architecture of Humanism*, which was published in 1914, considered it a "biological fallacy." According to Scott, styles did not evolve like species, nor were they the result of changes in construction, nor even less of ethical judgments; in his view styles were neither good nor bad. The scholar and poet, who was also an accomplished garden designer, was an aesthete. "Architecture, simply and immediately perceived, is a combination, revealed through light and shade, of spaces, of masses, and of lines," he wrote, anticipating Le Corbusier.* Scott placed the observer at the center of the experience and hence regarded changes in style as the result of human desires. Thus, the architects of the Renaissance, he observed, designed what they did simply because they liked forms of a certain kind. The historian John Summerson echoed this view when he described the invention of Gothic architecture: "[The pointed arch] was seized upon as essential, *not* because it was materially essential, but because the pointed arch struck that note of fantasy which was what the mind of the age desired." A pointed arch is not structurally more efficient than a round arch, and the lacy fan-vault ceiling, which seems like a more delicate version of the Romanesque vault, supports nothing but itself (the roof is carried on concealed timber trusses). Yet both the fan vault and the pointed arch are the essence of Gothic. Summerson's point is that changes in style are often influenced by changes in taste, a subject that will be explored in the final chapter.

---

*More pragmatically, Scott once defined architecture as "the art of organizing a mob of craftsmen."

Although art historians seek to categorize styles according to discrete periods, many buildings resist pigeonholing. Gothic did succeed Romanesque, yet round arches remained in use long after the pointed arch became fashionable, and cathedrals such as Laon and Noyon used both. Nor do styles necessarily wither and die. Venetian Gothic, a particularly ornate version with Byzantine and Moorish embellishments, remained popular in that city well into the Renaissance. When the Doge's Palace was badly damaged by fire, Palladio's proposal to rebuild the fifteenth-century Gothic façade in a classical style was rejected, and instead the original façade was restored. This was not an early example of historic preservation; rather, it was the expression of a popular preference for a particular style.

Venetians called Palladio's architecture *all'antica* (in the ancient manner), since he borrowed motifs from ancient Rome. Rome offered Palladio no models for country houses, palaces, and churches, however, and he had to adapt temple architecture to these new types of buildings. As Ackerman points out, an architect's search for a solution to an aesthetic problem is often the key impetus for the development of a style, but what appears to be a succession of steps *toward* a solution may actually be a succession of steps *away* from the original problem. In other words, art consists of possibilities as well as solutions, and as architects explore aesthetic questions they often make discoveries that open new and unforeseen avenues. In Palladio's case, the search for antique models led him to develop entirely new country-house designs that had nothing to do with Roman precedents—and would influence architects around the world for centuries.

STYLISTIC CONSISTENCY

There is another way in which the practitioner's view of style differs from the historian's. A historian uses style to categorize the past, while an architect uses it to organize the present. Whether he is designing in a specific historical style or pursuing a personal vision, an architect is obliged to be consistent, not simply when it comes to individual details—as we have seen with balustrades—but throughout. Imagine a Frank Lloyd Wright Prairie School house with Bauhaus door handles and tubular easy chairs, or the Farnsworth House furnished with Craftsman sofas and lamps. All architecture worthy of its name—whether it is traditional or modernist—invites us into a special world, a world with its own coherent visual logic. What creates that logic is a sense of style.

Louis Kahn's buildings have a very particular sense of style: distant, sometimes harsh, never cozy, always ascetic. The severe interior of the library at Phillips Exeter Academy is exposed brick and bare concrete. The teak cabinetwork might have added warmth except that its details are as austere as a Shaker meeting-house, and the individual study carrels are lined up like a row of

Louis I. Kahn, Library, Phillips Exeter Academy, Exeter, New Hampshire, 1972

monks' cells. Indeed, as in many of Kahn's buildings, the serene but stern atmosphere resembles a monastery.

The Seattle Public Library, designed by Rem Koolhaas and Joshua Prince-Ramus, is severe, too—the details are rough, sometimes even crude—but the impression is hardly monastic, more like an industrial building converted into a fashion-conscious urban hangout. The building's stylistic coherence lies in its jarring *in*consistency, its ability to jump from the banal to the theatrical. The canary-yellow escalators, the stainless-steel floors, and the stylish sitting furniture are bright accents in an interior whose arrangement often appears haphazard. Instead of ordered calm, which is what one expects in a library, one experiences disordered agitation. The advantage of this unusual approach is that nothing seems out of place, especially not the grungy Seattleites who happily occupy Koolhaas's unruly world and make it their own. The disadvantage is that the architects' single-

Rem Koolhaas & Joshua Prince-Ramus/OMA, Seattle Public Library, Seattle, 2004

Bing Thom Architects, Surrey City Centre Library, Surrey, British Columbia, 2011

mindedness sometimes works against them. On the exterior, the unrelieved glass grid closes off the building from the surrounding streets and makes it a somewhat forbidding presence in the city, a crystalline form awkwardly parachuted into the steeply sloping site.

The new library of Surrey, British Columbia, a few hundred miles north of Seattle, sits comfortably in its suburban surroundings. This is a community branch rather than a central library, but the architect Bing Thom likewise faced the challenge of designing a building for an unknown future, as the precise role of public libraries in a digital age remains something of a question mark. "The design evolves out of the need to provide a space for reading, studying, and above all, gathering as a community," he explained. "This building is very flexible and will accommodate all of these purposes, but does so in a way that will intrigue and entice the users through the building." Intrigue and entice—so, definitely not a monastery. The interior recalls Wright's Guggenheim Museum, with a sinuous parapet surrounding a central skylit space, although the floors are level instead of ramped. The geometry is fluid, as if the Guggenheim had been made of gelatin. Like Wright, Thom plays down the details and creates the impression of a seamless whole. Unlike Koolhaas, he does not shock—instead the calm interior accommodates many diverse activities while retaining its architectural aplomb.

The Surrey library received an LEED silver rating for sustainability. LEED stands for Leadership in Energy and Environmental Design, and is a rating system used in North America to measure the degree to which a building reduces the emission of greenhouse gases. In the case of the library, the use of natural light maximizes day lighting, which cuts down on artificial illumination and hence air-conditioning. At the same time, light is carefully controlled to avoid the overillumination problems of the Bibliothèque Nationale. External walls are only 50 percent glass to cut down on heat loss during the winter, and there is less glass on the west façade than on the east to reduce heat gain. The outward-sloping walls help to shade the glazing on the south side. Advocates of sustainability sometimes refer to "green architecture" as if it represented a new style. But while sustainability is a crucial concern, as with fire safety and earthquake resistance, it does not shape architectural form. Green buildings can be high-tech glass or bricks-and-mortar traditional. Or exposed concrete, as in Thom's minor masterpiece.

CLASSICAL DRESS

"Style is the dress of thoughts," wrote Philip Stanhope, the fourth Earl of Chesterfield, in a wonderful metaphor, "and let them be ever so just, if your style is homely, coarse, and vulgar, they will appear to as much disadvantage, and be as ill received, as your person, though ever so well-proportioned, would if dressed in rags, dirt, and tatters." The eighteenth-century British statesman was advising his son about elocution, but the distinction between content and delivery applies equally to architecture, as the Museum of Modern Art in New York, and the National Gallery of Art in Washington, D.C., demonstrate. The two museums opened within two years of each other (1939 and 1941 respectively). In New York the galleries are stacked vertically, while in Washington they are spread out on one level, but the most telling differences between the two buildings are the ways in which the architects deal with *similar* problems. Both façades are marble, but whereas at MoMA Edward Durell Stone and Philip Goodwin stretch out the material as tight as a drum, at the National Gallery John Russell Pope modulates the surfaces with reveals, moldings, and blank windows. While Stone and Goodwin signal the entrance with a curvy marquee-like canopy, Pope uses a columned temple portico. Instead of a mundane revolving door at sidewalk level as in the New York building, he has tall bronze doors at the top of broad exterior steps, and instead of a low-ceilinged lobby he provides a grand domed rotunda. Both buildings display their names, but whereas NATIONAL GALLERY OF ART is carved into the marble in classical Roman type, the Museum of Modern Art was originally identified by metal unserifed letters attached to the façade, and reading vertically rather than horizontally.* These differences are all matters of style. The National Gallery uses monumental classicism to communicate that this is a temple—or a palace—devoted to great art of the past. The Museum of Modern Art, by using commercial graphics and intentionally unmonumental forms without any historical connotations, sends the opposite message: Not Your Grandfather's Museum.

---

*MoMA's vertical sign, since removed, was an homage to the vertical sign of that modernist icon, the Bauhaus. Large vertical signs were not uncommon in American downtowns in the 1930s, but were used only for commercial buildings such as hotels, department stores, and movie palaces, not for cultural institutions.

*Philip L. Goodwin and Edward Durell Stone,
Museum of Modern Art, New York, 1939*

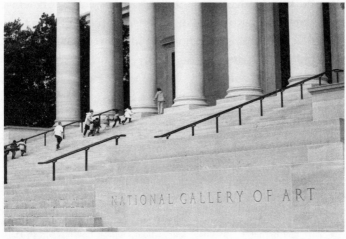

John Russell Pope, National Gallery of Art, Washington, D.C., 1941

A heated public controversy swirled around Pope's last commission, the Jefferson Memorial. His design was inspired by the Roman Pantheon, and while some critics maintained that an expensive monument was an unseemly use of public funds during the Depression, most of the debate had to do with style—that is, modernist versus classical. The director of the Museum of Modern Art, Harvard's architecture dean, and the editors of professional architectural periodicals, as well as many leading architects, supported the former. The Commission of Fine Arts, which had approved the National Gallery, disliked Pope's project, and even the architecture faculty of Columbia University turned on its most illustrious graduate. No less than Frank Lloyd Wright wrote to President Franklin D. Roosevelt and called the proposed memorial an insult to the memory of Jefferson. Roosevelt, however, remained an admirer of Pope's design and personally intervened to ensure that it was built.

Pope was sometimes—not always flatteringly—referred to as the "last of the Romans," and of his National Gallery of Art, Joseph Hudnut, the dean of Harvard's Graduate School of Design, wrote in 1941: "Surely the time cannot be far distant when we shall understand how inadequate is the death-mask of an ancient culture to express the heroic soul of America."* Yet, less than twenty-five years later, classicism reappeared in the national capital, and it did so precisely to express the country's "heroic soul." The location was inside the newly completed Department of State Building, an undistinguished International Style block. The two top floors contained executive offices and rooms for diplomatic receptions that Clement E. Conger, the State Department's cura-

---

*Hudnut greatly undervalued Pope's staying power. In 2007, on the occasion of its 150th anniversary, the American Institute of Architects commissioned a national survey to identify the public's 150 favorite American buildings. The Jefferson Memorial was ranked fourth, and the National Gallery thirty-fourth. No buildings by Walter Gropius or Marcel Breuer, the Bauhaus stars whom Hudnut had brought to Harvard, made the list.

tor, likened to a 1950s motel: "floor-to-ceiling plate glass, exposed steel beams, openings but no doors, support beams encased in fire proofing in the middle of rooms, wall-to-wall carpeting, and acoustical tile ceilings." To create what Conger considered an appropriate setting for international diplomacy, the State Department decided to furnish the rooms with authentic pieces of the early American period. This required an appropriate architectural setting, and the commission to redesign the interior was given to Edward Vason Jones.

Jones, who specialized in classical interiors, designed an entrance hall, portrait gallery, and several reception rooms, all in the Federal style; after his death, the work was continued by Walter Macomber, John Blatteau, and Allan Greenberg. In the 1980s, Greenberg redesigned a suite of rooms used for ceremonial occasions. The new centerpiece, the Treaty Room, is an elliptical space whose curved wall is articulated by pairs of freestanding Corinthian columns. According to Greenberg, "the delicate thinness of the acanthus leaves was influenced by Pope's Corinthian capitals at the National Archives, perhaps the most beautiful I've ever seen."

A small gilt facsimile of the Great Seal of the United States, of which the secretary of state is custodian, nestles among the acanthus leaves of the column capitals. The Treaty Room is full of such iconographic imagery. A compass rose at the center of the inlaid wood floor represents the harmony of nations from all four corners of the globe. Carved into the base of the egg-and-dart moldings that form the door surrounds are whorls that depict white roses, traditional symbols of peace, as well as the leaves and flowers of the tobacco plant, a reference to the Native American peace-pipe ceremony.

What attracts Greenberg to classical architecture is the same thing that attracted Pope—and Jefferson before him: the opportunity to work in a tradition that stretches back to the ancient Greeks and Romans. At the heart of this tradition are the orders,

Allan Greenberg Architect, Treaty Room, U.S. Department of State, Washington, D.C., 1986

the formalized system of columns and horizontal elements that forms the chief architectural feature of ancient temples. According to Summerson, the reason that the orders have fascinated architects for centuries is in part the authority of the Ancients and in part their surrounding mystique. There are five major orders—Tuscan, Doric, Ionic, Corinthian, and Composite—and there are rules about their proportions, design, and use. "The basic values of the orders is in two things," Summerson writes, "their limited plurality and their relative immutability." At the same time, he points out that these "ready-made bits of architecture" can be combined and recombined in a rich variety of ways.

Ideally the order controls the entire design. It delegates its authority by transmitting its vertical ratios and some of its profiles to the mass of the building. A secondary order may tangle with the first so that movement on two different scales may be harmonized or counterpointed. An order may announce itself in a portico, continue the conversation in pilasters, detached, half or three-quarters columns or mount a choreographic exposition of all four. It may be present all the time, caging the building in a total embrace; or part of the time; or none of the time, merely hinting at the mood of the building by the loan of some of its attributes.

In Pope's National Gallery the Ionic order appears in the giant columns of the porticos and the rotunda, although Pope's version of classicism is particularly severe: the columns are smooth stone drums without flutes, the entablature is highly simplified, and the cornice lacks projecting dentils. The rest of the building consists chiefly of blank walls (since the galleries are top-lit), although these are modulated with the barest hint of pilasters, so slight as to be almost invisible. The profiles of the portico entablature and cornice are pulled around the perimeter of the building, "continuing the conversation," in Summerson's words.

The News Building in Athens, Georgia, designed by Greenberg, is a workaday newspaper office and printing plant and hardly bears comparison with Pope's monumental museum. Yet the classical language is equal to the different circumstances: a similar temple portico marks the entrance to the offices, although the order is Doric rather than Ionic, and the smooth columns are precast concrete rather than Tennessee marble. Like Pope, Greenberg wraps the rest of the building—which is brick—with an entablature and lightly accented brick pilasters. The severe exterior of what is essentially an industrial box is sparsely adorned: an ornamental cast-iron frame surrounds the front door, cast-iron lion

Allan Greenberg Architect, News Building, Athens, Georgia, 1992

masks and anthemia (leaf-based motifs) embellish the utilitarian canopy of the loading dock. The interior of the entrance lobby, on the other hand, is richly polychromed, a nod to the late-eighteenth-century Greek Revival, of which so many fine examples still exist in the South.

There is nothing particularly complicated about Greenberg's design—a temple portico in front of a functional box, an arrangement used scores of times in museums, banks, and campus buildings. That is why the building is so immediately familiar and understandable: the main entrance is in the "front," the functional truck dock is on the "side," and an outdoor roof terrace with tables and chairs at the "rear." What makes this simple building satisfying are the proportions, the rhythm of the openings, and the details, which demonstrate what Summerson once observed: "Correct classical architecture is very difficult to design, but if well designed it is not difficult to understand."

NEW CLASSICISM

Pope's classicism is sometimes described as canonic, for it adheres closely to the five orders as described by the Roman author
Vitruvius and elaborated by Renaissance architects such as Alberti and Palladio. Paul Cret, on the other hand, had a looser
interpretation of classicism. Although he was a prizewinning
graduate of the École des Beaux-Arts, and believed that classicism was appropriate for American public buildings, Cret took it
for granted that the style needed to be adapted to the needs and
tastes of his time. He was one of several architects in the 1920s
who advocated a stripped classicism, or what he called "New
Classicism," dispensing with the orders but preserving a classical
sense of composition and symmetry. Perhaps the best example
is the Federal Reserve Board Building in Washington, D.C., a
commission that Cret won in a competition that included Pope,
Arthur Brown Jr., Egerton Swartwout, William A. Delano, and
James Gamble Rogers—all leading classicists. A decade later, in
a national competition for the Smithsonian National Gallery of
Art, Cret was the only one of ten finalists who was *not* a modernist (the winners were Eliel and Eero Saarinen).

Cret was stoical about the rise of modernism. "They triumph
now without modesty," he wrote in 1930, "as the classicists of
yesterday—Italianists, Neo-Greeks, or the Beaux-Art group—
triumphed from 1880 to 1910 over the Gothic Revivalists, the isolated individualists, and relics of the 'Dark Ages.'"* He described
the history of architecture as cyclical.

In Art there are two broad groups—the Classic and the
Romantic—and in the see-saw balancing between them

---

*The "relics of the Dark Ages" is presumably a reference to William Morris and the Arts
and Crafts movement.

which is recorded in the history of Art, it is now one, now the other, which is on the high end. The ascendancy group believes in good faith to have discovered the one and only Truth, and to have forever vanquished its adversary, until the limit of its ascent having been reached, there appears what they will call a Reaction, and the opposite group, a New Tendency, and the vanquished of yesterday become the victors of today.

According to Cret, despite modernism's claims for rationalism, its pursuit of individualism, its quest for utopian perfection, and its rejection of history were fundamentally romantic.

New Classicism is evident in Cret's design for the Folger Shakespeare Library. Folger had originally wanted an Elizabethan-style building, but his architectural adviser, Alexander Trowbridge, convinced him that Tudor half-timbering would look odd on Capitol

Paul Philippe Cret, Folger Shakespeare Library, Washington, D.C., 1932

Hill. Cret's design has no columns or other classical motifs, and the simplified pilasters—no capitals or bases—resemble fluted panels. The decorative grilles over the windows and the stream-lined moldings are clearly influenced by French Art Deco. Yet classical balance prevails. The wide blank band that surrounds the building at the roof is a sort of frieze; and a patterned strip at the cornice suggests a dentil molding. Like Cret's Federal Reserve Building, Bertram Grosvenor Goodhue's National Academy of Sciences, and Raymond Hood's RCA Building at Rockefeller Center, the severity of the architecture is balanced by artwork—in the case of Folger, nine bas-relief panels depicting scenes from Shakespeare's plays. The walls are inscribed with quotations from Samuel Johnson, Ben Jonson, and of course the Bard.

Folger did get his way in the interior. The theater is Elizabethan, the exhibition gallery resembles a hall in a seventeenth-century British country house, and the main reading room is modeled on Henry VIII's banqueting hall at Hampton Court, complete with a hammer-beam ceiling and Tudor paneling. The contrast between interior and exterior is slightly unsettling, and as Cret wryly observed, "has proved troublesome to those . . . holding with good reason that the interior and exterior treatment of a building must possess unity."

THE STYLE FOR THE JOB

Cret valued consistency, but he had no objection to working in different styles, designing Mediterranean houses, several neo-Gothic buildings at West Point, an Art Deco power plant in Washington, D.C., and red-tile-roofed buildings for the University of Texas at Austin that incorporate Spanish and Mexican motifs. Most architects of his generation were eclectics. The driving force for eclecticism was less the architects than their clients. This continues to be true, as clients variously demand Collegiate Gothic for campus buildings, Shingle Style for beach houses, steel-and-glass modernism for office buildings, and avant-garde modernism for art museums. Peter Bohlin designs minimalist glass stores for Apple, but for the headquarters of the animation studio Pixar, which is located in a warehouse district of a small Northern California town, he conceived a building that resembles an industrial shed, while for Bill Gates's estate on the edge of Lake Washington in Seattle, Bohlin and James Cutler designed a sprawling concrete-and-timber compound that is half-buried in the landscape.

The tradition of modern eclecticism dates back to Eero Saarinen, who coined the expression "the style for the job," which was one of the things that attracted corporate clients such as IBM, TWA, Bell Telephone, and CBS—they were assured unique buildings that reflected their corporate identities. While contemporary architects such as Michael Graves, Frank Gehry, and Renzo Piano have developed signature styles, others, such as Herzog and de Meuron, Jean Nouvel, and Moshe Safdie, adopt varying modes of expression depending on the client, the program, and the setting. This seems to be routine among younger architects. Asked if he had an architectural signature, David Adjaye, the designer of the National Museum of African American History and Culture, responded: "For my generation, the idea of a signature style seems a bit outdated."

Two recent Safdie projects illustrate the point; both are modernist, but modernist in different ways. The first, Marina Bay Sands in Singapore, is a casino resort complex whose most striking feature is a dramatic "sky park" platform that sits on top of three fifty-five-story hotel towers. It is a Saarinesque *parti*, so simple it is immediately understandable, and so unsubtly theatrical it becomes an unforgettable image. The second project, Crystal Bridges Museum, in Bentonville, Arkansas, built by Alice Walton to house her collection of American art, is almost the exact opposite: fragmented, self-effacing, nestled into the landscape. Influenced by the Louisiana Museum in Denmark, the

Arkansas museum is a casual arrangement of linked gallery pavilions surrounding water pools in a forest setting. Safdie compares the two projects, which opened the same year.

> Crystal Bridges is about the *particular* in architecture. The particular has to do with the program for a building. The particular is about the secrets embedded in the site and how, from an understanding of the site, a concept emerges. It has to do with building materials and methods which have to do with that particular place. Marina Bay, on the other hand, has to with the *general*. It has to do with the notion of mega-scale and cities. It has to do with how you build ten million square feet and create a public realm in the context of a dense, congested city.

Safdie makes no overt historical or regional references, yet he responds to the two settings—Singapore and the Ozarks—and

Safdie Architects, Crystal Bridges Museum, Bentonville, Arkansas, 2012

programs by using different forms, different materials, different structural systems, even different details. Marina Bay is hard, commercial, and rather slick; Crystal Bridges is intimate, hand-crafted, and intentionally unmonumental.

What attracts clients to a modern eclectic such as Safdie—or Saarinen before him—is precisely what disturbs many critics, who are uncomfortable with variety and much prefer stylistic consistency. Academics, too, tend to be more at home with con-sistency, which is more amenable to scholarly analysis, especially if it has theoretical underpinnings. Eclectics, on the other hand, think otherwise. "Architecture doesn't come from theory," wrote the Canadian architect Arthur Erickson. "You don't think your way through a building." Erickson's work demonstrates a wide stylistic range: romantic post-and-beam houses, a high-tech space-frame roof in Vancouver's Robson Square, a sculptural form in Toronto's Roy Thomson Hall, slick glass boxes in Ottawa's Bank of Canada building. The restless imaginations of eclectic architects make them appear artistically unreliable, for which they pay a price: Cret's and Saarinen's reputations fell precipi-tously after their deaths, as did that of Erickson, who died in 2007.

MODERN AND NOT MODERN

I saw Charles Moore's own weekend house in Orinda, California, in the mid-1960s. I was on a student architecture trip, and we drove up into the hills behind Berkeley, where Moore was teach-ing at the time. The modern buildings I was familiar with were characterized by flat roofs and expanses of glass, but the roof of this little structure was hipped, and while the glass corners opened up in a distinctly modern fashion, they were closed with what looked like barn doors. In fact, with its whitewashed wooden walls and weathered cedar shingles, the house resembled a little

Charles Moore, Moore House, Orinda, California, 1962

barn. Moore was unmarried, and the interior was an undivided "modern" space, with the shower out in the open under a large skylight. But the skylight was supported by four Tuscan—Tuscan!—columns. The result was both modern and not modern. As a conventionally trained twenty-one-year-old architecture student, I wasn't sure what to make of it.

Buildings like Moore's little house heralded the postmodernist movement, which attempted to fuse historical motifs with modernist ideology. Perhaps the most accomplished postmodern practitioner was James Stirling, whose Neue Staatsgalerie combines features of several styles with great invention and mastery. Recognizably neoclassical elements help to relate the new architecture to the original museum, but the addition is also a collage of modernist styles. Exposed structural steel, as brightly painted as a Rietveld chair, abuts traditional-looking masonry. Massive air vents are lifted from the Centre Pompidou, and fat shocking-pink balustrades seem to have migrated from the Las Vegas Strip. The bright green textured rubber floor recalls Pierre Chareau's

*James Stirling & Michael Wilford, Neue
Staatsgalerie, Stuttgart, 1984*

Maison de Verre, a modernist icon, while a wing housing the library has International Style ribbon windows above very un–International Style striped awnings.

Stirling saw architecture as a language, but he was not content merely to speak it properly. Something of an architectural bad boy, he wanted to stretch and enrich the modernist vocabulary with jokes, puns, slang, and wordplay. "For many of us working with the language of abstract modern architecture, Bauhaus, International Style—call it what you will—this language has become repetitive, simplistic, and too narrowly confining and I for one welcome the passing of the revolutionary phase of the Modern Movement," he told the audience in his 1981 Pritzker Prize acceptance speech. Sometimes, the strongest motivation for an architectural impulse can be boredom.

Postmodernism proved to be a short-lived style. In the hands of a witty designer such as Moore, or a student of history such as Stirling, or a conscientious architect such as Venturi, the result could be a fresh reinterpretation of the past. However, less knowledgeable architects tended to combine historical elements in an ad-hoc manner, irrespective of the context, like magpies indiscriminately hoarding bright objects. *Postmodernism* soon lost its original meaning and became a derogatory term, referring to any building with vaguely historical motifs, cartoonish forms, or pastel colors, and the public—as well as the profession—soon tired of the whole thing. Nevertheless, postmodernism played an important role in opening the door to both a reconsideration of modernism and a revival of classicism.

Some postmodern architects turned to a more thorough and considered application of historical styles. A recent monograph on the residential work of Robert A. M. Stern features twenty-six houses and includes more than a dozen different historical styles, most dating from the early twentieth century, the golden age of the American country house. For clients who are uncertain as to what type of house they want, the Stern office prepares precedent books, which show illustrations of different styles—Shingle Style, Arts and Crafts, American Colonial, Mediterranean, Norman, French Directoire—organized according to house types such as farmhouses or rustic lodges, or according to the domestic styles of a particular region such as Southern California or New England.

Stern has not designed any modern houses—yet—but his campus work displays a wider stylistic range. At Florida Southern College, a campus originally planned by Frank Lloyd Wright, three buildings by Stern are Wrightian only in the sense of having deep overhangs and angled geometry, otherwise their design is strikingly—and colorfully—contemporary. At the University of

Nevada's Las Vegas campus, which has grown haphazardly since its founding in 1957 and lacks a compelling architectural image, the Stern addition is a forceful modern building with large expanses of glass and a courtyard shaded by a pergola supporting photovoltaic panels. On the other hand, at Stanford University, a computer sciences building explores the Richardsonian Romanesque style of the original campus. At Rice University, Stern's school of business takes its architectural cues from the campus's idiosyncratic Byzantine-Romanesque style.

Stern was once asked if, when he used a historical style, he was trying to replicate the vocabulary of the past. He replied:

> Not to replicate; to speak. There's a difference. When you speak English you are not replicating Shakespeare's English, or Walt Whitman's English, or even Virginia Woolf's English. You have your own diction, but you're still using most of the same words, most of the same grammar. And you're trying to speak it as well as someone you admire before you.

The architectural language of Southern Methodist University in Dallas is redbrick Georgian Revival. When it was announced that Stern would be the architect of the George W. Bush presidential library on the SMU campus, it was widely assumed that he would continue that tradition. However, while the Bush library is related to the campus by its general massing and scale, its use of axes and symmetry, and its materials— brick with limestone trim—it's definitely not Georgian. "Right from the outset, Mrs. Bush [who chaired the design review committee] made it very clear, in her own way, that she wanted a building that would fit into the SMU campus, but that it should also have its own identity," says Graham Wyatt, a Stern partner.

Laura Bush requested that the building be modern, but also

*Robert A. M. Stern Architects, George W. Bush Presidential Center,
Dallas, 2013*

enduring. "She did not want a building that was the new-new
thing," says Wyatt, "that people would look back at in ten years
and say, 'Oh yes, that was 2013.'" The design is austerely modern
in its details yet its compositional strategy is balanced, calm, and
resolutely traditional. Wyatt says that the Stern team looked at
the civic architecture of the pre– and post–World War II era, and
the central lantern as well as the piers of the colonnaded entrance hearken back to Cret's New Classicism. The building is
largely brick—an unassuming material for a presidential library—
and it reminds me of another library, the last building that Eliel
Saarinen designed at the Cranbrook Academy of Art in 1942.
Stern included Saarinen's library in *Pride of Place*, his history of
American architecture, calling it "a quintessential American
dream house, establishing a sense of place, memory, and the
owner's personality, as it reaches out to establish a complex com-
munal vision that endures over time." Which is a pretty good description of the Bush presidential library.

WHY ARCHITECTS
ARE WARY OF STYLE

Stern is unusual in addressing the question of style directly; most architects are wary of the subject. The great British Arts and Crafts practitioner Mackay Hugh Baillie Scott explained why: "To consciously aim at achieving 'style' in design, either old or new, is to follow a Will o' the Wisp. For the pursuit of style, like the pursuit of happiness, must necessarily lead to disappointment and failure. Both alike are essentially by-products, and the quality of by-products is in direct ratio to the worthiness of the ideal pursued." Note that Baillie Scott did not deny that style exists, only that for the architect it represents a trap. "He who aims at style is he who would paint the lily rather than watering it," he wrote.

Paul Cret was a lifelong educator as well as a practitioner, and although he took classicism for granted, he believed that being overly concerned with style was harmful in learning how to be an architect. "In my opinion, the question of the styles must be absolutely excluded from the course in design; this question belongs properly to the history of architecture," he told his colleagues at the American Institute of Architects.

> Before studying the different expressions of architecture which constitute the styles, I think it imperative that the students be made familiar with the elements of architecture. For one who has not had this necessary preparation, the history of art becomes archaeology, that is to say, a science extremely interesting, but powerless to stimulate the mind toward the creation of new works of art—a science made for the scholar, not for the architect.

Cret's colleague George Howe, who with William Lescaze designed the first International Style skyscraper, Philadelphia's PSFS Building, saw style as purely historical. According to him there were three great styles, "embodied in the ancient Greek temple, the medieval European cathedral, and the seventeenth-century baroque church." But there he drew the line. "Modernism is not a style," he stated. "It is an attitude of mind." Perhaps he actually believed it, although looking back at the PSFS Building, it is obvious that a sense of visual style—what became known as the Streamline Moderne style of the 1930s—is an important part of this glamorous building. The idea that "modernism is not a style" is certainly hard to support today, when the International Style is revived by architects such as Richard Meier and Álvaro Siza, and the "skinny details" of early Southern California modernism show up in buildings such as Renzo Piano's California Academy of Sciences.

Piano is someone whose work exhibits a high degree of style. Yet he, too, is wary.

Yes. As an architect you do something and everybody thinks that this is your style. So if they love what you've done they want you to do again the same thing. Now this is the beginning of the end, of course, because then you are trapped in a sort of stylish cage, maybe sometimes a golden cage but it's still a cage. And this is terrible because one of the beautiful things about architecture is that it depends entirely on where you are, when, and doing what, you know. Architecture is really the mirror of the moment, and of the people you are working with, and so essentially of the client and the community . . . But you have to stay away from the notion of a style, in the sense of the rubber stamp. I mean that's terrible.

Like Cret and Baillie Scott, Piano regards style—even personal style—as an unconscious product of the design process. This is somewhat disingenuous, for like many architects he has developed habits of design, favorite details, and preferred materials—even a recurring color, which his publicists insist on calling Renzo Red. Nevertheless, it is not unreasonable for a designer to take his view, as the danger for the architect who becomes overly concerned with style is that he turns into a stylist. The difference between a designer and a stylist is analogous to the difference between Glenn Gould performing Bach and Victor Borge playing in the style of Bach. With Gould, we experience Bach's creation; with Borge, we merely recognize the composer's style. One is art; the other, however entertaining, is not.

9

THE PAST

High Hollow is the house that twenty-eight-year-old George Howe built for his growing family in 1914, on a steeply sloping site adjoining Fairmount Park in Philadelphia's Chestnut Hill. Howe was a wealthy young man, and this, his first built work, was based on his final project at the École des Beaux-Arts from which he had graduated the year before. The plan has all the refinement that one would expect from an *ancien élève*; what are unexpected are the details, or rather their absence. "All mouldings, ornaments, recesses, all those things that are commonly called 'architectural trimmings,' have been eliminated," wrote Paul Cret in *Architectural Record*. "These walls, built shortly before the war, seem to be old . . . And yet a remarkable fact is that the house is quite free from imitation of historic precedents in its details . . . No doubt many clients would be disappointed by their inability to tack a 'style' label to any portion of it."

Cret put his finger on it: High Hollow is curiously style-less. The seam-faced red and brown stone walls with red-brick trim, the steep slate roofs, and a striking round tower, are vaguely French, but this connection is blurred, like a distant memory. Although later owners clumsily redecorated the interior in a French period style, adding moldings and bric-a-brac, you can still experience Howe's architecture: the entrance hall with its checkerboard floor and dramatic stair, a beautiful oval study, and the grand living room. The living room floor is rustic Enfield tile from a local pottery, grayish yellow with a dull blue border; tall French doors slide into ingenious wall pockets. Howe went on to design many exceptional houses in a long career, but one sees the already steady hand of a talented architect in this early masterpiece, with its well-proportioned rooms, axial views, and integration into the natural landscape. "Were not the phrase 'modern art' somewhat discredited for having been a cloak to a multitude of sins," observed Cret, "I would see here a very typical example of what modern art ought to be; a logical continuation of the best traditions." Although Cret and Howe were friends, coming from the master, this was high praise.

In describing High Hollow's subtle charms, Cret saw no contradiction between modernity and tradition:

> The greatest pleasure will be found in discovering in these features, which at first seem to have been adopted without thought, a clever adaptation of the great principles of design; in realizing that this architecture, which owes so little to precedents, is true to the best traditions of art; in finding the soul of our art instead of the cast-off clothing of former time.

Cret obviously did not think much of architects who merely copied the past. He celebrated originality as the "soul of our art" while at the same time recognizing that the "great principles of design" were rooted in history. This was a subtle distinction, but then architects have always had a complicated relationship to the past.

Architects turn to history for the same reason that politicians read biographies of famous leaders: circumstances change, the problems are not the same, yet human nature—like materials and space—is a constant, and the hope is to glean something from the accomplishments of the past that will serve the present. Old buildings are best "read" firsthand, hence the tradition of the architectural tour. As long ago as the thirteenth century, the French master mason Villard de Honnecourt traveled to Chartres, Laon, and Reims to sketch their cathedrals; Inigo Jones and John Soane likewise compiled travel diaries. The eighteenth-century Grand Tour was a staple of aspiring British gentleman architects and their clients. Today, young graduates, with budget guides and cameras in hand, continue to visit Renaissance palazzos, Gothic cathedrals, and Greek temples. Architectural travel does not end with maturity—all the practicing architects I know travel in order to see places with their own eyes, to observe the effect of a specific form, a quality of light, or a particular dimension, and to learn how people behave in certain spaces.

This intimate relationship to the past sets the architectural profession apart, for while medicine and engineering both have recorded histories, neither doctors nor engineers consider a knowledge of the past—especially the distant past—to be an essential qualification for contemporary practice. In that regard, architects are more like lawyers who practice common law that is based on judicial precedents. Architectural precedents are not binding, of course, but they have frequently provided inspiration. Modern architects as different as Louis Kahn, Robert Venturi, and Michael Graves have drawn lessons from Renaissance Rome. Palladio went to the Eternal City to study its ancient ruins, Le Corbusier went to Vicenza to learn from Palladio, and a young Richard Meier went to Paris to study—and unsuccessfully apply for a job with Le Corbusier.

Retrospection begins in school. When I was a student, every school of architecture had its historian; the University of London had Nikolaus Pevsner, Columbia had James Marston Fitch, and Yale had Vincent Scully. The historian at McGill, where I studied, was Peter Collins, who had studied architecture at Leeds and worked for Auguste Perret in Paris. Collins wrote an important book on Perret and the early history of concrete, but he taught what today is disparagingly called a "survey course" in history—although it is hard to know a more effective way of learning about the past than chronologically.* We started with the ancients, then moved on to the Romanesque and Gothic; during the second year we covered the Renaissance; and the third year was devoted to French neoclassicism—which was Collins's great love—and the early twentieth century. Although McGill's design curriculum was influenced by the one that Gropius had installed at Harvard, there was an abiding sense—unlike at Harvard—that the past was important. Memorizing the names and dates of Greek temples for periodic slide tests struck me as a waste of time, but years later, when I saw the real thing, the buildings were all the more meaningful for being so familiar. We borrowed books from the library, but we all owned a copy of Banister Fletcher's dictionary-size A History of Architecture, first published in 1896. Like his father and coauthor, Fletcher was a practicing architect as well as a historian, and this comprehensive book never lost touch with the constructional foundation of architecture. As well as photographs, he included plans, elevations, sections, cutaway drawings, and details. My own copy—the seventeenth edition—had 650 pages of illustrations, almost half the book. Although Fletcher was not a revivalist—his 1937 Gillette factory in Brentford, a London suburb, is Art Deco in style—he saw the study of history as essential for all architects. "Greek architecture stands alone in being accepted as beyond criticism, and being an obligatory study for students of otherwise very different principles," he wrote.

*Sadly, most architecture schools have eliminated required courses in history, replacing them with elective seminars in so-called history-theory and thematic classes on selected topics.

REVIVALS

A prime indicator of architects' unique relationship to the past is the architectural revival. "An architectural revival is the physical expression of an architect's desire to demonstrate to his public that he wishes to remind them of an historic building form specifically because it existed in the past and which, for some subsequent period of time, fell out of general use," writes the contemporary British architect Robert Adam. "This revival could occur several times or once, it could be done wholly or partially, it could be done accurately or inaccurately; it is still a revival." The last point is important. Critics of revival architecture sometimes fix on a lack of historical verisimilitude as evidence that a revival is "inauthentic," but accuracy, as Adam writes, is not the point. Sometimes, merely creating an aura of a past period is enough.

Architectural revivals have occurred with clockwork regularity. The Renaissance revived Roman architecture; European neoclassicists revived Greek architecture; American architects revived Roman, Greek, and Renaissance architecture. One of the most enduring revival styles is Gothic. The heyday of cathedral building in northern Europe lasted from the twelfth to the thirteenth century, but Gothic churches continued to be built in Spain and Italy much longer than that, and Milan Cathedral, begun in the fourteenth century, was completed as late as the mid-1800s. In fact, there was never a period when Gothic disappeared entirely. Brunelleschi is considered a pioneer of Renaissance classicism, but his ribbed Duomo in Florence is more Gothic than classical; Christopher Wren rebuilt St. Paul's in the classical style, but he also built St. Mary Aldermary in London, which Pevsner judged the most important late-seventeenth-century Gothic church in England. The fan-vault ceiling of St. Mary is plaster rather than stone—so much for authenticity. In the

Porphyrios Associates, Whitman College, Princeton University, Princeton, 2007

mid-nineteenth century, Augustus Pugin led a major Gothic revival in Britain, Eugène Viollet-le-Duc did the same in France, and later Ralph Adams Cram was the leading advocate of Gothic in America. Twentieth-century Gothic structures on both sides of the Atlantic include Giles Gilbert Scott's Liverpool Cathedral, Marchand & Pearson's Peace Tower in Ottawa, and Cram's Cathedral of St. John the Divine in New York. Cram's partner, Bertram Goodhue, designed the exceptional Rockefeller Chapel at the University of Chicago in 1924, and six years later Goodhue's successor firm used the same Gothic style in the Oriental Institute next door. When Thomas Beeby designed an addition to the institute in the early 1990s, he adopted the style of his predecessors. Six years ago, Demetri Porphyrios completed Whitman College for Princeton in the Collegiate Gothic style that Cram had introduced to the university a hundred years earlier—thus, a revival of a revival.

THE ZEITGEIST

William Mitchell, former dean of the architecture school at the Massachusetts Institute of Technology, huffily told *The New York Times* that Whitman College signaled "an astonishing lack of interest in architecture's capacity to respond innovatively and critically to the conditions of our own time and place." Since revivals have a six-hundred-year track record, "astonishing" seems overwrought. Mitchell's "our own time and place" echoes Hegel's idea of the zeitgeist, or the Spirit of the Age, suggesting that each era produces its own distinctive architecture. But as Léon Krier has observed, while it is obvious that architecture can mark an epoch, it is less clear that the reverse is true; there are many historical periods that do not produce a distinctive architecture. Nevertheless, the notion of the zeitgeist persists. The University of Pennsylvania, for example, has adopted guidelines that instruct architects that the style of new buildings on the campus "should express the aesthetic ideas of our times, so that as we look back on them they also become a cultural record of ideas about architecture and campus life." Setting aside the questions of what *the aesthetic ideas of our times* actually mean and, if such ideas exist, whether they really change as often as the guideline implies, this is really code for "No historical styles allowed." Indeed, an award-winning architect who is known for his classical work told me that he was privately informed that the reason he was never considered for a commission at Penn was that the university built only "modern buildings."

The idea that architecture should be driven by the spirit of the age is relatively recent, deriving from the early days of architectural modernism. Le Corbusier explained in his 1923 classic *Vers une architecture*:

> The history of Architecture unfolds itself slowly across the centuries as a modification of structure and ornament, but

in the last fifty years steel and concrete have brought new conquests, which are the index of a greater capacity for construction, and of an architecture in which the old codes have been overturned. If we challenge the past, we shall learn that "styles" no longer exist for us, that a style belonging to our own period has come about; and there has been a Revolution.

Le Corbusier's proposition sounds plausible—new construction materials and methods require a new architecture; the old rules no longer apply; we are modern, so we should have our own modern style. But on reflection, the argument is less persuasive. Concrete was invented long ago by the Romans, but Roman builders had no difficulty combining the new material with ancient Greek forms. Reinforced concrete was invented in 1849, long before *Vers une architecture* was written, and architects such as Auguste Perret, for whom Le Corbusier worked, and Grosvenor Atterbury in the United States had already demonstrated how concrete could be used without "overturning old codes." Sullivan and Burnham had built steel-frame skyscrapers that expanded, but likewise did not upend, traditional rules.

Architects have always adapted old forms to new materials, and vice versa. Palladio built Roman columns out of brick, sometimes plastering them over to resemble marble, sometimes leaving the red brick exposed. Inigo Jones's Banqueting Hall in Whitehall was inspired by Palladio, but was built of dressed stone, not plastered brick. Jefferson's Doric columns in Monticello are wood. John Russell Pope's Ionic columns in the National Gallery rotunda are monolithic shafts of marble, not white but dark green Verte Imperial. For the Tuscan columns of the News Building in Athens, Georgia, Allan Greenberg made do with precast concrete. Today, in addition to wood, stone, and concrete, prefabricated classical columns can be had in cast stone, glass-reinforced gypsum, and glass-fiber reinforced plastic.

The other problematic question is exactly how to define "our own period." The industrial era celebrated by Le Corbusier in *Vers une architecture* lasted less than fifty years, and the transportation technologies that were the raison d'être for a revolutionary modern style—ocean liners, steam locomotives, flying boats, and Delage touring cars—all disappeared. According to Le Corbusier's own logic, his ideas about modern architecture were now obsolete and should be rethought, and, indeed, he turned from designing white Cubist boxes to rough concrete sculptural forms. Today, proponents of blob architecture and parametric design argue that a digital age requires its own architecture just as the industrial age did, but is a continuous architectural revolution really possible, let alone desirable? And granting that architecture is always a reflection of the moment, that moment may involve looking back, as well as looking forward. If the spirit of the age includes an interest in the past, as it has done so often, wouldn't looking back be the "modern" thing to do?

Steen Eiler Rasmussen raised the issue of the past in the first chapter of *Experiencing Architecture.* He included a photograph of a famous Danish actor dressed in a Renaissance costume of doublet and lace, riding a bicycle. "The costume, of its kind, is undoubtedly a handsome one, and the bicycle too is of the best. But they simply do not go together," Rasmussen wrote. "In the same way, it is impossible to take over the beautiful architecture of a past era; it becomes false and pretentious when people can no longer live up to it." There are a number of problems with this analogy. Rasmussen implied that Renaissance dress did not "go together" with a bicycle because the latter was a modern device, but the velocipede was invented in the early 1800s, and the first "safety bicycle" became popular well before the end of the nineteenth century. These early bicycles were pedaled by gentlemen in knickerbockers and straw boaters, and ladies in bloomers and sun bonnets, yet we do not consider it "false and pretentious" to ride a bicycle today dressed in shorts and a baseball cap. To maintain that the architecture of the past becomes false when people can no longer "live up to it" (or dress up to it?) ignores that people happily use old buildings all the time. It is not necessary to wear a blazer and flannels, as students did when Cram built Princeton's Collegiate Gothic colleges in the 1920s, to reside in Graduate College today; polo shirts and chinos will do just fine.

THE EVER-PRESENT PAST

Architecture, if it's well done, lasts a long time. With periodic maintenance and occasional refurbishment, buildings remain useful for hundreds of years. They are not disposable, which makes them special in our throwaway culture. None of my students has ever seen a steam-powered locomotive in regular service or flown in a dirigible, yet they can still walk through the concourse of Grand Central Terminal, or visit the observation platform of the Empire State Building, whose mast was originally intended for mooring airships. Cuisine, dress, even behavior, changes from one generation to the next; I don't dress, or eat, or behave like a person of a hundred years ago. I don't drive a hundred-year-old car, but I do live in a hundred-year-old house. I don't think of my home as an antique, exactly, it's just a house that happens to be old. The casual, daily experience of old buildings may explain why the public has accepted—sometimes even demanded— architecture that reminded them of the past.

Le Corbusier, Rasmussen, and Mitchell would have us believe that people experience buildings as unique expressions of distinct historical periods. My built Philadelphia is a hodgepodge of old and new. Apart from streets and streets of row houses of every vintage, the city includes the Athenaeum as well as Thirtieth Street Station, the venerable Academy of Music and the Kimmel Performing Arts Center, the Neo-Grec Philadelphia Museum of Art as well as the recently completed Barnes Foundation. I may pause to reflect on the fact that the Athenaeum kicked off the Renaissance Revival in the United States, or that Thirtieth Street Station was the last of the grand railroad stations, and I have my likes (the Academy) and dislikes (Kimmel). But like most people I don't think of buildings as representing historical periods; they are simply places in the urban landscape. Moreover, I do not expect that every building added to that landscape must be radically different. It's nice that I. M. Pei's Society Hill towers stick out, but it's also nice that Robert A. M. Stern's 10 Rittenhouse Square fits in. Pei's towers are fifty years old, but to most people they still look "modern," while Stern's brick-and-limestone building is brand-new, but most would describe it as "traditional." Like the people in the street, some buildings are dressed in the latest fashions, some in nondescript dress, and others—this is Philadelphia, after all—are a throwback to another time. I like seeing the architectural equivalent of a gentleman in a seersucker suit, or a lady in a proper hat, from time to time. It would be boring if everyone dressed the same.

Historic revivals are not unique to architecture, although in the other arts they occur less regularly. One field that is similar, as far as revivals are concerned, is typography, whose long history curiously parallels that of architecture. The first movable type used by Gutenberg in the mid-fifteenth century was based on a medieval script, called blackletter, and widely used in Germany, the Netherlands, England, and France. The successor to blackletter was roman, developed by Renaissance typecutters in Italy, who copied ancient lettering from surviving Roman monuments— the first typographic revival. The roman typeface spread all over Europe. Claude Garamond, an early sixteenth-century Parisian typecutter, developed several popular fonts based on roman models. "Garamond's romans are stately High Renaissance forms with humanist axis, moderate contrast and long extenders," writes the Canadian typographer Robert Bringhurst. The Garamond typeface later itself experienced several revivals. In 1900, Original

Garamond was introduced at the Paris World's Fair; in 1924, the Stempel foundry in Frankfurt issued a Garamond typeface; in 1964, the famous typographer Jan Tschichold designed Sabon, named after a fifteenth-century French typefounder and based on Garamond; and in 1977, a digital version of Garamond was released. The sixteenth-century type experienced yet another revival when, from 1984 to 2001, Apple used Garamond as its corporate font.

The font of my word processor as I write this is Times New Roman, which Bringhurst describes as a historical pastiche, with a "humanist axis but Mannerist proportions, Baroque weight, and a sharp, neoclassical finish." The typeface was commissioned by the London *Times* in 1931, and although the newspaper no longer uses the original Times New Roman, the typeface has become one of the most widely used in history, thanks to its default position in Microsoft Word. Times New Roman, like most book and newspaper fonts, is a serif typeface—that is, the letters have small marks at the ends of the strokes, a feature introduced by ancient Roman letter carvers. Unserifed—or sans serif—letters also date back to ancient Greece and Rome, but unserifed printing type did not appear until the early nineteenth century—in London—and was used only in advertising signs and newspaper headlines. Unserifed type was revived in the twentieth century, since its geometrical purity suited the Bauhaus aesthetic; Futura, designed by Paul Renner in the 1920s, is a typical modernist font. When I was a student, we used Letraset press type on our drawings, and the font of choice was Helvetica, a Swiss unserifed typeface. The most recent revival of unserifed type is due to a technological change: unserifed letters are easier to read on low-resolution electronic screens and have become the standard font on all digital devices.

Typesetting technologies have changed radically in the last five hundred years, yet as Bringhurst points out, this does not necessarily mean that the basis of typographical design has altered:

Typographic style is founded not on any one technology of typesetting or printing, but on the primitive yet subtle craft of writing. Letters derive their form from the motions of the human hand, restrained and amplified by a tool. That tool may be as complex as a digitizing tablet or a specially programmed keyboard, or as simple as a sharpened stick. Meaning resides, in either case, in the firmness and grace of the gesture itself, not in the tool with which it is made.

Architecture is likewise not founded on the techniques or materials of construction but on the enclosure of space and ultimately on the human activity it houses. As in typesetting, there are no absolutes, no moral imperatives. There are rules, but these derive from practice rather than theory, sometimes very old practice. That is why the past continues to influence architects. The root of the word *tradition*, as Tschichold pointed out, is the Latin *tradere*, which means to deliver, one generation handing over to the next.

CONVENTIONS

Jan Tschichold observed that the root of *convention* is the Latin *conventionem*, which means "agreement." "I use the word convention and its derivative, conventional, only in its original and never in any derogatory sense." Revivalist architects tend to follow conventions. As we have seen, Robert A. M. Stern has designed many campus buildings in revival styles—Georgian, Gothic, Richardsonian Romanesque—generally as a way of complementing neighboring buildings. His choice of the Federal style for the McNeil Center for Early American Studies at the University of Pennsylvania arose from a different motive. The longtime benefactor of the program insisted that the center's new home reflect

Robert A. M. Stern Architects, McNeil Center for Early American Studies, University of Pennsylvania, Philadelphia, 2005

its academic mission, and the university softened its stylistic guideline. Federal is an American version of the Adam style that was popular in the United States from 1780 to 1820. Although the Penn campus has no Federal buildings, Philadelphia is the site of some of the finest Federal architecture in the country. Stern modeled his design on the university's original medical school, designed by Benjamin Henry Latrobe in the early 1800s (and long since demolished). The result is a brick box with uncomplicated massing, a flattened tripartite composition, no classical details, and a low hipped roof.

Stern was looking back, but not only to the nineteenth century. The top of the McNeil Center has a parapet wall pierced by square window-like apertures. This detail is not Federal but is derived from Louis Kahn, a longtime presence at the university. The apertures are based on Kahn's Phillips Exeter Academy Library, as are the brick jack arches. The connections to two of the city's great architects—Latrobe and Kahn—to the nineteenth-century home of the university, and to the redbrick traditions of

Philadelphia, combine to make this little building a rich exercise in historical memory.

While Stern's design made explicit links to the past, at the University of Miami, Léon Krier designed an octagonal lecture hall that has no immediate precedent yet appears distinctly classical, although it does not slavishly follow stylistic conventions. The interior of the auditorium is a steeply raked hall surmounted by an industrial-looking dome supported on exposed steel beams. The whitewashed exterior has no orders and no classical detail; a tiered tower resembles a columbarium. The effect is both primitive and slightly mysterious. "Alone among architects working in a traditional syntax, Krier has extended the vocabulary of classicism through bold use of proportion and a free interpretation of tropes and motifs," writes Alexander Gorlin.

Mannerists call up rules, too, but usually in order to distort

Léon Krier/Merrill Pastor, Jorge M. Perez Architecture Center, University of Miami, 2006

them. Robert Venturi and Denise Scott Brown's work is full of
bent conventions and deformed precedents: odd column spac-
ings, capitals that don't quite meet their architraves, moldings
that are awkwardly located in the "wrong" place. One of their favorite strategies is to play with scale. The entrance to Gordon Wu
Hall at Princeton has heraldic motifs drawn from Elizabethan
domestic interiors. "The entrance enhances the identity of this
otherwise recessive building through the bold symbolic pattern
adorning it," Venturi writes, "which refers to Elizabethan/Jaco-
bean motifs often found over fireplaces and appropriate within
the context of a quasi-Elizabethan precinct of the campus." But
at Wu Hall, these motifs are vastly enlarged and moreover flattened out, as if a steamroller had run over them.

Even an architectural revolutionary such as Le Corbusier,
once he was done challenging the past, came to terms with tradition. His designs after 1950, such as the Jaoul houses in Paris
and the Sarabhai residence in Ahmedabad, India, have rough
brick walls and tiled Catalan vaults in a modern interpretation
of Mediterranean vernacular architecture. His most sculptural
work, the chapel at Ronchamp, contains many oblique Mediterranean references: whitewashed walls, rough details, Cycladic
towers.

The experience of a building, especially an abstract modernist
building, is enriched when it includes allusions to the past. Louis
Kahn's Richards Medical Building distinguished between what
the architect called "servant and served spaces," brick shafts containing staircases and ducts, and the laboratories themselves.
This rather obscure notion—there is no real parallel between
people climbing stairs and air traveling through exhaust ducts—is
probably lost on most observers, but no one who has ever visited
the Tuscan hill town of San Gimignano (as Kahn did in 1928)
will miss the connection between the tall brick shafts and medieval towers. Another Kahn design that benefits from a link to the
past is the Kimbell Art Museum. Long, vaulted rooms for dis-

Louis I. Kahn, Kimbell Art Museum, Fort Worth, 1972

playing art date back to the Renaissance, and by the eighteenth century, the vaulted *galleria*, usually top-lit, was a staple of palace planning. Kahn was no revivalist, yet his vaulted, top-lit galleries are a modern interpretation—and a masterly one—of this old convention.

The lanterns and vaulted rooms of Venturi's addition to the National Gallery are a direct acknowledgment of John Soane's Dulwich Picture Gallery, although the scale of the latter is much smaller, and Soane's use of detail is actually *less* conventionally classical than Venturi's. Norman Foster at the Sainsbury Centre for Visual Arts in Norwich makes no direct references to the past, yet his design resonates with history in subtle ways, as Reyner Banham pointed out. The long, shedlike building, which resembles an airship hangar, is less than twenty miles away from the site of an old Royal Navy Air Service airship station. At the same time, the simple linear building in its parklike setting has reminded many of a Greek temple; one critic called it

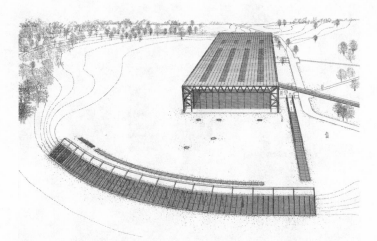

Foster Associates, Sainsbury Centre for Visual Arts, University of East Anglia, Norwich, 1978

East Anglia's Parthenon. Thus, the Sainsbury Centre conjures up two opposing images of the past, one relatively recent and one ancient.

Some architects ignore the past altogether, willfully solving old problems in new and unexpected ways. The novelty of these buildings attracts attention, but buildings that cut loose from the past pay a price; their novelty can quickly become stale. In that regard, I find London's Tate Modern, which is housed in a converted power station, to be a more interesting building than the de Young Museum in San Francisco, precisely because at the Tate, Herzog and de Meuron's often relentless innovation is tempered by Giles Gilbert Scott's 1940s architecture.* Similarly, Frank Gehry's Disney Hall is more compelling than the Bilbao Guggenheim Museum, because the traditional, wood-lined con-

*Scott, the architect of Liverpool Cathedral and Battersea Power Station, was also the designer of the iconic British red telephone box.

cert hall sets up an interesting dialogue with the stainless-steel sail shapes that surround it. The New World Symphony Center, where Gehry shoehorns a rambunctious sense of sculptural fun into a conventional South Beach white box, is likewise more nuanced than his buildings that are unfettered by such self-imposed constraints.

REMEMBERING THE PAST

One type of architecture that deals explicitly with history is the memorial, since its sole function is to commemorate an event or a figure from the past. Five outstanding twentieth-century memorials illustrate how architects have used different means to achieve this difficult task.

THE CENOTAPH

The Cenotaph in London has inspired replicas and copies across the British Empire, yet the iconic monument came about almost by accident. In 1919, the British government planned a national holiday to celebrate the signing of the peace treaty that formally ended the Great War. The central event of Peace Day was to be a victory parade through London. When the British learned that the French, who were holding a similar parade in Paris, were erecting a temporary funerary memorial next to the Arc de Triomphe to honor the fallen, they decided that the London parade should have a similar structure. The prime minister, David Lloyd George, turned to Sir Edwin Lutyens, Britain's foremost architect. Since Peace Day was less than three weeks off, Lutyens had to work quickly, and he is said to have made his first sketch the same day. He proposed a memorial based on an archaic funerary device that dates from ancient times and commemorates a dead personage who is buried elsewhere: a cenotaph (the word is from the Greek meaning an empty tomb). Lutyens's design is of the utmost simplicity: a stepped plinth, a base, and a tall shaft supporting a coffin. There are no military decorations or allusions to war, no patriotic sentiments, no mention of God or country. The only inscriptions are the dates MCMXIV–MCMXIX, and the words, said to be suggested by Lloyd George, THE GLORIOUS DEAD.

The temporary structure built of wood and plaster was located in the middle of Whitehall, the broad street that runs through the center of the government precinct of Westminster. The parade of Allied forces took place on July 14, 1919. Then something unexpected happened. For days after the peace pa-

Edwin Lutyens, Cenotaph, London, 1919

rade, long lines of people formed at Lutyens's memorial, leaving flowers and paying their respects. After four years of devastating human losses, the British public felt neither the thrill of victory nor pride in military prowess, simply a deep sense of bereavement. "No feature of the Victory March in London made a deeper impression than the Cenotaph," observed *The Times*. "Simple, grave and beautiful in design, it has been universally recognized as a just and fitting memorial of those who have made the greatest sacrifice; and the flowers which have been daily laid upon it since the march show the strength of its appeal to the imagination."

So strong was the public outpouring of support, and so loud the calls to preserve the memorial, that within two weeks the cabinet decided that the Cenotaph should be rebuilt on the same spot in Portland stone. The temporary memorial had included live laurel wreaths and actual silk flags, three on each side, and for the permanent monument Lutyens wanted to have the wreaths and flags carved in stone, which would have reduced their impact as nationalistic symbols. He got his stone wreaths, but the cabinet insisted on keeping the real flags. He also made several other small but crucial modifications. The vertical surfaces are very slightly battered, and the horizontal surfaces are imperceptibly curved. Lutyens based his work on the optical refinements found in ancient Greek temples, and these subtle enhancements give the memorial a marked solidity and humanist grace. The Cenotaph is just over thirty-five feet tall, yet because it occupies a prominent position in the center of an important street, and because of its delicate severity, it makes a strong impression. Like all good memorials, it leaves plenty of room for the onlooker to find meaning. Memorials should neither preach nor moralize. The Cenotaph also achieves an essential quality— timelessness. Memorials are intended to last forever, and it helps if they look as if they had been there forever, too.

LINCOLN MEMORIAL

The Lincoln Memorial, at the west end of the National Mall in Washington, D.C., was dedicated in 1922, three years after the Cenotaph, but this project had a much longer gestation. In 1901, the Senate Park Commission, which was replanning and extending the Mall, proposed culminating the west end of the great axis with a memorial to Abraham Lincoln, facing the Washington Monument across a long reflecting pool. Charles McKim, a member of the commission, proposed a giant open-air colonnade supporting an attic story bearing the text of the Gettysburg Address. A bronze statue of the president was to stand outside on a terrace overlooking a fountain and the reflecting pool. "This extraordinarily elegant solution created multiple stages of transcendence," writes the historian Kirk Savage. "Lincoln as a human figure was elevated above the historic strife suggested by the fountain, and his words were in turn removed from their historical context of creation and lifted to a nearly sacred status at the top of the composition. It was no longer the man himself who was the pinnacle of the monument but his aphorisms, which outlived him."

Many in Congress resisted the high cost of what would have been the most expensive American memorial ever built, while others objected to the site. McKim died in 1909, his design unrealized. In 1912, the memorial finally received the congressional go-ahead. Henry Bacon, McKim's protégé, and John Russell Pope, an up-and-coming young architect, were invited to submit proposals. Pope's design consisted of a huge open-air Doric colonnade encircling a statue of the president; Bacon's winning design resembled a temple.

Although Bacon's memorial is often compared with the Parthenon, it includes several distinctly untemplelike features. The entrance to a Greek temple is always at the narrow end, but Bacon turned the building ninety degrees and placed the entrance in the center of the long façade. Moreover, he made the entrance

Henry Bacon, Lincoln Memorial, Washington, D.C., 1922

simply a break in the wall—no door—creating a sense of unobstructed access. The message is that this is a *democratic* temple, open to all. Bacon also eliminated the pitched roof—and the pediments—which are traditional features of Greek temples. The Lincoln Memorial has a flat roof, or rather, it is surmounted by a boxy attic—a nod to McKim's original design—that hides a large skylight. Thus the Greek model is transformed.

The interior of the memorial is divided into three chambers. The east and west walls carry the full texts of Lincoln's two most famous wartime speeches: the Gettysburg Address and the Second Inaugural. The central chamber contains Daniel Chester French's colossal marble statue of the president. Behind and above the statue, carved into the wall, is the inscription IN THIS TEMPLE, AS IN THE HEARTS OF THE PEOPLE FOR WHOM HE SAVED THE UNION, THE MEMORY OF ABRAHAM LINCOLN IS ENSHRINED FOREVER.* Ancient Greek temples often contained a cult statue;

---

*The author was Bacon's friend the art critic Royal Cortissoz.

the Parthenon housed Pheidias's ivory-and-gold goddess Athena. On the face of it, this is an odd model for a memorial to a democratically elected president, especially one as homespun as this one. French was obviously aware of this anomaly, for there is nothing Olympian about his somber Lincoln. The president is sitting rather than standing, and he looks resolute, though tired, rather than triumphant. "The gentleness, power, and determination of the man has been wonderfully expressed by the sculptor," wrote Bacon, "not only in the face but also in the hands which grip the arms of the massive seat."

Like Lutyens, Bacon incorporated subtle optical refinements based on ancient Greek practice. "The columns are not vertical, being slightly tilted inward toward the building, the four corner columns being tilted more than the others," he wrote. "The outside face of the entablature is also inclined inward, but slightly less than the columns underneath it." Unlike the Cenotaph, the Lincoln Memorial incorporates a complex narrative—of sacrifice, suffering, and national redemption. The thirty-six columns of the peristyle represent the number of states in the Union at the time of Lincoln's death. The names of the states, and their dates of entry into the Union, are inscribed in the frieze. A second frieze, surrounding the attic, contains the names of the forty-eight states that existed at the time of the memorial's dedication. The immense funerary tripods that flank the steps outside, eleven feet tall and carved from single blocks of marble, symbolize Lincoln's ultimate sacrifice.

The Lincoln Memorial did not meet with universal approval. Many critics thought that it was too wedded to the past, and that an ancient temple was an inappropriate—and un-American— symbol. "One feels not the living beauty of our American past, but the mortuary air of archaeology," wrote Lewis Mumford. Bacon might have answered that the architecture of the world's first democracy was a suitable model for a memorial to Lincoln, but the truth was that he was a confirmed classicist, and whether he was designing a railroad station or a library—or a memorial—he used the language of Greece and Rome. He might have simplified that language, as Lutyens did, or designed a more original form, as McKim had done. On the other hand, the juxtaposition of the colossal brooding Lincoln and his two speeches continues to be moving, and the memorial has taken its place as a national symbol of human struggle and emancipation.

CHÂTEAU-THIERRY

During the summer of 1918, the fourth year of the First World War, the Aisne-Marne salient was the site of heavy fighting. In July, Germany launched its last great offensive, known as the Second Battle of the Marne, against the French army and eight untested divisions of the newly arrived American Expeditionary Force. The German offensive drove forward and reached as far as Château-Thierry, only fifty-four miles from Paris. The Allied forces stopped the advance, and their counterattack drove the exhausted Germans back beyond their original front line, hastening the end of the war. There were twelve thousand American dead and wounded. After the war, each of the Allies built military cemeteries, but they also built commemorative memorials on battlefield sites. The dramatic site of the monument commemorating the Aisne-Marne campaign is what the doughboys called Hill 204, overlooking the town of Château-Thierry and the Marne River.

There are two kinds of war memorial. Some, like the Cenotaph, commemorate events that happened elsewhere; others, like a battlefield memorial, mark the actual spot. The architect of the Château-Thierry Monument, Paul Cret, elected to let the site speak for itself and to make the memorial extremely simple: a roofed double colonnade, 50 feet high and about 150 feet long, dead straight and standing on a broad terrace. An access road approaches the monument from the rear and arrives at a large paved semicircle. Facing this platform, in the center of the colonnade, are two heroic-size allegorical female figures representing the United States and France. One figure holds a sword, the other a shield; their fingers are intertwined. The dedication, in both English and French, reads: THIS MONUMENT HAS BEEN ERECTED BY THE UNITED STATES OF AMERICA TO COMMEMORATE THE SERVICES OF HER TROOPS AND THOSE OF FRANCE WHO FOUGHT IN THIS REGION DURING THE WORLD WAR. IT STANDS AS A LASTING SYMBOL OF THE FRIENDSHIP AND COOPERATION BETWEEN THE FRENCH AND AMERICAN ARMIES. On the opposite side of the memorial, a terrace looks eastward over the Marne Valley. A compass rose in the paving orients the visitor to the chief locations where the fighting took place. On this side, the colonnade is adorned with a giant American eagle and the inscription TIME WILL NOT DIM THE GLORY OF THEIR DEEDS. The sculptor, Alfred-Alphonse Bottiau, collaborated with Cret on several projects, and like him had served in the French army during the war.*

The Château-Thierry Monument was designed more than a decade after the Lincoln Memorial, and it represents a different approach to the classical past. The architecture is spare and austere. Traditional columns are replaced by massive square piers without bases or capitals, but scribed with grooves to suggest fluting. The piers are so close together that the voids are barely wider than the solids; the effect is more like a massive stone wall with slots than a traditional colonnade. The plain architrave, which is engraved with the names of individual battle sites, merely continues the plane of the piers. The effect is almost utilitarian; even the dedication is in a contemporary-looking unserifed typeface, rather than in a classic roman font. The Doric frieze—palm leaf triglyphs (symbolizing victory over death) alternating with oak

---

*Cret was awarded a Croix de Guerre for his military service; he became a U.S. citizen in 1927.

Paul Philippe Cret, *Château-Thierry Monument, Château-Thierry, France, 1937*

leaf metopes (symbolizing longevity)—is the only classical motif. Above the frieze is a narrowly projecting cornice adorned by bronze medallions, not the usual leonine decoration but lupine— wolves' heads. The cornice is surmounted by a low plain attic. The style of the memorial, according to Cret, "though inspired by a Greek simplicity of treatment is not, however, an archaeological adaptation but follows, rather, the American traditions of the post-colonial period, and develops them in the spirit of our own times." Interestingly, many of the simplifications that Cret introduced were in response to a request by his client, the American Battle Monument Commission (chaired by General Pershing), which considered Cret's first design for the Château-Thierry Monument too imposing. Cret complied, and later continued to explore this stripped classicism in buildings such as the Folger Library and the Federal Reserve.

It is difficult to look at this evocative memorial today with an unprejudiced eye. In the 1930s, Hitler's architects, Paul Troost and Albert Speer, copied Cret's stripped classicism, so that for many today the style is synonymous with Nazism. That is a shame. Compared with Bacon's literal interpretation in the Lincoln Memorial, Cret's allusions to history are light-handed, and they give the Château-Thierry Monument a severe modernity. Seen from the town, the giant hilltop colonnade suggests an immovable bulwark, or perhaps a line of soldiers firmly standing their ground.

GATEWAY ARCH

St. Louis's Gateway Arch started life in the 1930s as a city boosters' idea for downtown revival. A plan to replace a forty-block area of nineteenth-century commercial buildings with a riverfront park had been around for decades, but its supporters believed that linking the project to a national memorial to Thomas Jefferson and westward expansion, and creating jobs during the Depression, would garner federal support. They were right. In due course, Franklin D. Roosevelt signed an executive order approving the memorial, instructing the National Park Service to acquire the land, and allocating almost $7 million in WPA and PWA funds to the project. That was 1935, but as usual Congress was slow to apportion the money, the Second World War intervened, and it was another dozen years before the project could begin.

The designer of the memorial was chosen by a national competition, organized by none other than George Howe. "I was called in as professional adviser to divest the event of local implications," he later explained, "and possibly as a sort of missing link between past and present." While modernism was in the air, no major modernist monument had yet been built in the United States, and many in the architectural establishment doubted that it could. As the first modernist to be made a fellow of the American Institute of Architects, the Beaux-Arts-trained Howe was an inspired choice. He balanced the jury between traditionalists and modernists, including Fiske Kimball, the director of the Philadelphia Museum of Art who had recently chaired the commission that had built the Jefferson Memorial, and Louis La Beaume, a local classicist, together with Richard Neutra and William W. Wurster, both California modernists. The competition attracted more than 170 entries. Howe's presence ensured that many of the younger generation of modernists entered, including Edward Durell Stone, Wallace K. Harrison, Charles Eames, Louis Kahn, Gordon Bunshaft, and Minoru Yamasaki, as well as such senior figures as Walter Gropius and Eliel Saarinen. None of these was among the five finalists, however, although neither were there any classicists.

Howe's competition brief for the second stage called for a "striking element, not only to be seen from a distance in the landscape, but also as a notable structure to be remembered and commented on as one of the conspicuous monuments of the country." Some of the finalists included vertical elements such as a pylons, but

Eero Saarinen & Associates, Gateway Arch, St. Louis, 1968

only Eero Saarinen responded directly to the call for an iconic form, proposing a giant arch of stainless steel, which combined innovation with tradition in a way that won over both factions of the jury. In any case, his entry was by far the best. *Architectural Forum* found the other finalists "somewhat disappointing," and concluded that "American architects are uncomfortable and unsteady on projects of this scale."

Saarinen's soaring arch suited the eighty-acre site beside the broad Mississippi River. Although the shape of the arch is sometimes described as a parabola, it is actually an inverted catenary arch, a form derived by hanging a chain from two fixed points at the same height and inverting the resulting shape. A catenary arch is extremely efficient, since the thrust is contained within the curve. That makes it sound like a work of engineering, but Saarinen was trained as a sculptor before he studied architecture, and his approach, whether he was designing an armchair or a building, was never purely technical. He wanted the triangular cross-section arch to narrow as it rose, which resulted in a flattened, or weighted, catenary, whose height—630 feet—was equal to its span.

Thanks to delays in land acquisition and fund-raising, construction did not begin until 1962—a year after Saarinen's death—and by the time the memorial was complete, the design was already two decades old. Yet Saarinen's sculptural form remains as fresh as ever, and demonstrates conclusively that modernism is compatible with monumentality. The arch is unabashedly modernist—absolutely abstract, with no symbolic decoration, not even an inscription—yet it is familiar. Triumphal arches originated in Roman times, and since the Renaissance, gates and arches have been important urban symbols. The St. Louis arch is not processional, but as Saarinen rather offhandedly observed, it symbolizes "the gateway to the West, the national expansion, and whatnot."

VIETNAM VETERANS MEMORIAL

To celebrate its 150th anniversary, in 2007 the American Institute of Architects commissioned a national opinion poll that
asked the public to name its favorite buildings in the United
States. The four most popular buildings turned out to be the Empire State Building, the White House, Washington National Cathedral, and the Jefferson Memorial. The list continued in a
similar retro vein: the Golden Gate Bridge, the U.S. Capitol, the
Lincoln Memorial, the Biltmore Estate, and the Chrysler Building.

The AIA survey suggests that the American public has a
marked antipathy to modern design—there are no Pritzker Prize
winners in the top fifty—yet there is one contemporary design
among the top ten: the Vietnam Veterans Memorial.* The story
of how the designer, Maya Lin, a twenty-one-year-old Yale architecture student, beat out almost fifteen hundred entries to win a
national competition is the stuff of legend. The concise competition brief had only four simple requirements: the memorial should
be reflective and contemplative in character; it should harmonize
with its surroundings; it should contain the names of those who
had died in the conflict or who were still missing; and it should
make no political statement about the war.

Given the requirement that more than 58,000 names be recorded on the memorial, it was obvious that a large vertical surface would be required. Lin's brilliant concept was to create this
surface belowground.

> I imagined taking a knife and cutting into the earth, open-
> ing it up, an initial violence and pain that in time would
> heal. The grass would grow back, but the initial cut would
> remain a pure flat surface in the earth with a polished,
> mirrored surface, much like the surface on a geode when

---

*The only other modernist design near the top of the list was Saarinen's Gateway Arch,
in fourteenth place.

you cut it and polish the edge. The need for the names to be on the memorial would become the memorial; there was no need to embellish the design further. The people and their names would allow everyone to respond and remember.

Simple as the design is, there are several important refinements. The two "cuts" are in a V shape, with a ramped walk descending ten feet to a low point at the apex of the V, and rising again along the other side. The two arms are oriented to the Washington Monument and the Lincoln Memorial. Although the Vietnam memorial is often referred to as a wall, Lin envisioned it differently. She imagined the polished granite as a thin surface and resisted all suggestions to make it thicker and more monumental. The other important detail is the order of the names. Lin arranged the names chronologically, by dates of death—not alphabetically. Moreover, rather than simply listing the names from left to right across the memorial, she arranged the sequence to begin at the apex of the V, continue to the east end, then recommence at the far west end. "Now the chronological sequence began and ended at the apex so that the time line would circle back to itself and close the sequence," she explained. "A progression in time is memorialized. The design is not just a list of the dead." The sequence begins with the date 1959 and ends with 1975, marking the year of the last fatality. Two short inscriptions are the only references to the subject of the memorial.*

Lin's design is abstract but it is not without meaning. The highly polished mirrorlike granite is black—the traditional color

---

*The two inscriptions are: IN HONOR OF THE MEN AND WOMEN OF THE ARMED FORCES OF THE UNITED STATES WHO SERVED IN THE VIETNAM WAR. THE NAMES OF THOSE WHO GAVE THEIR LIVES AND OF THOSE WHO REMAIN MISSING ARE INSCRIBED IN THE ORDER THEY WERE TAKEN FROM US, and OUR NATION HONORS THE COURAGE, SACRIFICE AND DEVOTION TO DUTY AND COUNTRY OF ITS VIETNAM VETERANS. THIS MEMORIAL WAS BUILT WITH PRIVATE CONTRIBUTIONS FROM THE AMERICAN PEOPLE. NOVEMBER 11, 1982.

Maya Lin, Vietnam Veterans Memorial, Washington, D.C., 1982

of mourning. Listing the names of the dead is likewise traditional; Lin has said that she was inspired by John Carrère and
Thomas Hastings's 1901 Yale Memorial Rotunda, whose walls
are inscribed with the names of all alumni killed in military service. In that sense, the Vietnam memorial resembles a large
tombstone. The funereal theme is further emphasized by the descent belowground, the underworld being a concept common to
many ancient mythologies. These references to the past are subtle but unmistakable.

From a distance, Maya Lin's design resembles one of Robert
Smithson's earthworks. Like all good memorials, the Vietnam
memorial can be appreciated as art, but it is definitely a memorial, although an unusual one. It does not commemorate the
war—which, after all, the United States lost—nor, in spite of its
name, does it commemorate all the veterans who served. Like the
Cenotaph, it memorializes only the dead, although in Lutyens's
case the dead are "glorious," whereas in the Vietnam memorial

they are merely absent. Unlike the Château-Thierry Monument, Lin's design is almost completely nondidactic. "These people died" is all it says, leaving us to fill in the blanks. For this memorial has a different purpose than teaching about the past; in Kirk Savage's words, the Vietnam memorial is "the nation's first 'therapeutic' memorial." Lin herself has described the memorial as cathartic. "I remember one of the veterans asking me before the wall was built what I thought people's reaction to it would be," she recalled. "I was too afraid to tell him what I was thinking, that I knew a returning veteran would cry."

James Stirling once remarked, "Architects have always looked back in order to move forward." Looking back takes different forms. In his design of the Cenotaph, Edwin Lutyens took the influence of history for granted, although his remarkable talent allowed him to find new meaning in the old forms. Henry Bacon's deep respect for the ancient world was more literal, although like the Cenotaph, the Lincoln Memorial is enriched by its connection to the past. Paul Cret acknowledged history, although he was more interested in how architecture could be changed to suit the modern world than in merely referring to a previous era. Both Eero Saarinen and Maya Lin were aware of the past, as the forms of their memorials—a gateway, a wall—suggest, even if as modernists their interpretations were highly abstract.

The architectural advantage of looking back is that it engages the memory as well as the eye. The Cenotaph would be considerably impoverished if it were merely a block of Portland stone. If the Lincoln Memorial were just a walled enclosure, the moving contrast between the ancient temple and the statue of the all-too-human president would be lost. And as so many banal walls-of-names memorials have subsequently demonstrated, the power of the Vietnam memorial lies not in its abstraction but in its understated evocation of the past.

Looking back may be prompted by different sentiments—
nostalgia, reverence, admiration—or simply by the recognition
that we owe a debt to our ancestors. The alternative, only looking
forward, produces what are sometimes called visionary buildings,
but nothing fades as quickly as yesterday's vision of tomorrow.
That is why old science-fiction films tend to elicit chuckles rather
than admiration, just as old visionary buildings—houses shaped
like soap bubbles or rock crystals—will soon look merely eccentric and will not acquire the status of old friends.

10

TASTE

Before she became the grande dame of American letters, Edith Wharton wrote *The Decoration of Houses*. The subject is the history of décor from the sixteenth to the eighteenth century, but the aim of Wharton and her coauthor, the architect Ogden Codman Jr., was polemical rather than scholarly. They denounced the clutter of contemporary Victorian homes and called for a return to architectural principles of classical Italian and French interiors. "Rooms may be decorated in two ways," they advised, "by a superficial application of ornament totally independent of structure, or by means of those architectural features which are part of the organism of every house, inside as well as out." Clearly favoring the latter, they extolled the décor of the "golden age of architecture," and deplored the present-day excesses of what they called the "gilded age of decoration." Both Wharton and Codman spent their summers in Newport, Rhode Island, which had some of the most extravagant examples of overdone interior decoration, much of it in the mansions built by members of the Vanderbilt family. "I wish the Vanderbilts didn't retard culture so very thoroughly," Wharton wrote heatedly to her coauthor. "They are entrenched in a sort of Thermopylae of bad taste, from which apparently no force on earth can dislodge them."

Wharton and Codman acknowledged the "vagaries of taste,"

but believed that taste in décor was not a matter of personal feeling, as it was in painting or music. "With architecture and its allied branches the case is different," they wrote. "Here beauty depends on fitness, and the practical requirements of life are the ultimate test of fitness." Certainly they were not functionalists, but they saw utility as the bedrock of architecture—and decoration. "The essence of taste is suitability," Wharton wrote in *French Ways and Their Meaning.* "Divest the word of its prim and priggish implications, and see how it expresses the mysterious demand of the eye and mind for symmetry, harmony, and order." Wharton practiced what she preached in her celebrated home, The Mount, built under her direction, and whose rooms she and Codman decorated. That peripatetic houseguest Henry James described Wharton's home as "an exquisite French chateau perched among Massachusetts mountains—most charming ones—and filled exclusively with old French and Italian furniture and decorations."

Elsie de Wolfe, who invented the profession of high-society

Drawing Room, The Mount, Lenox, Massachusetts, 1902

interior decorator, was influenced by Wharton's ideas on décor, and the two were acquainted although not close—Wharton disapproved of de Wolfe's flamboyant lifestyle. In 1913, de Wolfe published *The House in Good Taste*, a collection of her articles from women's magazines. This decorating handbook is full of sage advice on practical matters such as heating (fireplaces are more agreeable than steam heat), electric lighting (make sure it is located where you need it), closet organization (don't waste space), and furnishing small apartments (stay away from massive armchairs). But the thread that runs through the book—as the title implies—is the importance of taste. Taste is what will guide us through the myriad decisions that are required to furnish a home, whether they have to do with paint colors, furniture styles, or the best place for a writing desk.

De Wolfe believed that taste, like good manners, had to be learned. "How can we develop taste?" she asked. "We must learn to recognize suitability, simplicity and proportion, and apply our knowledge to our needs." Suitability—that word again—had as

Elsie de Wolfe, Trellis Room, Colony Club, New York, 1907

much to do with aesthetics as with convenience and comfort. De Wolfe believed in visual rather than stylistic consistency in interiors, often mixing styles, and she was open to the avant-garde, writing admiringly of the black-and-white décor of the Viennese architect and designer Josef Hoffmann. Above all, she championed simplicity—less furniture, limited colors, fewer knickknacks. Her ultimate goal was what she called the Modern House. "Before very long we shall have simple houses with fire-places that draw, electric lights in the proper places, comfortable and sensible furniture, and not a gilt-legged spindle-shanked table or chair anywhere." Her thinking anticipated Bauhaus modernism—assuming the Bauhauslers had been able to come to terms with chintz and trelliage.

ENTHUSIASM FOR FORM

Geoffrey Scott's *The Architecture of Humanism* appeared a year after *The House in Good Taste*. It is a different sort of book, but written by someone with a similar sensibility—Scott worked as a secretary for Codman and Wharton, and knew de Wolfe well. He subtitled his book *A Study in the History of Taste*, and argued that while architects were influenced by function, materials, and engineering, their work was also the result of taste, which he defined as "the disinterested enthusiasm for architectural form." This is the same point that John Summerson made about Gothic builders being attracted to pointed arches, but the historic period that influenced Scott's thinking was the Italian Renaissance.

> The architecture of the Renaissance is pre-eminently an architecture of Taste. The men of the Renaissance evolved a certain architectural style, because they liked to be surrounded by forms of a certain kind. These forms, as such, they preferred, irrespective of their relation to the mechanical means by which they were produced, irrespective

of the materials out of which they were constructed, irrespective sometimes even of the actual purposes they were to serve. They had an immediate preference for certain combinations of mass and void, of light and shade, and, compared with this, all other motives in the formation of their distinctive style were insignificant.

There is abundant evidence for Scott's claim. Renaissance architects designed the same ornamental pilasters, whether these were carved stone, plastered brick, or painted frescos. Symmetry was adhered to, both in elevation and plan: if an enclosed staircase was required on the right of a space, then a matching volume had to occur on the left, even if all it enclosed was an empty—and unneeded—closet. If symmetry mandated an extra window, then a window was added—irrespective of functional needs; when an actual window was not feasible, a false window would do. A trademark Renaissance motif was the arch, which was used irrespective of structural spans—if more strength was required an iron tie bar was added.

Scott did not explain where Renaissance taste came from—he was a critic rather than a historian, and his prime purpose in writing was to influence contemporary opinion. He believed that architecture had become overintellectualized, and he was as skeptical of academic classicism as he was of John Ruskin and the Romantic Movement. He ignored contemporary architects, even Lutyens, whose version of classicism he might have admired. Nor did he take issue with such modernist theorists as Adolf Loos and Walter Gropius. Perhaps, sequestered in Florence, Scott was simply unaware of—or uninterested in—current architectural fashions. Or maybe he was being shrewd, for by avoiding topical references, his book acquired a timeless quality which partly accounts for its longevity.

Scott resisted the impulse to formulate an alternative aesthetic theory. "What we feel as 'beauty' is not a matter for logical demonstration," he wrote. Scott can be maddeningly obscure, and the closest he came to practical advice was to recommend a greater firsthand familiarity with humanist architecture, which would presumably develop one's taste. He recognized that to many this sounded capricious and inconsequential; nevertheless, he called for the primacy of aesthetics, and for responding to buildings with the eyes and heart rather than with the intellect.

On this last point, Paul Cret was in total agreement. He once described the goal of architectural education as "the development of what artistic sense the student may possess in a latent state— the education of his taste and the opening of his eyes to the beauty of form." Cret emphasized that this process should not be mechanical. "To be really deep and effective, this (slow) passage through successive stages in which one learns how to appreciate some new things and despise others, must be a personal one, else the intellect only, and not the feelings will be touched and permanently influenced."

Cret may have been thinking of his time at the École des Beaux-Arts. The school was divided into *ateliers*, or studios, each consisting of sixty to seventy students of all levels, newcomers as well as upperclassmen, all under the tutelage of a *patron*, an eminent practicing architect. When the planner and architect Andrés Duany attended the École in the early 1970s, the curriculum was much changed but the *atelier* system was still in place. Duany recalls that since the *patron* came to class only on Saturday mornings, the bulk of teaching was done by the senior students. Another surviving feature of the old École was the *charrette*, an intense work period when students prepared final drawings of their design assignments, the junior students regularly assisting their senior classmates. "During the *charrettes*, the upper-level students sometimes fed their assistants in the many good, affordable restaurants that were nearby," Duany writes. "There they learned about cheese and wine and the flamboyance of dress and manner required of an *ancien élève* . . . Socialization was not just the transmittal of architectural culture," he emphasizes, "but also of manners, mannerisms, and taste."

Most schools of architecture devote the first year of the curriculum to design exercises whose aim is less to impart specific practical knowledge than to develop visual and conceptual abilities—that is, to develop taste. The Bauhaus institutionalized this practice in the *vorkurs*, or preliminary course, which was started by Johannes Itten and later taught by László Moholy-Nagy and Josef Albers. Students explored color, texture, and graphics through a series of exercises, producing collages, mobiles, and a variety of color and form studies. According to the art historian Leah Dickerman, "These compositions also stand as a first effort, repeated in many iterations through the Bauhaus, to define a primary visual language for all artistic practice."

An early application of the Bauhaus visual language was the director's office that Walter Gropius designed for the Weimar Bauhaus in 1923. The room is conceived as a walk-in Constructivist sculpture. The same geometry governs the design and placement of the furniture, the rug, and a wall hanging. A structure suspended in the center of the room is an unshaded tubular lighting fixture, whose functional inadequacy, as Reyner Banham pointed out, is attested to by the desk lamp, which was not part of the original design. The lamp, like the furniture and the textiles, was made in the school's workshops. Although the office was a demonstration of the new unity of art and industry, the handmade nature of its contents—as well as its design—clearly gave precedence to art. A visitor perched on the Gropius-designed armchair would have to peer awkwardly around the in-out tray and across the corner of the desk to speak to Herr Direktor. Hardly Wharton's idea of fitness.

When I was a student at McGill, our *vorkurs* was called Elements of Design, and was taught by Gordon Webber, who had been a student of Moholy-Nagy at the Chicago Institute of Design. One afternoon a week we painted color charts, constructed

Walter Gropius, director's office, Bauhaus,
Weimar, 1923

three-dimensional mobiles of wire and string, and built "feely boxes." The last were cardboard boxes with a hole large enough to insert your hand, and stuffed with a variety of tactile materials: fur, steel wool, rocks, sandpaper, a wet sponge. The highlight of the class was when our professor would sample the boxes, a procedure accompanied by many oohs and ahs.

We considered Webber's playful class a welcome relief from our demanding lecture courses in structural steel and reinforced concrete, but Elements of Design had a serious purpose. Somewhat akin to the goal of military basic training, the goal of the course was to "break down" our visual prejudices (for many of us, formed by our suburban upbringings) and to "build up" a new set

of aesthetic values. Values, not rules. We were never actually forbidden to design a traditional pitched roof or a bow window, but
we came to instinctively understand that these did not belong to
the approved modernist vocabulary. Modernist design was challenging, however. For my first studio assignment, I adapted one of
Marcel Breuer's houses, which I admired, and was soundly
scolded; I learned it was strictly forbidden to copy. On the other
hand, imitating drawing styles was acceptable. Le Corbusier's
minimal drawings were particularly popular, since they were easy
to reproduce. I learned how to draw his stick-figure people and
spindly trees. One of my classmates had a set of metal Corbusian
lettering stencils, whose military-style type could turn any drawing into an *hommage* to the master.

Six years of indoctrination had its effect. Although I had grown
up in a suburban bungalow with pastel-colored walls, when I
graduated I could not imagine painting the walls of my apartment
any other color than flat white. Wall-to-wall carpeting was out,
too; small colorful rugs were okay, but a bare wood floor was best.
Wood-and-canvas director's chairs completed the décor. However, the only constant in taste is that tastes change. A few years
later, postmodernism was in the air, and after visiting a Bavarian
Rococo church, I added a blue sky and puffy clouds to my bedroom ceiling; the walls stayed white. A decade later, that changed,
too, when I pasted up striped wallpaper in our guest room, feeling
deliciously like a bourgeois traitor to my Corbusian roots. Re-
searching *Home*, I came across Elsie de Wolfe, who introduced
me to the field of interior decoration, and my taste broadened. I
acquired a wing chair, still my favorite reading spot. I was particularly taken with the celebrated home of the Swedish painter
Carl Larsson, and I painted the wooden ceiling of our dining
room cobalt blue. A decade later, we sponge-painted our bedroom
walls to create a textured finish. The walls and ceilings of our
current house are all the same color, a warm yellowish white, like
old parchment, with sand added to the paint to produce a rough

finish. I sponge-painted the bathrooms—one ocher, one pink—to camouflage the plastered-over cracks, but also because the battered appearance reminds me of an old Italian villa.

One can look back on one's youthful taste with amusement. Who was that young man in the Nehru jacket with the long sideburns and the Zapata mustache? In time, discarded fashions can be left in the back of the closet, and grooming can change, as can décor. But architecture remains. Part of the attraction of old buildings is that they are a testimony of who we once were, what we believed in, our values as well as our tastes. We can look back with admiration, respect, or awe. Or puzzlement. What were those Victorians thinking when they indiscriminately piled up layer upon layer of startling ornament? Did the modernists really think that "streets in the air" would be as good as streets on the ground? Did the Brutalist architects of the 1960s believe that the public would ever warm to their cold, ponderous concrete creations? How on earth could the postmodernists use those insipid pastel colors? But there's no accounting for taste.

ARCHITECTURAL TASTE

I'm pretty sure that Itten would have disputed the claim that his *vorkurs* had anything to do with taste. Indeed, since Scott, few architects have seen taste as a legitimate concern. The modern dismissal of taste is the result of the current belief that intellectual theories are the foundation for design, as well as the profession's understandable desire to distance itself from the frivolity of fashion. When Richard Rogers was designing the Lloyd's of London building, he wrote: "Taste is the enemy of aesthetics, whether it is found in art or architecture. It is abstract, at best elegant and fashionable, it is always ephemeral, for it is not rooted in philosophy or even craftsmanship, being purely a product of the senses. As such it can always be challenged and is always being superseded, for how can one judge whose taste is best? Yours, mine, or someone else's?"

Unlike Scott and Cret, Rogers is suspicious of taste precisely *because* it is governed by the senses. But can taste really be dismissed so summarily? Isn't an architect's preference for a certain way of dressing, for example, an indication of taste, and wouldn't the same visual taste be likely to influence the design of a building? Frank Lloyd Wright, who wore flowing neckties and capes, went so far as to design some of his own clothes, which were as original and as theatrical as his buildings. As one might expect, Mies van der Rohe dressed more conservatively, but his handmade suits were as meticulously crafted as *his* buildings. That bohemian firebrand Le Corbusier also wore well-cut suits, although usually accompanied by a jaunty bow tie.* Architectural dress is a balancing act between communicating sobriety (I am a responsible builder) and creativity (I am also an artist). Some architects assert the latter by sporting fashion accessories such as colorful socks, an insouciant scarf, or a pair of off-beat eyeglasses. The last was pioneered by Le Corbusier, who had extremely poor eyesight (he was blind in one eye) and made thick, perfectly round framed glasses (later emulated by Philip Johnson and I. M. Pei) his trademark.

Architecture being visual, it's natural that architects should be concerned with fashion. When I was a young architect I wore tweed jackets with hand-woven ties—lots of textures and earth colors. Today, young architects favor all black, which makes them resemble clerics—perhaps they see themselves as spreading the gospel of Good Design, or maybe it's just a practical way of appearing stylish on a limited budget. Not all contemporary architects subscribe to this somber dress code. Richard Rogers is usually photographed in intensely colored collarless shirts; for

---

*There is a photograph of Le Corbusier and Mies together, taken in the 1920s. Le Corbusier sports a dashing short coat, a bow tie, and a derby. Mies is wearing a homburg, a capacious double-breasted ulster, and spats.

formal occasions, the shirts are white. Norman Foster dresses like a very successful business executive in a creative field. Renzo Piano is an unusual dresser for an architect: his clothes are neither black, nor colorful, nor stylish, and surprisingly not Italian but casually American—pullovers, chinos, tieless button-down shirts. Gap rather than Prada.

Taste may be ephemeral, as Rogers claims, but his own architectural taste has remained remarkably consistent over the years. In the Reliance Controls Electronics Factory, a landmark project designed with Norman Foster when both men were in their early thirties, the workers' canteen was furnished with Eames chairs. Forty-five years later, Rogers uses similar chairs in the staff cafeteria of 300 New Jersey Avenue, an office building in Washington, D.C. The choice is revealing. The Eames DSR Chair, designed by Charles and Ray Eames, is a molded plastic seat on spindly wire legs. The chair, geared to mass production, perfectly encapsulates a certain kind of taste: innovative, progressive, unfettered by history. Although this modernist icon appeared in 1948, it's still in production—and likely will be in 2048, when the original will officially qualify as an antique.

The Washington office building also demonstrates Rogers's abiding taste for bright colors: the columns in the atrium are canary yellow, the structural masts are emerald green, and as for the Eames chairs, they are bright red. This partiality to color was evident in the Centre Pompidou, whose exterior is a riot of color-coded pipes and ducts—blue for air, green for water, and yellow for electricity—as well as red elevators and escalators.

The Centre Pompidou is one of those unusual buildings that emerge aesthetically fully formed. Critics, assuming there was nothing left to explore, described it as the swan song of high tech. But in the following decades, in a series of remarkable buildings (Lloyd's of London, Madrid's Barajas Airport, the Bordeaux Law Courts), Rogers showed conclusively that this is not the case.

Another Rogers obsession is complicated, lightweight struc-

*Rogers Stirk Harbour + Partners, 300 New Jersey
Avenue, Washington, D.C., 2010*

ture. The glass atrium roof of 300 New Jersey Avenue is carried
on trusses that extend out to unusual-looking masts. Dennis Austin, one of the design team, explains:

> The mast columns at the entrance support the ends of the
> trusses. They are essentially nine-story unbraced columns,
> so we studied a mast outrigger form to provide stability
> over its height. The mast is a simple six-inch column with
> a series of arms which provide mid-length support (the ef-
> fect is that the six-inch column is fooled to think it is really
> a five-foot-diameter column at mid-length). They were
> originally painted light gray so as not to call attention to

themselves; however, when Richard saw how beautifully they were fabricated, he felt that they should be painted a bright green—which we did.

Rogers's last-minute decision to change the color of the masts sounds capricious, but he regularly uses colors to distinguish the main structural elements of his designs—he wants us to understand how things work. On the other hand, his predilection for garish colors such as bright orange, magenta, chrome blue—never pastels—*is* a matter of taste. Rogers's use of color can be iconoclastic. The atrium of 300 New Jersey Avenue could have been all one color, white or gray, which would have suited a high-end office building that houses an international law firm. But by using unexpectedly bright colors, Rogers undermines the solemnity and self-importance that usually attaches to corporate architecture.

One of the powerful early influences on Rogers was Charles and Ray Eames's house and studio in Santa Monica. Built in 1949, the house uses prefabricated factory-made materials such as open-web steel joists, corrugated steel decks, and standardized windows in an artful way that is both industrial-looking and casual. The exterior black-painted steel frame is filled with glazed and colored panels. The inspiration is obviously Mies, but the architecture is much too relaxed, too cozily cluttered, and too unmonumental to be called Miesian.

Norman Foster, who also visited the Eames House as a young man, shared Rogers's interest in lightweight structures (and also used Eames chairs in many projects), although his taste in color is more sedate. With the notable exception of a few early buildings such as the Willis Faber office building, which has bright green rubber flooring on the main level, and the Renault Distribution Centre, whose exposed structure is entirely painted a bright canary yellow, Foster's interiors have tended to be monochrome. The Sainsbury Centre for Visual Arts, for example, is

*Foster + Partners, Crescent Wing, Sainsbury Centre for Visual Arts,
University of East Anglia, Norwich, 1991*

predominantly gray and silver—the Eames chairs in the student
cafeteria are white. The Hongkong Bank is a sober (charcoal
gray) version of the Centre Pompidou that likewise reveals its
structural bones. But this turned out to be one of Foster's last
"Gothic" structures. Over the years—unlike Rogers—he has
moved away from dramatic engineering to a seamless integration
of structure, skin, and mechanical services. An early example is
an addition to the Sainsbury Centre, designed a decade after the
original building. If the original Sainsbury Centre could be said
to reflect the early twentieth-century engineering aesthetic of a
dirigible shed, the Crescent Wing is more like the Italian sail-
plane that Foster flew at the time: precise, streamlined, and very
sleek. Foster was always a minimalist, but today his minimalism
has become opulent, almost luxurious.

Renzo Piano was also Rogers's partner—on the Centre

Pompidou project—but when he struck out on his own, it be-came evident that his taste was more conservative, too. Piano's first major work, the Menil Collection in Houston, is completely monochrome—the steel structure is painted white, the sun-shades are white concrete, and the cypress siding is painted gray. Using wood in a high-tech design is unexpected, and it gives the engineered building a distinctly handcrafted look. This combina-tion of craft and technology has become a Piano trademark, and later buildings have incorporated iroko wood, terra-cotta panels, laminated timber, and fabrics. The New York Times Building is one of the few office buildings I know whose lobby floor is wood—white oak—rather than granite or marble. That, and the use of marmorino (hand-laid Venetian plaster) on the walls, humanizes the commercial environment. The marmorino is a warm marigold color. Piano occasionally introduces bright ac-cents, although unlike Rogers, he is not a natural colorist, and the results sometimes feel forced. The bright-red-painted steel on the new wing of the Los Angeles County Museum of Art appears contrived. Reacting to the strident colors of the terra-cotta skin of

Renzo Piano Building Workshop, New York Times Building, New York, 2007

Central St. Giles, *The Independent*'s Jay Merrick asked: "Can this shouty polychromatic architecture really be the work of the 72-year-old designer whose museums have become masterful demonstrations of fine-boned modernist decorum?"

Rogers, Foster, and Piano share, in Scott's phrase, an "enthusiasm for certain forms," particularly those forms found in modern engineered structures such as aircraft hangars, drilling platforms, factory sheds, and transmission towers. While each has interpreted this enthusiasm somewhat differently, it is the common thread that runs through their work. Architects such as Gehry, Herzog and de Meuron, and Nouvel produce individual works whose unusual forms garner attention, but Rogers, Foster, and Piano have redefined entire categories of buildings: airport terminals, office towers, civic buildings, museums. Their particular combination of technological innovation and structural refinement seems to capture, dare I say it, the spirit of the age. Or maybe we have simply all come to share their taste.

THE ARCHITECT'S HOUSE

In 1971, while a graduate student, I visited Marcel Breuer's house in New Canaan, Connecticut, which he had designed twenty years earlier. We had lunch with the illustrious architect, sitting around a square, granite-topped dining table. The chairs were his classic Cesca sidechairs, chrome tubing, wood, and rattan, dating from the time that he was furniture master at the Bauhaus. His modernist taste was evident in the large plate-glass windows, the white-painted brick fireplace, and the spare décor, but these were combined with an unexpected rusticity: fieldstone walls, a rough flagstone floor, and a broad-planked cypress ceiling. Not for nothing did Philip Johnson call Breuer a "peasant mannerist."

There is a long tradition of architects designing houses for themselves: Wright's sprawling compound in Spring Green, Aalto's summer house on Muuratsalo Island, Moore's little barn in Orinda, and, of course, Johnson's glass house. An architect's choices are generally circumscribed by the particularities of a project: the demands of the program, the limitation of the budget, the constraints of regulations, and, not least, the likes and dislikes of the client. But in his or her own home, the taste of the architect is, if not completely free, certainly less inhibited. Even if a house is not a self-conscious design statement—as Johnson's was—it is always architecturally revealing.

VILLA CORBEAU

Marc Appleton is neither a modernist nor a mannerist. He studied architecture at Yale under Charles Moore and worked for Frank Gehry, but when he struck out on his own, he realized that neither Moore's postmodernism nor Gehry's modernism appealed to him. "When I thought about the Southern California architecture I most admired, much of it had been created by classically trained architects from the early twentieth century," he told an interviewer. "What I appreciated most was these folks seemed flexible and adept at working in varied styles, without imposing an overriding personal stamp on their buildings. This appealed to me, and, coupled with the fact that as a young architect I began with restoration and remodeling of older buildings, sent me off in different directions." The different directions included exploring the many regional domestic styles of Southern California: Spanish Colonial Revival, English Arts and Crafts, and Mediterranean.

The home that Appleton built for himself and his wife, Joanna Kerns, in Montecito, California, is named Villa Corbeau, in part to honor the crows that hang around the site, and in part as a tongue-in-cheek reference to Le Corbusier—Corbu. The form of the house is a simple box. The roof is hipped and covered in clay tiles, and the stucco walls are cream-colored with slightly irregular surfaces and softened corners. The only architectural gesture on the

Appleton & Associates, Villa Corbeau, Montecito, California, 2002

façade—which is more or less symmetrical, with regularly placed wooden casement windows of different sizes—is an unadorned stone door-surround with a projecting cornice. The gravel court-yard in front of the house encircles a large California live oak.

The interior is equally artless. Some of the floors are rough limestone from France, others are recycled oak boards, and the ceiling beams in the living room are reused hand-hewn timbers. The plan is simplicity itself. A stair hall divides the lower floor in two, with the living room on one side, and a large kitchen and dining area on the other. The wood paneling in the living room is orderly but unremarkable, the wood windows have divided lights. The dining area opens onto an outdoor gravel patio shaded by an iron pergola. "The overgrown garden will eventually resemble a Mediterranean country house gone to seed," says Appleton. In all, the building looks like a recently renovated Tuscan farmhouse, or perhaps like a house designed and built by an experienced but unschooled Tuscan mason.

Living room, Villa Corbeau

"I was inspired by the Santa Barbara Mediterranean Revival," explains Appleton, whose grandparents built Florestal, a nearby estate designed by George Washington Smith. "But I didn't want to do another Spanish Colonial house, and Joanna liked Tuscan and Provençal farmhouses." What makes his house traditional is less its style than Appleton's taste. He obviously admires old, unpedigreed buildings. "What I like about vernacular architecture is the way that it simplifies classical traditions," he says. At the same time, he doesn't feel the need to make a self-conscious architectural statement. "As I designed it, the house got simpler. We got rid of shutters, for example. There's not a lot of frosting or detail," he adds.

Effortless Appleton's architecture may be, but by ascetic modernist standards, it is almost sybaritic. The décor is simple rather than austere; the furniture in the living room is ample and comfortable rather than "designed"—there are no Eames chairs. Equally unmodernist is a pleasant sense of clutter, both literally— the mantelpiece is crowded with objects—and also visually: the space abounds in patterns, colors, and textures. This is a room of which Elsie de Wolfe would approve.

THE WAREHOUSE

Michael Graves likewise finds inspiration in the Mediterranean. To reach the front door of his house, you pass under a drooping wisteria bower into an open-air anteroom that is animated by the low sound of a bubbling fountain in a water-filled stone trough, a nineteenth-century replica of a Roman sarcophagus. The pink-stucco building is hidden away in the center of a downtown block in Princeton, New Jersey. The original two-story structure was built in the 1920s as a warehouse where students could store their belongings for the summer. Graves bought the dilapidated structure and over several decades transformed it into a rambling, highly personal home that he calls the Warehouse.

Although zoning regulations prevented Graves from adding to or altering the footprint of the L-shaped plan, he transformed a utilitarian building by the judicious placement of new openings, and the addition of landscape elements—a pergola, a rectangle of lawn, a gravel courtyard. Two five-foot-high terra-cotta olive oil jars stand at the edge of the courtyard. Graves seems haunted by Italy, especially Rome, which he first experienced as a Rome Prize winner. "What I took from Rome isn't so much classicism,

Michael Graves & Associates, Graves House, Princeton, New Jersey, 1970–present

Living room, Graves House

or Baroque, or even the medieval architecture that's there," he once told an interviewer. "One of the glories of Rome is that it works with all these periods in such a fluid and magnificent way." This fluidity is visible in his own house, which combines a highly simplified version of classicism, with Cubist-inspired forms and his own characteristic palette of muted, painterly colors. Graves's designs can sometimes look perilously like cartoonish versions of themselves; that is not the case here. There are no jokes or visual puns, no architectural wordplay; there is only calm, order, and beauty.

The interior plays with space and light in a way that suggests John Soane and nineteenth-century neoclassicism. This impression is heightened by the Biedermeier furniture and Graves's collection of nineteenth-century Grand Tour souvenirs, including drawing instruments, Temple of Vesta inkwells, and other architectural curios. The paintings (some real, some replicas painted by Graves), the furnishings—some old, some designed by the architect—the objects, and the décor are all of a piece. Not since the great early-twentieth-century Viennese designer Josef Hoffmann, whom Graves admires, has a modern architect orchestrated such a *Gesamtkunstwerk*, or total work of art.

BOHLIN HOUSE

There are no Grand Tour souvenirs in the home that Peter Bohlin built for himself and his wife, Sally, in Waverly, a small town near Scranton, Pennsylvania. A framed sketch by Erik Gunnar Asplund—the Karl Johan School in Göteborg—hangs in the bedroom. "I admire Asplund and especially Sigurd Lewerentz, who saw the traps in modernism and avoided them," says Bohlin. At first glance, his house, covered in unprepossessing gray siding with white trim, looks ordinary. The central portion is an 1800-era gable-roofed structure that has been enlarged by adding several wings. At second glance, the architect's modernist sensibility gently asserts itself. Traditional construction details are simplified and refined, a bay window is larger than expected, a wall oddly overlaps a dormer, and a tall freestanding brick chimney painted white brings to mind Louis Kahn—or Marcel Breuer. The casual entry sequence is carefully orchestrated: from a walled car court the space slides under a trellis and between the house and an outbuilding, which frame a view to a meadow. Throughout, the house responds to the surrounding landscape. The deck of a guesthouse cantilevers over the pond to make a sort of Zen viewing platform. Zen-like, too, is a pristine lap pool set in the meadow next to a little wooden barnlike pool house. Bohlin describes the small cluster of buildings as "a calm, soft place that recalls childhood memories of unpretentious houses and a northern landscape of walls, forest, fields, and water."

Bohlin describes himself as a "soft modernist" and, perhaps because of his Swedish ancestry, has a pragmatic, unpolemical, and unsentimental Scandinavian attitude to design. Things are

Bohlin Cywinski Jackson, Bohlin House, Waverly, Pennsylvania,
2001

what they are. In his house, a section of cement-block wall that was part of an earlier addition is simply painted over; slivers of the nineteenth-century wooden structure are exposed in unexpected places; the raised stone hearth of the fireplace is supported on small I-beams. The eat-in kitchen and the living room are casually combined, and the dining room, which doubles as a work area, is in a space that resembles a porch, with closely spaced exposed roof joists and floor-to-ceiling glazing. Bohlin manipulates scale as purposefully as Appleton and Graves, although to different ends, not as part of a classical language, but to affect the experience of the interior space.

The porch looks into a birch grove. Every window in the house frames a particular view. When hardware is required—light fixtures, door handles, drawer pulls—it is out in the open, but does not call attention to itself. The walls and ceilings are mostly white, and natural materials abound: a recycled southern pine floor, honed marble kitchen countertops, a sisal rug, and classic

Living room, Bohlin House

1920s-era Thonet bentwood-and-rattan dining chairs—a long-time favorite of architects. The furniture is an eclectic modernist mix: a nondescript couch with colorful Josef Frank throw pillows, Aalto stools, butterfly chairs, an Eames rocking chair. This low-key home is definitely different architecturally from Apple's dramatic glass cube, yet it is governed by the same pared-down taste: intelligent, somewhat ascetic, demanding, and founded in construction rather than intellectual speculation.

GEHRY HOUSE

Berta and Frank Gehry's home likewise incorporates an old house, a 1920s gambrel-roofed cottage on a small corner lot in Santa Monica. "I looked at the old house that my wife found for us to live in, and I thought it was kind of a dinky little cutesy-pie house," Gehry recalls. "We had to do *something* to it. I couldn't live in it." He set out to make the house more to his taste.

Armed with very little money I decided to build a new house around the old house and try to maintain a tension between the two by having one define the other, and to have the feeling that the old house was intact within the new house, from the outside and from the inside. Those were the basic goals.

From the exterior, the impression is of a construction site: angled walls of corrugated sheet metal resemble construction hoarding, unpainted plywood looks like a temporary barrier, and—most famously, for Gehry is something of a showman—chain-link fencing envelopes part of the pink cottage. Nor was the old house exactly left "intact." Many of the walls and ceilings were stripped of the original lath and plaster to reveal the wooden studs and rafters beneath; elsewhere plaster was replaced by plywood.

Following a 1990s renovation, the interior has lost some of its rough edges—the exposed joists have been covered with a wood-

Frank O. Gehry & Associates, Gehry House, Santa Monica, California, 1977–78, 1991–94

Dining room and kitchen, Gehry House

strip ceiling, some of the plywood walls have been plastered, the rolled asphalt kitchen floor is now asphalt pavers, and the director's chairs in the dining room have been replaced by Gehry-designed bentwood chairs. But this is still the home of a bohemian. Books are everywhere; so is modern art, hanging and stacked against the walls.

The use of low-cost materials was influenced by more than merely a restricted budget. Like Foster and Rogers, Gehry is partial to certain modern forms, but they are the forms of everyday life rather than of advanced technology. "It just seems so obvious to me, that one should use chain link, because it's such a pervasive material," he once said. This is slightly disingenuous, since to most people it is not obvious at all. Gehry has a definite iconoclastic streak, and chain-link fencing used sculpturally is a calculated affront to mainstream taste, as is the raw plywood on the exterior, and a front door that is a smooth panel of unpainted galvanized metal, as prosaic as a warehouse fire exit.

In the late 1970s, when Gehry was designing his house, what were other architects doing? James Stirling and Michael Wilford had just won the competition for the Staatsgalerie addition in Stuttgart with a historical collage, Piano and Rogers were celebrating technology at the Centre Pompidou, and in the East Building of the National Gallery, I. M. Pei was demonstrating that there was still life left in mainstream modernism. The Gehry house shares none of their architectural concerns—it contains no historical references, no fancy hardware, no elegant details. With its cheerful disdain for conventional architectural refinement, the house is a milestone both in the architect's career and in the development of contemporary architectural taste.*

"Each age finds its own expression in material things, and the faculty we use to identify those things we find palatable or repellent we call taste," writes the British design critic Stephen Bayley. In other words, taste is about making choices, it's about what we *dis*like as well as what we like. Appleton likes the casual classicism of Italian farmhouses and adapts it to modern living; Graves interprets the same classicism in a more personal fashion; Bohlin likes his old house in Waverly and accepts its limitations; Gehry doesn't like his pink cottage and subverts it. The self-effacing Appleton dislikes standing out, Gehry and Graves dislike fitting in. Bohlin seems somewhere in between.

The homes—and tastes—of these four architects reflect the wide range of contemporary architectural expression. The low-key Villa Corbeau is a reminder that classicism is here to stay. After centuries of revivals, and revivals of revivals, this is hardly surprising. As long as architects—and their clients—are drawn

---

*In 2012, the American Institute of Architects gave the Gehry House its Twenty-Five Year Award.

to age-old traditions, classicism will continue, even if it is used to design a refined Tuscan farmhouse. Since classicism is a cumulative tradition, it only becomes richer over time, offering the architect an array of examples—grand, modest, elaborate, simple. The contemporary classicist is able to draw on John Russell Pope and Edwin Lutyens as well as Andrea Palladio—or on the rural Tuscan vernacular.

No one would ever confuse the Warehouse with a Tuscan farmhouse; the architect's hand is too apparent. Graves avoids ornament, creating a composition of volumes that is classical in its symmetrical and axial arrangement, but modern in its unembellished simplicity. At the same time, Graves's painter's taste for color undermines the severity. This personal interpretation of classicism is part of a long tradition, found in the work of John Soane and Paul Cret in the past, and the late Aldo Rossi and Léon Krier today.

Frank Gehry, the iconoclast, pushes the limits. But this is not 1923, when Le Corbusier could write of revolution and overturning old codes, and Gehry's exploration is personal rather than prototypical. Instead of avant-garde—a portent of the future—his vision is quirky and personal. When Gehry was seventeen and living in Toronto, he heard a talk by Alvar Aalto, and years later made a pilgrimage to the Finn's office in Helsinki. "He was away but I was allowed to sit in his chair." Gehry, like Aalto, is an intensely intuitive modernist. "If I think too much about a design, I tend to discard it," he says.

Peter Bohlin seems to look forward *and* backward. Unlike most classicists, he accepts the revolution that was modernism, but is unwilling to observe all its confining rules—"traps," he calls them. He doesn't embrace the past, but does cast a fond backward glance from time to time. He is unwilling to treat architecture as a medium of personal expression, preferring to root his designs in the constraints of site, materials, and construction. I don't want to make him sound too diffident. The wall that defines the front of his property in Waverly is the straightest, most precise, most perfect dried-laid stone wall I have ever seen. It says Architect's House just as unmistakably as Gehry's unconventional façade on a quiet street corner in Santa Monica.

CHANGING TASTES

In 1972, Robert Venturi, Denise Scott Brown, and Steven Izenour published *Learning from Las Vegas*, a polemical book whose theme was that architects should be more attuned to the tastes of mainstream America. "Billboards are almost all right," they proclaimed, championing a Pop Art sensibility that somewhat unconvincingly aimed to fuse the vulgar with the highbrow. A few years later, the editors of *VIA*, a student publication of the University of Pennsylvania, referred to Venturi's book in an interview with Michael Graves. Why was Graves's formal architectural vocabulary so different—they called it a breach—from the taste of average Americans, they wanted to know? Graves, whose style had only just begun to shift from Corbusian modernism to a more figural classicism, gave an interesting answer:

> I would like to respond by discussing the issue of popular culture. Popular culture gets its strength, it seems to me, through its transitory nature. It is probably interesting to us because it is short-lived, a part of fashion or trends, and probably has a commercially oriented base. It must change or be supplanted by other trends and fashions. It must be made over to feed its commercial orientation. It gets its strength from being here today and gone tomorrow. Its symbols are, in fact, transitory. To codify elements of the popular culture is to make them static, which is contrary to their ephemeral nature.

Graves was making a sharp distinction between architectural and popular taste, although it was not the distinction between good taste and bad that Edith Wharton might have drawn. Instead, he differentiated between ephemeral popular culture and—by implication—the long-lasting values of architecture.

Neither the architect nor his interviewers could have imagined that it would be Graves—not Venturi—whom the popular culture would lionize. A few years later, in a feature article in *The New York Times Magazine*, the newspaper's architecture critic Paul Goldberger called Graves "the architect of the hour." Goldberger did not use the word *taste*, but he made it clear that his subject had connected with the American public in a profound way. "Graves has burst into a kind of celebrity shared by no other architect of his generation," Goldberger wrote. "We are at a moment when we have come to reject the sleek austerity of modernism, a style that never served very well as anything but a symbol of corporate anonymity. We want architecture to serve as a symbol, to stand for cultural values and civic grandeur, but we tend to remain fairly uncomfortable with modernism's obvious opposite, the literal re-use of historical style. If we seek a hero, we want one who seems to bring us something we have not seen before."

Graves became that hero. He was commissioned to design public libraries and museums, office buildings and civic centers, and was effectively the house architect for the Disney company. When the Washington Monument was being renovated, it was Graves who designed the distinctive scaffolding that, illuminated at night, became a tourist attraction in its own right. He produced a wildly successful whistling teakettle, and for the mass market he designed not high-end flatware and crystal but everyday objects such as kitchen whisks and dustpans. Graves did not exactly adopt popular culture as Venturi wanted architects to do, but popular culture definitely adopted him.

By the late 1990s, the Guggenheim Museum in Bilbao had captured the public's imagination, and Frank Gehry was the new architect of the hour; moreover, Goldberger's analysis was up-turned. The "sleek austerity of modernism" made a resounding comeback in the shape of Norman Foster's Swiss Re building in London—the Gherkin, corporate but hardly anonymous—and in numerous museums, many designed by the globe-trotting Renzo Piano, whose sleek austerity became the new museum norm. When Richard Meier led a wave of all-glass condominium towers in New York, some observers declared modernism the winner in the condo style wars. Then Robert A. M. Stern's 15 Central Park West became the most successful residential real estate project in the city's history, demonstrating that the days of the "literal re-use of historical style" were far from over. A few years later Gehry reasserted himself with the tallest—and most abstractly curvaceous—residential tower in the city.

These shifts in popular taste displaced Graves from center stage. However, like Richard Rogers, he remains true to his personal vision, which is the ultimate lesson: the public's taste may change, but an architect should hold firm. Indeed, it is this sense of deep personal conviction—not style, or craft, or taste—that is the test of the best architecture. Louis Kahn never courted popularity; a building was what it wanted to be. The uncompromising Paul Rudolph followed his architectural muse even when she ceased to be popular. And the indifferent Mies van der Rohe proclaimed, "I don't want to be interesting, I want to be good."

There are many ways to be good. Architecture is not a religion, and there is no right and wrong, although there is certainly good and bad, practical and impractical, beautiful and ugly. But taste—"those things we find palatable or repellent"—is hard to escape, hence the Gothic-classical debates of the nineteenth century, the classical-modernist dispute of the early twentieth, and the modernist-traditional contretemps of today. Since architecture is not a science, there can be no ultimate proof, which may explain the ferocity of the argument.

"Every worthwhile building—like all works of art—has its own standard," observed Steen Eiler Rasmussen. "If we contemplate it in a carping spirit, with a know-it-all attitude, it will shut itself up and have nothing to say to us." He wrote that more than fifty years ago, and in a multicultural world, a global world of many and varied tastes, it is more true than ever. Diversity is not merely accepted by the public, it is demanded—in fiction, in music, in movies, in food, so why not in architecture? We are happy with corporate minimalism in an office building, expressionism in a concert hall, and tradition at home. Or maybe minimalism at home, tradition in the concert hall, and expressionism in the office—it all depends.

While I find it hard to excuse a building that fails at a functional level, or that ignores its setting, or that is badly built, that does not mean that I cannot appreciate a variety of design approaches. What I have called a conceptual toolkit can help us to understand this variety. The media have a tendency to focus on what is new and unexpected, but it is important to understand that architectural innovation, whether it is willful and questions established conventions, or considered and embraces old rules, never occurs in a vacuum. The architect takes a position with respect to history and style, details and structure, and plan and setting. This position, as I have tried to show, can vary. This does not mean that it always leads to success; the world is full of pretentious experiments and banal re-creations. Yet architectural diversity is a good thing. An architect must hold strong convictions in order to create, but as users of architecture we should open our minds—and our eyes—to the richness of our surroundings. And allow the buildings to speak to us.

GLOSSARY

Many of the terms included here are concerned with classicism, which over its long history has accumulated a rich terminology that may be unfamiliar to the reader. Modernist architecture has had less time to develop a lexicon, and while some architects have tried to invent new terms, they tend to be in the category of professional jargon. I have avoided the contemporary fashion for rushing to identify new styles—"isms"—as they appear. Stylistic labels such as Gothic, Baroque, Rococo, even Art Deco, were coined long after the periods they describe. In any case, it is always better to try to understand a building than to be satisfied with merely pigeonholing its designer.

acroterion: An architectural ornament or sculpture placed at the apex or the extremities of a *pediment.* In Chicago's Harold Washington Library, the acroteria include owls, symbols of wisdom.

ancien élève: A former student of the *École des Beaux-Arts.*

anthemion: A classical decorative motif based on a plant, with curling leaves or petals.

architrave: The lowest portion of a classical *entablature.* A door or window surround that uses the same profile may also be called an architrave.

Art Deco: The name is derived from the Parisian Exposition Internationale des Arts Décoratifs et Industriels Modernes of 1925, which introduced Jazz Age

furniture and décor by designers such as Paul Poiret and
Émile-Jacques Ruhlmann. The glamorous and sophisticated
style influenced Paul Cret at the Folger Library, Raymond
Hood at Rockefeller Center, and William Van Alen at the
Chrysler Building. One of the great Art Deco cities of North
America is Montreal (the ballyhooed Art Deco buildings of
Miami's South Beach are an impoverished, commercialized
version of this urbane style).

Arts and Crafts: The Arts and Crafts movement originated in Britain in the
second half of the nineteenth century, led by figures such as William Morris
and Charles Voysey. Sometimes called Craftsman in America, the style is associated with potters, weavers, and furniture makers, especially Gustav Stick-
ley. Arts and Crafts houses were often *Shingle Style.* Leading practitioners
were Frank Lloyd Wright (in his Prairie period) and, in California, Charles
and Henry Greene, Bernard Maybeck, Julia Morgan, and Ernest Coxhead.

atelier: Literally, studio. The *École des Beaux-Arts* was divided into fiercely
competitive ateliers, each headed by a prominent practicing architect. The
term has survived as a somewhat affected name for an architect's office, as in
Ateliers Jean Nouvel and Studio Daniel Libeskind.

attic: An attic is a storage space under a pitched roof where you keep old
trunks. In a classical building, an attic (from Attica) story is a floor added
above the *entablature,* which has the effect of reducing the apparent height of
a building. A square pier with a simplified capital, based on the no longer ex-
tant Choragic Monument of Thrasyllus in Athens, is sometimes referred to as
the Attic order.

baluster: The vertical spindle, or stick, of a *balustrade.* May be
plain or elaborately shaped. Since the 1970s, advances in glass-
manufacturing technology have allowed balustrades to be fabricated entirely from sheets of tempered glass, which eliminates
the need for balusters. Glass balustrades are visually neat although vulnerable to sticky-fingered children. Stretched wires
can also be substituted for balusters.

balustrade: The railing of a stair or gallery, consisting of *balusters* supporting a
banister.

banister: The handrail of a *balustrade*. Best when shaped to fit the hand.

Baroque: The period, beginning in the late sixteenth century, when architects took Renaissance classicism in a theatrical and rhetorical direction. This era coincides with Baroque music, but if architecture really is frozen music, as Goethe claimed, then I'm not sure what flamboyant Borromini and Bernini share with Purcell and Bach.

Bauhaus: The famous German art school that existed from 1919 to 1933, moving from Weimar to Dessau, and lastly in Berlin. The school was founded by Walter Gropius, and included such eminent artists as Paul Klee, Wassily Kandinsky, and Josef Albers (illustrated). Although the Bauhaus is sometimes called a school of architecture, that subject was taught only after 1927. Architects who taught at the Bauhaus included Marcel Breuer, Hannes Meyer, and Mies van der Rohe.

bond: Brick walls consist of "stretchers" (bricks laid lengthwise) and "headers" (bricks laid crosswise). Running, or stretcher bond, consists of only stretchers, and is used for one-brick-thick veneer walls. For thicker walls, different bonds can be used. In Flemish or Dutch bond, stretchers and headers alternate, creating a decorative pattern (illustrated). In English bond, a row of stretchers alternates with a row of headers, while in American or common bond, a single row of headers is laid every five to seven stretcher courses.

Brutalism: From the French *béton brut* (raw concrete). The term was coined by Alison and Peter Smithson and refers to a style that favors exposed concrete, heavy monumental forms, and rugged details. Notable buildings include Paul Rudolph's Yale School of Art and Architecture and Gerhardt Kallmann and Michael McKinnell's Boston City Hall. Brutalism was popular among architects—though not with the public—between 1950 and 1970. Architects who use exposed concrete today, such as Tadao Ando and Moshe Safdie, tend to give it a mirror-smooth finish—not brutal.

cantilever: A simple beam is supported at both ends; a cantilevered beam is supported only at one end and projects like a diving board. Masonry construction does not lend itself to cantilevers, and wood cantilevers are relatively small (balconies and galleries). Steel and reinforced concrete make large cantilevers possible. Exaggerated cantilevers are a hallmark of many recent buildings, such as the Clinton Presidential Library.

charrette: A term that originated in the *École des Beaux-Arts* where carts (*charrettes*) were used to transport the large drawings from the *atelier* to the main building on the rue Bonaparte for evaluation by the professors. Tardy students who touched up unfinished drawings during the journey itself were said to be working *"en charrette."* The term came to refer to any intense design session with a looming deadline.

classicism: A classical building uses an architectural vocabulary derived from the Greco-Roman architectural tradition. Together with *Gothic,* classicism is one of the two great architectural traditions of Western culture.

Colonial Revival: A style based on the white clapboard New England architecture of the period preceding the Revolutionary War. The Colonial Revival was stimulated by the Philadelphia Centennial Exposition, which included reconstructions of Colonial homes. During a famous 1877 trip, four young architect friends—Charles Follen McKim, William Rutherford Mead, Stanford White, and William Bigelow—traveled in Massachusetts and New Hampshire, sketching colonial-era houses. The famous firm founded by the first three did much to popularize the Colonial style, which remains a staple of American domestic architecture to this day.

Composite order: A Composite capital combines features of *Corinthian* (acanthus leaves) and *Ionic* (volutes). The most opulent of the five orders, Composite was invented by the Romans; the oldest surviving example is found on the Arch of Titus.

Corinthian order: The capital of a Corinthian column consists of two rows of stylized acanthus leaves that somewhat resemble female tresses, leading some to consider this order as feminine, as opposed to the sturdy masculine Doric. Sir Henry Wotton, who coined this famous line about architecture, "Well-building hath three conditions: Commoditie, Firmeness, and Delight," described the Corinthian order as "lascivious . . . decked like a wanton courtesan."

cornice: The uppermost part of a classical *entablature.* More generally, the projecting ledge that crowns a building, a door, or a window. The function of a cornice is to throw water free of the building's wall; visually, a cornice provides a satisfying sense of termination to a building.

curtain wall: A nonstructural wall that is attached to—hangs from—the exterior of a building. The first glass-and-metal curtain wall dates from the 1860s, but the curtain wall emerges in its characteristic modern guise in Chicago in 860–880 Lakeshore Drive, a pair of apartment towers designed by Mies van der Rohe in 1948.

deconstructivism: The term *deconstructivism* came to the fore in the late 1980s thanks in part to a Museum of Modern Art exhibition organized by Philip Johnson and Mark Wigley that featured the work of Peter Eisenman, Rem Koolhaas, Daniel Libeskind, Frank Gehry, Zaha Hadid, and others. Deconstructivism is vaguely related to French literary theory, and even more vaguely to the Russian Constructivist movement of the 1920s. Although the architects named above rejected the label, the term stuck, at least for a time, probably because the buildings it described really do look deconstructed— that is, as if they are falling apart. The critic Charles Jencks compared deconstructivism to post-punk music, "an informal style appealing to a substantial taste for the discordant and ephemeral, the unpretentious and tough . . . urban anomie raised to a high art."

dentils: Literally, teeth. The small, spaced decorative blocks in the cornice of a classical building, whose origin is likely the projecting ends of rafters, from the time when Greek temples were constructed of wood. Dentils occur in the *Ionic, Corinthian* and *Composite* orders, and are sometimes used alone in the "stripped classical" style.

Doric order: Because of its sturdy proportions, this austere order is often described as masculine, compared with feminine *Corinthian.* The extremely simple Doric capital resembles an upside-down soup plate. Greek Doric is considered the foundation of all the classical orders. Roman Doric sometimes adds a base to the column.

École des Beaux-Arts: The Parisian school of architecture that traces its origins to 1671, and which dominated architectural education in the late nineteenth and early twentieth centuries. Students from around the world attended the École, which taught a rigorous method of design using symmetry, axes, and hierarchical composition. Among the American *anciens élèves* were Richard

Morris Hunt, H. H. Richardson, Louis Sullivan, Charles McKim, Thomas Hastings, Bernard Maybeck, and Julia Morgan.

entablature: A beam-like element that spans between the columns of a classical temple. An entablature is subdivided into *architrave, frieze,* and *cornice.*

entasis: The swelling taper of a classical column. The taper is not straight but gently curved, and it generally begins one-third of the way up the column. Pointing to a straight column in a modernist building, Allan Greenberg observed: "That's not a column, it's a post."

esquisse: A preliminary design sketch by an *École des Beaux-Arts* student made in isolation during a twelve-hour period. In the case of a major design assignment (*projet rendu*), the student was given an additional two months to develop the design, but was not allowed to substantively diverge from the esquisse.

façade: The front, or face, of a building. An elevation is an architectural drawing that represents a façade in strict two-dimensional projection.

Federal: The American version of the Adam style that was popularized by the Scottish brothers Robert and James Adam. Although the heyday of Federal was from 1780 to 1820, the style resurfaced during the Colonial Revival of the late nineteenth century. Federal buildings are similar to Georgian, often using brick with stone trim, but with more attenuated classical details.

flutes: The shallow grooves cut into classical columns are called flutes. Columns can be fluted or smooth. Flutes are usually vertical, although there are surviving examples of Roman columns with spiral flutes, such as those at Aphrodisias and Sardis in Turkey.

frieze: The central portion of a classical *entablature*, in the *Doric order* consisting of *triglyphs* and *metopes*. More generally, a frieze is a decorative horizontal band, usually above eye level, that may be painted or sculpted. The frieze of Otto Wagner's St. Leopold's Church in Vienna consists of alternating bronze wreaths and crosses.

Georgian: The British architectural style that coincides with the reigns of Georges I–IV (1720–1840). Greatly influenced by the simple classicism of Palladio, these decorous brick buildings depend chiefly on proportion and symmetry for their architectural impact. In America, many Colonial buildings are Georgian, and after a revival in the early 1900s, the style has never gone out of fashion.

gerberette: A short-propped cantilevered beam invented by the nineteenth-century German bridge engineer Heinrich Gerber. Peter Rice introduced a modern version made out of cast steel in his structural design for the Centre Pompidou.

Gothic: The cathedral architecture that developed in medieval Europe in the twelfth century, characterized by pointed arches. Gothic represents the "other" Western architectural tradition. There have been several Gothic revivals, and for many Gothic remains the archetypal style for churches and campus buildings.

high tech: More an attitude than a style, high tech emerged in the 1970s in the work of such architects as Norman Foster, Richard Rogers, and Renzo Piano. High-tech buildings tend to be steel, emphasize lightweight structure and structural connections, often have long spans, and incorporate new building materials and techniques. Although these buildings feature structure, they are not simply exposed construction. The British engineer Frank Newby once sarcastically defined high tech as "the use of redundant structure for decorative purposes."

International Style: The formative era of modernist architecture. The term was coined by Henry-Russell Hitchcock and Philip Johnson in 1932, and was a loose umbrella for a wide variety of approaches, causing confusion ever since. The International Style was typified by concrete construction, modular structure, and flat roofs, all anticipated in Le Corbusier's 1914 Domino project (illustrated).

Ionic order: The Ionic order is said to have originated in Asia Minor in the middle of the sixth century B.C. The distinguishing features are the two spiral forms (volutes) on the capital that resemble ram's horns or seashells. The Ionic order is considered matronly, compared with *Doric*, although not as feminine as *Corinthian.*

mannerism: The period (1520–60) between the Renaissance and the *Baroque,* when architects such as Michelangelo and Giulio Romano pushed the boundaries of *classicism,* often in an unharmonious, exaggerated direction. Ever since, *mannerism* refers to any architecture that knowingly breaks rules; Robert Venturi has called himself a "modern mannerist."

maquette: A scale model. Architects make models in a variety of scales and materials: clay, paper, wood, plastic. Study models are rough and used during the design process; presentation models are more elaborate and intended for the client or the public; full-size mock-ups of parts of the building test details, appearance, and performance.

Mediterranean Revival: A modern eclectic style that combines features of Spanish and Italian domestic architecture: arches, roughly plastered walls, tiles. First appeared in Southern California in the 1920s.

megastructure: A 1960s idea to design housing complexes, college campuses, even parts of cities, as single structures that integrate functional spaces with circulation and infrastructure. Urban megastructures proved unrealizable, but a number of megastructure universities were built: the University of East Anglia (Denys Lasdun) in England, Simon Fraser University (Arthur Erickson) and Scarborough College (John Andrews) in Canada, and the University of Berlin (Candilis, Josic & Woods). Although megastructures were supposed to control future growth, the idea faltered as succeeding architects tended to take their own course.

metope: The alternating square space between *triglyphs* in a Doric *frieze.* Metopes were sometimes painted with decorative figures, or carved like the famous metopes of the Parthenon that depict the battle between the Centaurs and the Lapiths.

modernism: The architectural movement that began in the early twentieth century and broke conclusively with the classical and Gothic traditions that had shaped Western architecture for centuries. Modernism, in its original form, lasted fewer than fifty years. It was briefly derailed by *postmodernism,* but a later revival returned modernism to favor.

neoclassicism: An architectural movement, beginning in the mid-eighteenth century that, in reaction to the *Rococo* style, turned to the more severe classical architecture of ancient Greece and Rome. Karl Friedrich Schinkel in

Germany and John Soane in Britain are two celebrated neoclassicists. Neo-classicism lasted a long time and developed into the Greek Revival and *Federal* styles.

oculus: Literally, eye. Refers to circular windows or openings, especially in the tops of domes, as in the Roman Pantheon, Andrea Palladio's Villa Rotonda, and John Russell Pope's National Gallery of Art.

order: An order is the total assembly of pedestal, column, and *entablature*. There are nominally five orders: *Doric* and *Ionic*, which originated in Greece; *Corinthian*, which is Roman; and *Tuscan* and *Composite*, which were identified by Renaissance scholars and whose origin is also Roman. The orders vary in their proportions, the design of their capitals, and associated details. Over the centuries, there have been many heterodox orders, such as Benjamin Latrobe's corncob capital in the U.S. Capitol, and the Mogul-influenced order that Edwin Lutyens designed for the Viceroy's House in New Delhi.

parti: Literally meaning a decision, this was originally a term of the *École des Beaux-Arts* that referred to the position taken by the architect with respect to the solution of a particular building program. For example, Paul Cret described the parti of his Pan American Union building: "In a word, the public is to be accommodated more like guests in a large residence than like crowds attending a paid function in a public hall." Today, the term is used more generally to describe the idea behind a design.

pediment: The gable end of an ancient temple. The triangular form is often used ornamentally on classical buildings, both in loggias and porticos, and in a smaller version atop doors and windows. There are many variations of this characteristic form: broken pediment (illustrated), curved pediment, seg-mental pediment, open pediment, and a swan-neck pediment. Large pediments are sometimes filled with sculptural figures. The pediment of Gunnar Asplund's Karl Johan School in Göteborg, Sweden, has playful figures in brick; the pediment of Michael Graves's Team Disney Building in Burbank, California, includes Dopey, one of the Seven Dwarfs.

peristyle: A continuous colonnade, either surrounding a classical building, as in the Lincoln Memorial, or a courtyard, as in the White House Rose Garden. The cloister is a medieval version of the peristyle.

pilaster: The representation of a column in a wall. Pilasters are used to visually break up a wall, or to emphasize door or window openings, but they are always purely ornamental and merely suggest structure. Pilasters are rectangular; half-round or three-quarter-round representations are called attached columns.

postmodernism: A short-lived architectural movement of the 1970s that introduced historical elements—sometimes exaggerated or distorted—into modern buildings. Early practitioners included Charles Moore and Robert Venturi. The first large postmodern buildings were the Portland Building (Michael Graves) and the AT&T Building (Philip Johnson and John Burgee).

reinforced concrete: The most common modern building material, consisting of Portland cement concrete reinforced by steel bars. Reinforced concrete has the advantages of being relatively cheap, fireproof, and simple to construct. It can be cast on-site (in situ) or prefabricated in a factory (precast). Most of the early pioneers of reinforced concrete, which was invented at the end of the nineteenth century, were French: the engineers François Hennebique and Eugène Freyssinet, and the architect August Perret. The acme of concrete architecture was *Brutalism.*

revival: An architectural revival is "the physical expression of an architect's desire to demonstrate to his public that he wishes to remind them of an historic building form specifically because it existed in the past," according to Robert Adam. Revivals have occurred regularly throughout the history of architecture.

Rococo: A highly ornate eighteenth-century style emerging at the end of the *Baroque* period. Lighthearted and intimate, Rococo was most popular in Catholic Europe, and never gained favor in Britain, where *rococo* meant old-fashioned or overly decorated.

Romanesque: The medieval architectural style that preceded *Gothic,* characterized by rounded arches. Despite its name, this style has little to do with ancient Rome, and developed independently in northern Europe (in Britain it is called Norman). A Romanesque Revival occurred in the nineteenth century. The heavy style lent itself not only to churches but also to libraries, city halls, and department stores. The foremost American practitioner of the Roman-

esque Revival was Henry Hobson Richardson; the work of his many followers is known as Richardsonian Romanesque.

scale: In architectural parlance, size and scale are not the same. Size is the actual dimension of something, while scale is the visual relationship between that thing and the human observer. Thus, a small building may have a large scale and appear bigger than it actually is, and vice versa.

Shingle Style: Named by Vincent Scully, the style refers to domestic American architecture of the last quarter of the nineteenth century. Influenced by the simplicity of American Colonial architecture, architects such as H. H. Richardson, McKim, Mead & White, and Peabody & Stearns built rambling summer houses with large roofs, simple massing, and straightforward details, the roofs and walls covered with wood shingle. A revival of the Shingle Style in the 1980s was led in large part by Robert A. M. Stern.

Spanish Colonial Revival: A style based on the early Spanish buildings of Southern California, typically with red clay-tile roofs, loggias, patios, arcades, wrought ironwork, and patterned ceramic tiles (illustrated). Introduced by Bertram Goodhue at the Panama-California Exposition held in San Diego in 1915, the Spanish Colonial style was popularized by George Washington Smith in Santa Barbara and Wallace Neff in Los Angeles. Spanish Colonial in Florida has different roots, more Spanish and less Colonial. When John Carrère and Thomas Hastings built re- sort hotels in St. Augustine, they adopted the Spanish Renaissance style, and Moorish Spain was the predominant influence on the eclectic work of Addison Mizner in Palm Beach. An early biographer, Alva Johnston, characterized Mizner's architecture as "Bastard-Spanish—Moorish—Romanesque—Gothic—Renaissance—Bull-Market—Damn-the-Expense Style."

Stripped classicism: This austere style dispenses with the *orders* and combines classical composition with simplified details. It is found in American public buildings of the 1930s, and is sometime referred to as WPA Moderne or Depression Modern. The leading practitioner was Paul Cret, whose work includes the Folger Shakespeare Library and the Federal Reserve Board Building. Stripped classicism was adopted by certain prewar German and Italian architects, hence is often (mistakenly) associated with Fascism and Nazism.

torus: From the Latin meaning "cushion." A large bulging molding, often found at the bases of columns.

trelliage: Latticework used as interior decoration to suggest an arbor or trellis, popularized by the decorator Elsie de Wolfe.

triglyph: Triglyphs alternate with *metopes* in a *Doric frieze.* The triglyph has vertical grooves and is thought to represent the ends of beams, a reminder that Greek temples were originally constructed entirely of timber.

Tuscan order: The plainest of the orders, developed by the Romans, is a simplified version of *Doric,* never fluted; in truth, it's very hard to tell the two apart. Tuscan is often used in barns and stables, or in military buildings.

vernacular: Term used to distinguish the work of untutored builders from that of formally trained architects. Vernacular architecture can be traditional (a Shaker barn) or contemporary (a highway diner). A milestone event in the modern awareness of vernacular building was Bernard Rudofsky's *Architecture Without Architects,* a book based on a 1964 Museum of Modern Art exhibition.

Vitruvius: Marcus Vitruvius Pollio was an obscure first-century B.C. Roman architect whose *Ten Books on Architecture* was rediscovered in the fifteenth century in the Abbey of St. Gallen. This unique surviving Roman handbook on the art of building became an invaluable aid for Renaissance builders seeking to revive ancient architecture. Often referred to simply as "Vitruvius," this is the oldest and most influential architectural book ever written.

NOTES ON SOURCES

This is not a scholarly work, so I have not burdened it with reference notes. However, I have relied on many books and articles, and for readers who wish to pursue a subject further I include these brief bibliographical notes. In the text, I follow convention and credit individual architects with the design of particular buildings, but the reader should be aware that architecture is a collaborative endeavor and in many cases—especially in today's large practices that routinely involve scores if not hundreds of people working on many concurrent commissions—partners, associates, and consultants make significant contributions.

INTRODUCTION

Steen Eiler Rasmussen's *Experiencing Architecture,* written in Danish and translated by Eve Wendt, first appeared in 1959 (MIT Press, 1964). Norbert Schoenauer is the author of several books, including his magnum opus, *6,000 Years of Housing,* now in its third revised edition (W. W. Norton & Co., 2000). James Wood's admirable *How Fiction Works* (Farrar, Straus and Giroux, 2008) influenced my general approach.

1. IDEAS

John F. Harbeson's classic 1926 guide to the teaching methods of the École des Beaux-Arts, *The Study of Architectural Design,* was recently republished with a new introduction by John Blatteau and Sandra L. Tatman (W. W. Norton & Co., 2008). Another good source of information about the École is Joan Draper's

"The École des Beaux-Arts and the Architectural Profession in the United States: The Case of John Galen Howard," in *The Architect: Chapters in the History of the Profession*, Spiro Kostof, ed. (University of California Press, 1977). *Philip Johnson: Writings* (Oxford University Press, 1979) collects many of his essays and lectures. Franz Schulze's *Mies van der Rohe: A Critical Biography* (University of Chicago Press, 1985) is the standard biography; the story of Mies's visit to Johnson's house is recounted in *The Philip Johnson Tapes: Interviews by Robert A. M. Stern*, Kazys Vernelis, ed. (Monacelli Press, 2008). Peter Blake makes cogent observations on the Johnson house in his gossipy memoir, *No Place Like Utopia: Modern Architecture and the Company We Kept* (Alfred A. Knopf, 1993). The best way to experience Fallingwater is to visit the house, which I did one memorable evening for dinner; the second-best way is to leaf through *Fallingwater*, Lynda Waggoner, ed. (Rizzoli, 2011). Neil Levine's *The Architecture of Frank Lloyd Wright* (Princeton University Press, 1996) is an illustrated overview of the architect's work. Cees de Jong and Erik Mattie's two useful volumes, *Architectural Competitions: 1792–1919* and *Architectural Competitions, 1950–Today* (Benedikt Taschen, 1994), document the subject. John Peter's interesting *The Oral History of Modern Architecture: Interviews with the Greatest Architects of the Twentieth Century* (Harry N. Abrams, 1994) includes interviews with virtually all the major figures of early modernism. Background on the African American museum competition is based on press releases, minutes of meetings of the Commission of Fine Arts, and the author's conversation with Dr. Lonnie G. Bunch, director of the museum, and Don Stastny, professional adviser to the competition. The Bibliothèque Nationale de France is discussed in an unpublished paper by Shannon Mattern, "A Square for Paris, a National Symbol, and a Learning Factory: Dominique Perrault's Bibliothèque Nationale de France" (see WordsInSpace.net). Patricia Cummings Loud's excellent *The Art Museums of Louis I. Kahn* (Duke University Press, 1989) describes the construction of the Yale Center for British Art as well as the Kimbell Art Museum. Carter Wiseman's *Louis I. Kahn: Beyond Time and Style* (W. W. Norton & Co., 2007) is a good general introduction to the architect's life and work.

2. THE SETTING

I have told the full story of Moshe Safdie's National Gallery of Canada in *A Place for Art: The Architecture of the National Gallery of Canada* (National Gallery of Canada, 1993). Jack Diamond's work is documented in *Insight and On Site: The Architecture of Diamond and Schmitt* (Douglas & McIntyre, 2008), while the saga of Mariinsky II is recounted by Don Gillmor in "Red Tape," *The Walrus* (May 2010). The acoustician Leo Baranek's classic is *Concert and Opera Halls: How They Sound* (Acoustical Society of America, 1996). I wrote about Seiji Ozawa Hall in "Sounds as Good as It Looks," *The Atlantic Monthly* (June 1996). *Edwin Lutyens: Country Houses* (Monacelli Press, 2001) contains archival photographs of the great architect's work. Colin Amery's *A Celebration of Art & Architecture* (National Gallery, 1991) recounts the story of the National Gallery's Sainsbury Wing. Robert Venturi's *Complexity and Contradiction in Architecture* (Museum of Modern Art, 1966) remains a classic; the reader is also directed to *Architecture as Signs and Symbols: For a Mannerist Time* (Belknap Press of Harvard University, 2004) by Venturi and Denise Scott Brown.

3. SITE

Frank Lloyd Wright wrote many books, most of which make for a hard slog today, but for the layman, and especially for the prospective home-builder, *The Natural House* (Horizon Press, 1954) remains an excellent source of wise advice. Christopher Alexander et al.'s classic *A Pattern Language: Towns, Buildings, Construction* (Oxford University Press, 1977) is an invaluable reference. Esther's McCoy's *Five California Architects* (Reinhold Publishing Corp., 1960) is an important history of early modernism in that state (the five architects are Bernard Maybeck, the Greene brothers, Irving Gill, and Rudolf Schindler). Brendan Gill's lively biography is *Many Masks: A Life of Frank Lloyd Wright* (G. P. Putnam's Sons, 1987). My parents' North Hero summer cottage is documented in Robert W. Knight's *A House on the Water* (Taunton Press, 2003). Jeremiah Eck's *The Distinctive House: A Vision of Timeless Design* (Taunton, 2003) is a useful source of information on domestic design. John W. Cook and Heinrich Klotz, *Conversations with Architects* (Lund Humphries, 1973), includes spirited interviews with Philip Johnson, Kevin Roche, Paul Rudolph, Charles Moore, Louis Kahn, and the Venturis. The Smithsons' building at St. Hilda's College is discussed by Robin Middleton in "The Pursuit of Ordinariness," *Architectural Design* (February 1971).

4. PLAN

The best English translation of Palladio's *The Four Books on Architecture* is by Robert Tavernor and Richard Schofield (MIT Press, 1997). Leon Battista Alberti's *On the Art of Building in Ten Books* has been ably translated by Joseph

Rykwert, Neil Leach, and Robert Tavernor (MIT Press, 1991). I describe my encounter with the Villa Saraceno in detail in *The Perfect House: A Journey with the Renaissance Master Andrea Palladio* (Scribner, 2002). Marcus de Sautoy's interesting book is *Symmetry: A Journey into the Patterns of Nature* (HarperCollins, 2008). The Frank Gehry conversation with Tom Pritzker took place at the Aspen Ideas Festival in 2009 and is available on YouTube. The Stern quotation is in his introduction to *Robert A. M. Stern: Buildings and Projects, 1999–2003*, Peter Morris Dixon, ed. (Monacelli Press, 2003).

5. STRUCTURE

John Summerson's *The Classical Language of Architecture* (Thames & Hudson, 1980) is an excellent overview of the subject. The best contemporary handbook on classical architecture is Robert Adam's *Classical Architecture: A Comprehensive Handbook to the Tradition of Classical Style* (Harry N. Abrams, 1990). Mary Beard's *The Parthenon* (Harvard University Press, 2003) is an interesting history of the building. For an informed discussion of the practical origins of classicism, one cannot do better than J. J. Coulton's *Ancient Greek Architects at Work: Problems of Structure and Design* (Cornell University Press, 1977). Edward R. Ford's exhaustive *The Details of Modern Architecture* (MIT Press, 1990) and *The Details of Modern Architecture: Volume 2, 1928–1988* (MIT Press, 1996) have provided much of the technical information in this chapter. Frank Lloyd Wright's essays on materials are contained in *The Essential Frank Lloyd Wright: Critical Writings on Architecture*, Bruce Brooks Pfeiffer, ed. (Princeton University Press, 2008). Lewis Mumford's observations on the Unité d'Habitation and the Guggenheim Museum are in his interesting collection of essay and reviews, *The Highway and the City* (Harcourt, Brace & World, 1963). Lisa Jardine's *On a Grander Scale: The Outstanding Life of Sir Christopher Wren* (HarperCollins, 2002) is an informative biography.

6. SKIN

Le Corbusier's 1923 classic, *Vers une architecture*, was recently republished in a new English translation by John Goodman, *Towards a New Architecture* (Getty Research Institute, 2007). Mies van der Rohe spoke about the Lake Shore Drive apartments in a rare interview in *Architectural Forum* (November 1952). *Canadian Centre for Architecture: Building and Gardens*, Larry Richards, ed. (Canadian Centre for Architecture, 1989), documents the genesis of the CCA Building. James Stirling was quoted by Norman Foster on the occasion of Stirling receiving the RIBA Gold Medal for Architecture in *Architectural Design Profile: James Stirling* (Academy Editions, 1982).

7. DETAILS

Roger Scruton's *The Aesthetics of Architecture* (Princeton University Press, 1979) includes a provocative discussion of the use of architectural details. Several houses discussed in this chapter are described in *Robert A. M. Stern: Houses and Gardens*, Peter Morris Dixon, ed. (Monacelli Press, 2005), for which I wrote the introduction. Koolhaas is quoted by Edward R. Ford in *The Architectural Detail* (Princeton Architectural Press, 2011). I wrote about the Harold T. Washington Library in "A Good Public Building," *The Atlantic Monthly* (August 1992).

8. STYLE

Lester Walker's *American Shelter: An Illustrated Encyclopedia of the American Home* (Overlook Press, 1981) is a charmingly illustrated guide. James Ackerman's views on style are contained in *Distance Points: Essays in Theory and Renaissance Art and Architecture* (MIT Press, 1991). The story of the Jefferson Memorial is recounted by Nicolaus Mills in *Their Last Battle: The Fight for the National World War II Memorial* (Basic Books, 2004). John Summerson's *Heavenly Mansions: And Other Essays on Architecture* (W. W. Norton & Co., 1963) contains his observations on the origins of Gothic, and much else besides. His essay "Classical Architecture" is in *New Classicism*, Andreas Papadakis and Harriet Wilson, eds. (Academy Editions, 1990). The best single source for Paul Cret's writings is *Paul Philippe Cret: Architect and Teacher*, Theo B. White, ed. (The Art Alliance Press, 1973). Robert A. M. Stern's description of the Cranbrook library is from *Pride of Place: Building the American Dream* (Houghton Mifflin, 1986), based on his PBS television series of the same name. David Adjaye's interview with Belinda Luscombe of *Time* (September 11, 2012) can be viewed on www.style.time.com. Moshe Safdie's quote about the particular and the general is from a public conversation with the author that took place at the University of Pennsylvania, April 3, 2012. George Howe's remark about historical styles was made during a 1953 lecture to the Philadelphia Art Alliance, and is quoted by Helen Howe West in *George Howe: Architect, 1886–1955, Recollections of My Beloved Father* (W. Nunn Co., 1973). Renzo Piano talks about the perils of style in a BBC Radio 3 interview with John Tusa.

9. THE PAST

Cret's article on High Hollow is "A Hillside House," *Architectural Record* (August 1920). Banister Fletcher is quoted from the fifth edition of *A History of Architecture on the Comparative Method* (Charles Scribner's Sons, 1905). Robert Adam's important essay "The Radiance of the Past" is in *The New Classicism*. William Mitchell's comment on Whitman College is contained in Fred Bernstein, "Dorm Style: Gothic Castle vs. Futuristic Sponge," *The New York Times* (November 20, 2002). The Penn directive on architectural style is part of "Design Guidelines and Review of Campus Projects" (University of Pennsylvania, undated). Robert Bringhurst, the distinguished Canadian typographer, is the author of *The Elements of Typographic Style* (Hartley & Marks, 1992). Jan Tschichold's essays on typography are gathered together in *The Form of the Book* (Hartley & Marks, 1991). The best source of information on the Cenotaph remains Allan Greenberg's "Lutyens's Cenotaph" in the *Journal of the Society of Architectural Historians* (March 1989). The Lincoln Memorial is discussed by Kirk Savage in *Monument Wars: Washington, D.C., the National Mall, and the Transformation of the Memorial Landscape* (University of California Press, 2005), which also analyzes the Vietnam Veterans Memorial. Elizabeth Greenwell Grossman writes about the Château-Thierry Monument in "Architecture for a Public Client: The Monuments and Chapels of the American Battle Monuments Commission," in the *Journal of the Society of Architectural Historians* (May 1984). She is also the author of *The Civic Architecture of Paul Cret* (Cambridge University Press, 1996), a valuable reference to the architect's work. The Gateway Arch is discussed by Jayne Merkel in *Eero Saarinen* (Phaidon Press, 2005); the March 1948 issue of *Architectural Forum* describes the St. Louis competition. Maya Lin's description of her design is from her 1982 retrospective essay "Making the Memorial," published in *The New York Review of Books* (November 2, 2000).

10. TASTE

An excellent recent illustrated history of The Mount is Richard Guy Wilson's *Edith Wharton at Home: Life at The Mount* (Monacelli Press, 2012), with photographs by John Arthur. Edith Wharton and Ogden Codman Jr.'s *The Decoration of Houses* (Charles Scribner's Sons, 1897) remains an erudite history of interior decoration. Elsie de Wolfe's *The House in Good Taste* (The Century Co., 1913), ghostwritten by Ruby Ross Wood, is less scholarly, but is full of useful advice and is still worth reading. An architect who wrote at length about taste was the always stimulating Geoffrey Scott in *The Architecture of Humanism: A Study in the History of Taste* (Peter Smith, 1965; orig. pub. 1914). Andrés Duany describes the Beaux-Arts atelier in "The Beaux Arts Model," in *Windsor Forum on Design Education*, Stephanie E. Bothwell et al., eds. (New Urban Press, 2004). The Bauhaus is discussed in detail in *Bauhaus: Workshops for Modernity, 1919–1933*, Barry Bergdoll and Leah Dickerson, eds. (Museum of Modern Art, 2009), and in Nicholas Fox Weber's *The Bauhaus Group: Six Masters of Modernism* (Knopf, 2009). Richard Rogers is quoted on taste in Bryan Appleyard's *Richard Rogers: A Biography* (Faber and Faber, 1986). Marc Appleton's work is described in *New Classicists: Appleton & Associates, Architects* (Images, 2007), for which I wrote an introduction. *Graves Residence: Michael Graves* (Phaidon, 1995) describes the Warehouse in detail. The Graves quote on Rome is contained in a charming short film by Gary Nadeau, made for *Dwell*. Peter Bohlin describes his home in the preface to *12 Houses* (Byggförlaget, 2005). Frank Gehry is quoted from *The Architecture of Frank Gehry* (Walker Art Center, 1986). Stephen Bayley's *Taste: The Secret Meaning of Things* (Pantheon, 1991) remains a rare if uneven examination of the subject. The student interview with Graves is in *VIA IV: Culture and Social Vision* (MIT Press, 1980). Paul Goldberger's article on Michael Graves is "Architecture of a Different Color," *The New York Times Magazine* (October 10, 1982).

ACKNOWLEDGMENTS

I have tried to follow Steen Eiler Rasmussen's example and write only about buildings that I have had the opportunity to visit. While this has obliged me to neglect some important examples, I hope it has made my impressions more insightful. With one or two exceptions, I have avoided writing about unbuilt works. Although some of the examples cited are recent, many are older, reflecting my conviction that buildings are best judged in the fullness of time. If I have included some of my own youthful efforts, it is not because they bear comparison with the great works of architecture but only because I am intimately familiar with their development. Making architecture, as well as thinking and writing about it, has influenced my views, and a tip of the hat to my steadfast clients: Jacques Renaud for my first commission, a house on the Balearic island of Formentera; my parents for the North Hero cottage; Bill Sofin for sundry projects in Montreal; Robert Verrall of the National Film Board of Canada; the esteemed glassblower Erwin Eisch in Frauenau, Bavaria; and Frank Dumont, Jim and Jacqueline Ferrero, and Emmanuel Leon, for residences in rural Quebec. My experience as a registered architect was preceded by apprenticeships with Allan Mackay, Moshe Safdie, Edouard Fiset, Luis Villa, and Norbert Schoenauer.

Conversations with practitioners over the years have informed this book, and I want to acknowledge Robert Adam, Louis Auer, John Belle, Jean-Louis Bévière, John Bland, John Blatteau, Jack Diamond, Andrés Duany, Jeremiah Eck, Norman Foster, Allan Greenberg, Frank Hamilton, Michael McKinnell, Alvaro Ortega, William Rawn, Ian Ritchie, Jaquelin T. Robertson, Moshe Safdie, Edward Satterthwaite, Donald Schmitt, Adrian Sheppard, Robert A. M. Stern, Bing Thom, Stuart Wilson, and Graham Wyatt. Architects who facilitated visits to their projects have included Marc Appleton, Alvin Holm, Roger Seifter and Randy Correll of Robert A. M. Stern Architects, Denis Austin of Rogers Stirk Harbour + Partners, Spencer de Grey and David Jenkins of Foster + Partners, Michael Heeney of Bing Thom Architects, and Thomas Beeby of HBRA. My particular thanks to Joanna Kerns and Marc Appleton, Michael Graves, Sally and Peter Bohlin, and Berta and Frank Gehry for generously allowing me into their homes.

First Lady Laura Bush invited me to serve on the George W. Bush Presidential Center design committee, which provided an invaluable opportunity to observe the design process from the client's side of the table, and to learn from my fellow committee members Deedie Rose and Roland Betts. Lonnie Bunch and Don Stastny answered questions about the competition for the National Museum of African American History and Culture. I followed the design development of this project as a member of the U.S. Commission of Fine Arts, on which I served from 2004 to 2012. My fellow commissioners, in particular Michael McKinnell and David Childs, sharpened my critical faculties through their perceptive observations during our project reviews. The commissioner Pamela Nelson organized visits to the Baron House and the Rachofsky House in Dallas. Thomas Luebke, secretary of the CFA, provided useful information on Paul Cret. My friend Winnie Lear shared memories of living in George Howe's High Hollow. My thanks also to Vikram Bhatt, Robert Campbell, David De Long, Edward R. Ford, Mark A. Hewitt, David Hollenberg, Bonnie Kate Kirn, Calder Loth, Shannon Mattern, and Michelangelo Sabatino, for their help and suggestions. Ten years ago, my Penn colleague Richard Wesley proposed that I teach a freshman seminar on architecture, a happy experience that lasted a decade and stimulated me to think about some of the basic issues of the art. Jacob Weisberg invited me to be architecture critic for *Slate*, a seven-year gig where some of the ideas in this book first saw the light of day. My thanks also to the excellent editors who in years past provided me with regular opportunities to write about architecture: Constance Rosenblum of *The New York Times*, Bill Whitworth of *The Atlantic*, Lex Kaplen of *Wigwag*, and John Fraser and Kenneth Whyte of *Saturday Night*. For help in acquiring images, my thanks to Marc Appleton, John Arthur, Tom Beeby, Jack Diamond, Peter Morris Dixon, Jeremiah Eck, Philip Freelon, Allan Greenberg, Jonathan Grzwacz, Humberto Gunn, Katy Harris, Natalia Lomeli, Enrique Norten, Elizabeth Plater-Zyberk, Jenny Stephens, Jennifer Varner, Ben Wintner, and, of course, the invaluable Wikimedia Commons.

Eric Chinski of Farrar, Straus and Giroux provided stimulating editorial advice from the beginning, and his many suggestions have helped to give the book its final shape. John McGhee was a valuable copy editor; Jonathan D. Lippincott produced a handsome design. Andrew Wylie, my agent, saw the potential of this book when it was merely the glimmer of an idea. Thanks are due, as always, to my wife, Shirley Hallam, for her invaluable editorial suggestions, and for reading the manuscript aloud—several times.

W.R.
The Icehouse, Chestnut Hill, Philadelphia
April 2011–November 2012

INDEX

Page numbers in *italics* refer to illustrations.

ILLUSTRATION CREDITS

19 Photograph by Piotrus. Licensed under the Creative Commons Attribution-ShareAlike 3.0 Unported license.

20 Photograph by Jack E. Boucher, National Park Service.

21 Photograph by Carol M. Highsmith.

26 (top) Photograph by Figuura. Licensed under the Creative Commons Attribution-ShareAlike 3.0 Unported license.

26 (bottom) Photograph by Hans A. Rosbach. Licensed under the Creative Commons Attribution-ShareAlike 3.0 Unported license.

29 Photograph by Gnangarra. Licensed under Creative Commons Attribution 2.5 Australia License.

31 Photograph by taxiarchos228. Licensed under the GNU Free Documentation License, Version 1.2.

38 Courtesy of Freelon Adjaye Bond/SmithGroup, Architects.

42 Photograph by Tangopaso.

44 Photograph by Mike Peel. Licensed under Creative Commons Attribution-ShareAlike 2.5.

52 Photograph by Bobak Ha'Erinder. Licensed under the terms of the GNU Free Documentation License, Version 1.2.

53 Photograph by RaynaultM. Licensed under the terms of the GNU Free Documentation License, Version 1.2.

57 (top) Courtesy of Gehry Partners.

57 (bottom) Photograph by Neal Jennings. Licensed under the Creative Commons Attribution-Share Alike 2.0 Generic license.

60 Courtesy of Diamond Schmitt Architects.

61 Photograph by Ryan Kaldari.

63 Photograph by Daderot. Licensed under the terms of the GNU Free Documentation License, Version 1.2.

67 (top) Photograph by Pepíček. Licensed under the terms of the GNU Free Documentation License, Version 1.2.

67 (bottom) Photograph by Andreas Praefcke.

71 (top) Photograph by the author.

71 (bottom) Courtesy Jewish Museum, New York.

74 Photograph by Katsuhisa Kida/ FOTOTEC. Courtesy of Rogers Stirk Harbour + Partners.

76 Photograph by Richard George. Licensed under the terms of the GNU Free Documentation License, Version 1.2.

82 Photograph by the author.

162 Photograph by Argos'Dad. Licensed under the Creative Commons Attribution-ShareAlike 3.0 Unported license.

163 Photograph by GanMed64. Licensed under the Creative Commons Attribution 2.0 Generic license.

166 (top) Photograph by the author.

166 (bottom) Photograph by the author.

167 Photograph by the author.

168 Photograph by Antoine Tavenaux. Licensed under the Creative Commons Attribution-ShareAlike 3.0 Unported license.

169 Photograph by the author.

171 Photograph by the author.

174 Photograph by Fb78. Licensed under the Creative Commons Attribution-ShareAlike 2.0 Germany License.

175 Photograph by Undine Prohl. Courtesy of TEN Arquitectos.

176 Courtesy of Freelon Adjaye Bond/SmithGroup Architects.

182 Photograph by the author.

183 Photograph by the author.

184 Photograph by the author.

186 (top) Photograph by the author.

186 (bottom) Photograph by the author.

188 Courtesy of Eck MacNeely Architects.

189 Photograph by Daniel Kovacs. Licensed under the Creative Commons Attribution-ShareAlike 3.0 Unported license.

191 (top) Photograph by Brian Oberkirch. Licensed under the Creative Commons Attribution-ShareAlike 2.0 Generic license.

191 (bottom) Photograph by the author.

193 Photograph by the author.

195 Photograph by the author.

196 Photograph by the author.

198 Courtesy of Eck MacNeely Architects.

199 Photograph by Andreas Praefcke. Licensed under the Creative Commons Attribution 3.0 Unported license.

200 Photograph by the author.

201 Photograph by the author.

205 Photograph by the author.

207 Photograph by Daderot.

212 Photograph by Leonel Ponce. Licensed under the Creative Commons Attribution 2.0 Generic license.

213 Photograph by the author.

214 Photograph by the author.

217 (top) Photograph by The Grotto, Wikipedia Loves Art participant. Licensed under the Creative Commons Attribution-ShareAlike 2.5 Generic license.

217 (bottom) Photograph by Jamie Adams. Licensed under the Creative Commons Attribution-ShareAlike 3.0 Unported license.

220 Courtesy of Allan Greenberg Architect.

222 Photograph by Tim Buchman. Courtesy of Allan Greenberg Architect.

224 Photograph by AgnosticPreachersKid. Licensed under the Creative Commons Attribution-ShareAlike 3.0 Unported license.

227 Photograph by the author.

229 Photograph by the author.

230 Photograph by the author.

233 Courtesy of George W. Bush Presidential Center.

242 Photograph by Peter Dutton. Licensed under the Creative Commons Attribution 2.0 Generic license.

250 Photograph by Peter Aaron/OTTO for Robert A. M. Stern Architects

251 Photograph © 2006 Thomas Delbeck. Courtesy of University of Miami School of Architecture.

253 Photograph by Andreas Praefcke.

254 Courtesy Foster + Partners.

256 Photograph by Green Lane. Licensed under the Creative Commons Attribution-ShareAlike 3.0 Unported, 2.5 Generic, 2.0 Generic, and 1.0 Generic licenses.

259 Photograph by Leon Weber. Licensed under the Creative Commons Attribution-ShareAlike 3.0 Unported license.

263 Photograph by gvallee.

265 Photograph by Bev Sykes. Licensed under the Creative Commons Attribution 2.0 Generic license.

269 Photograph by Hu Totya. Licensed under the Creative Commons Attribution-ShareAlike 3.0 Unported, 2.5 Generic, 2.0 Generic, and 1.0 Generic licenses.

274 Photograph by John Arthur.

285 Photograph by the author.

287 Nigel Young/Foster + Partners.

288 Photograph by the author.

291 Photograph by the author.

292 Photograph by Matt Walla. Courtesy of Appleton & Associates Architects.

293 Courtesy of Michael Graves & Associates.

294 Courtesy of Michael Graves & Associates.
296 Photograph by the author.
297 Photograph by the author.
298 Photograph by the author.
299 Photograph by the author.
307–18 All illustrations in the glossary are courtesy of the author.